D0712757

WITHDRAWN
UTSA LIBRARIES

Adult Learning and la Recherche Féminine

Adult Learning and la Recherche Féminine

Reading Resilience and Hélène Cixous

Elizabeth Chapman Hoult

ADULT LEARNING AND LA RECHERCHE FÉMININE

Copyright © Elizabeth Chapman Hoult, 2012.

All rights reserved.

First published in 2012 by
PALGRAVE MACMILLAN®
in the United States—a division of St. Martin's Press LLC,
175 Fifth Avenue, New York, NY 10010.

Where this book is distributed in the UK, Europe and the rest of the world,
this is by Palgrave Macmillan, a division of Macmillan Publishers Limited,
registered in England, company number 785998, of Houndmills,
Basingstoke, Hampshire RG21 6XS.

Palgrave Macmillan is the global academic imprint of the above companies
and has companies and representatives throughout the world.

Palgrave® and Macmillan® are registered trademarks in the United States,
the United Kingdom, Europe and other countries.

ISBN: 978–0–230–33883–8

Library of Congress Cataloging-in-Publication Data

Hoult, Elizabeth.
    Adult learning and la recherche féminine : reading resilience and
Hélène Cixous / Elizabeth Chapman Hoult.
        p. cm.
    ISBN 978–0–230–33883–8 (hardback)
    1. Adult learning. 2. Transformative learning. 3. Feminism and
education. 4. Cixous, Hélène, 1937– I. Title.

LC5225.L42H677 2011
374—dc23   2011024442

A catalogue record of the book is available from the British Library.

Design by Newgen Imaging Systems (P) Ltd., Chennai, India.

First edition: January 2012

10 9 8 7 6 5 4 3 2 1

Printed in the United States of America.

Library
University of Texas
at San Antonio

For my mother, Lilian Margaret Chapman
January 20, 1925–April 1, 2011
with love and thanks

Contents

Preface

To begin (writing/living) we must have death.[1]

—Hélène Cixous

This writing began with death. Ten years ago I was teaching a Masters in Education program to a group of experienced teachers. All the sessions took place in the twilight hours, after the end of the working school day, and the program was delivered in a classroom of one of the participating schools. It was situated in an urban area that was characterized by multiple deprivation indicators. The course content included generic educational theory with an onus on reflection and a particular focus on school leadership. The reading list consisted mostly of standard, evidence-based work, and there was a strong influence on school-improvement and school-effectiveness literature, which emphasizes the transformative potential of education to change the life chances of children and young people from socially and economically disadvantaged backgrounds. I had just completed my own MA at the Institute of Education, University of London, and I was immersed in the emerging literature that challenged the sociology of pessimism. Texts such as the Paul Hamlyn Foundation's *Success Against the Odds: Effective Schools in Disadvantaged Areas* (1996) and MacGilchrist et al.'s *The Intelligent School* (1997) were key readings. Such texts, with their evangelical insistence that the effects of poverty and underachievement could be overturned by teachers who refused to collude with low expectations and by school principals who changed the culture of their schools from one of complacency and cynicism to one of dynamic openness in which everyone—including principals—saw themselves as learners, were quickly appropriated by the Blair government as totems for improvement in the new classless society. Such literature is now sometimes regarded skeptically, and its simplicity is questioned.[2] At the time, though, it appeared to offer hope for change.

The teachers were mostly tired and often jaded in the sessions. The neighborhoods in which their schools were based experienced many of the concomitants of poverty—complex and multiple problems, including drug-dependency, crime, and a pervasive lack of aspiration. The local authority presided over an anachronistic, selective school system, which seemed to reward preexisting advantage with more of the same. Underachievement was endemic. The realities of the teachers' daily lives were far more complex and exhausting than the neat models offered by the management of change literature we studied, and the vacuum between theory and practice was often a talking point. One of the teachers—Deborah—stood out. Although she took a skeptical and often healthily cynical approach to the literature, she was energetically critical in the best sense and always optimistic about what could be achieved. She was dynamic and passionate about teaching and learning, and she had a positive effect on the rest of the group. Midway through the course, her husband was diagnosed with terminal pancreatic cancer. His diagnosis was sudden and his decline was rapid. Within just four months, he entered hospice care and then he died, leaving Deborah to carry on and look after her two teenage daughters. It was a shock to the group. Deborah took a year off. From the time of his diagnosis she had made it clear that it was her intention to return to her studies as soon as it was practical to do so. She was determined to get back into the course and she did so, graduating with flying colors. During this time, other members of the group had fallen by the wayside—the course had an average attrition rate for a part-time, in-service professional development course, and this was no surprise. The reasons for withdrawal given by those teachers who did not complete it were the usual ones—promotion, more demands at home, and just not keeping up with the work. I was accustomed to counting and accounting for student withdrawals. Funding bodies have an interest in measuring attrition, and this means that enquiries into why students drop out are numerous in studies of higher education. Research typically works backwards to try to understand why the students drop out. Such research seemed to me then, and it seems to me now, to be asking the question the wrong way round. It assumes that the education system is already functioning correctly and therefore that any student who is unable or unwilling to comply with it is somehow deficient. The effect is at once highly idealistic about the potential of education to transform lives and highly punitive to teachers and institutions that fail to deliver on this expectation. Part-time study is tiring and demanding, and why people drop out should be no mystery. It was much more interesting to me to ask why someone like Deborah should want to continue. That set me thinking, why is it that some adult learners are so resilient and successful against the odds? That was where I began.

Acknowledgments

I would like to thank my family, friends, and colleagues for their generous support for this book. In particular, I would like to thank the following: John Moss, Ian Wellard, Linden West, Rayya Ghul, Mandy Cooper, Ben Knights, Viv Griffiths, and Ian Marsh for their helpful comments on the drafts. Brooke Hopkins, Andrew King, and Jane Stevens all took my thinking about *The Winter's Tale* into new and exciting areas, and I am grateful to all of them for sharing their insights with me. Paul Skinner kindly shared his knowledge of Mamet and Russell and introduced me to the art of writing a play and Pete Webster helped me understand the Pygmalion story from a sculptor's point of view. Thanks also to Lesley Malkin for her very thorough help with the compilation of the book and to Burke Gerstenschlager and Kaylan Connally at Palgrave Macmillan for supporting the project.

Most of all, I give thanks to Simon for his love and support for the work since its inception, and to the adult learners who shared their stories of resilience with me and allowed me to include them in the study.

Statement of Confidentiality

A differentiated approach to anonymity is taken in this book. All names have been changed to pseudonyms for the main cohort of interviews included in Chapters Five, Six, and Seven. The name of the main institution featured in those chapters has also been changed to the pseudonym Kingsley College. The names of the destination universities, as well as the buildings and societies associated with the higher education institutions featured in the study, have also been fictionalized. The nature of the higher education institutions and where they sit in the hierarchy of universities is relevant, and so I have provided some idea of their nature in the endnotes. When interviewees have named other people, such as tutors, friends, and teachers from their school days, I have used pseudonyms.

A different approach to anonymity is taken to the auto/biographical material and a full account of the reasons for the approach is given in Chapter Eight. Briefly, additional permission was sought and gained from family members mentioned in the auto/biographical material to use their real names. Given the proximity of their relationship to me, it seemed nonsensical to anonymize them. My mother is the subject of Chapter Eight, and given the content of her interview, not only was the right to approve and edit the transcripts given to her (as were all the interviewees), but this was extended to the analysis of the chapter itself. This is explained more fully in Chapter Eight.

CHAPTER 1

Ecdysis

Resilient adult learners are the firebirds of the education system. Understanding what makes them flourish is a matter of immense importance. Resilience makes the difference between the endless repetition of the cycle of poverty, exclusion, and failure, and the disadvantaged person's ability to break free from that cycle through a return to education. Resilience is the mysterious and elusive quality that explains why some people are able to withstand massive disadvantage and yet still succeed, while others fall by the wayside.

In the sense that it is most commonly understood, resilience means the ability to recover strength and spirits quickly after a setback. It derives from the Latin verb *resilire*—to spring back or rebound. All the learners in this book do this in one way or another; they leap back after being knocked down—they get back into the fight. In order to survive the academic system, many of them also need to challenge and defy it. The nexus between resistance and persistence is, therefore, the place where resilience resides. These learners are resilient in that they carry on and succeed despite "common sense" predictions that they might drop out, and they are defiant in that they defy gloomy predictions about their educational trajectories. With this in mind, Daniel Challener's broad definition of the resilient (child) learner, as "one who faced considerable challenges—more than those of an average child—yet ultimately was able, as an adult, to function as an independent, caring individual"[1] (1997, p.7), might be transposed to an equally broad definition with regard to the adult learners who are the subject of this book. That is to say, a resilient adult learner is one who has faced considerable challenges—more than those of the average student—yet is ultimately able to succeed and to thrive academically.

Reading and Writing Resilience

The term "adult learners" embraces the group of learners who are also sometimes called mature students, returners, or older learners. In the original study that informed this book, I conducted a series of interviews with a range of resilient adult learners. Three examples of these are included in this book, in chapters five, six, and seven. The adult learners in the study have all overcome disadvantages, setbacks, and opposition in order to survive and to succeed. Resilience is performed by them in response to restrictions that can be loosely grouped into three categories:

1. the ability to succeed academically despite a lack of capital;[2]
2. the ability to return to, or to continue, learning after or during difficult and traumatic personal circumstances;
3. the ability to exist and remain successful in an academic field without fully complying with the habitus[3] (i.e., illegitimately).

Access to higher education for the most disadvantaged communities can be improved with the removal of structural and financial barriers. It is much harder to provide the right kinds of support for those learners once they are in the system though. A UNESCO communiqué[4] on higher education draws attention to the importance of learner support: "In the past ten years, tremendous efforts have been made to improve access and ensure equity. This effort must continue. Access alone is, however, not enough. Much more needs to be done. Efforts must be made to ensure the success of learners."[5] But how can we do that when the relationship between success and talent seems so nuanced and complicated? The creation of institutional diversity policies is only part of the answer. The UNESCO report is quite clear—our thinking about equity must go much further than the issue of access; higher education must provide the right sorts of "educational support for those from poor and marginalized communities.[6]" This is where the real work begins. Understanding the complex ways in which a disadvantaged learner makes sense of the higher education institution and negotiates his or her way through it toward graduation is a vast undertaking. What I aim to do in this book is to get as close as possible to the higher education experience for a particular type of minority learner—mature students—by reading it in ways that go beyond the usual methods and epistemologies of social science. This is not an attempt to replace the work that has been achieved in the fields of education and psychology with regard to resilience.[7] Rather, it is an attempt to read resilient learning through texts not normally included in educational research studies—myth, poetry, drama, and autobiography, alongside empirical data—in order to see if new ways of understanding the phenomenon might emerge and complement existing findings.

The links between successful learning and intended outcomes are far from simple. It is certainly possible to reap enormous benefits from a learning event without completing the prescribed course or even meeting any assessment criteria. Here, though, success is broadly, and perhaps prosaically, understood as the completion of a program of study and the achievement of its intended learning outcomes as they are understood by the academic management system. However, success is not understood as being constituted in the attainment of full inclusion in the academy and conformity to its rules. For most of the learners whose experiences are explored here, success tends to take place in an energetic area just outside of the mainstream. The tension between the pain and loneliness of exclusion and the resistance of full inclusion is central to many of the accounts of resilient adult learners in the original study.

This book charts the course of a five-year project that explored resilience in adult learners. I count myself as a resilient learner descended from, as it turned out, a lineage of resilient learners. This research project became a transformational learning journey. My starting point for the investigation was quite conventional for a piece of research in education—the collection of empirical data and subsequent analysis. However, as I read and reread the passionate accounts of returning to education as a profoundly liberating experience that had allowed the interviewees to escape the economic and social inequalities of their early lives, I was presented with my own theoretical dilemma regarding how to write such transformational learning in ways that allowed me to get as close as possible to it without inscribing the inequalities and power imbalances that are too often part of the academic project.

Adrienne Rich's 1972 poem "Diving Into the Wreck" speaks to me—more powerfully than anything else I have ever read—about the dilemma faced by the researcher who wants to write in a way that refuses to play academic and philosophical power games, while at the same time acknowledging that the only tools available are the ones associated with those games. In that poem, a deep sea diver sets out on a quest to find

the wreck and not the story of the wreck
the thing itself and not the myth.[8]

Rich charts the course of the diver as s/he gets closer to understanding the wreck and its treasures. As she does so, she must lose those structures that give her a sense of security. The tension for the diver is that the very equipment that allows her to get as close as possible to her subject is exactly what separates her from it. The majority of educational research is carried out and "written up" in ways that conform to the conventions of academic writing. This usually involves the employment of certain "authority moves."[9]

As I got deeper into the study, I found that this safety equipment became increasingly cumbersome and that, far from giving me access to the experience of resilient adult learning, it had the effect of separating me from it. By writing about these people as "subjects" of a research study, I seemed to turn living and breathing resilient people—"the treasures that prevail"[10] of Rich's poem—into excavated artifacts held up for academic examination. I urgently needed to find another way of researching and writing resilience.

Eventually, the search for an authentic way of reading and writing resilience led to a reengagement with deconstruction—and in particular with the works of Hélène Cixous—which, when I used it to read the data on adult learners, opened the texts up in new and surprising ways and allowed me to write in a way that at least went some way to representing resilient adult learning more faithfully.

This book, therefore, deliberately challenges the more conventional social scientific models of reading and writing, in which the literature review sets out the possibilities for thought within a field; the account progresses along a linear path; and writing up is regarded as a neutral and transparent act. Instead, I offer here an alternative research approach, which I will call "*la recherche Féminine*," after Hélène Cixous's notion of *l'écriture Féminine*.[11] Cixous's long commitment to a writing practice that breaks through generic, political, social, and psychological constraints provided me with a method for writing about resilient adult learning in new ways. Similarly, her output, which includes plays, prose-poetry, and autobiography, as well as philosophical writing, allowed me to include a much wider range of sources in the breadth of data I examined and created. Later on in the chapter I will return to a more detailed explanation of what Cixous's work offered the study.

There is a deliberate attempt here to *put into practice* the principles of a particular version of post-structuralist[12] literary theory, rather than to just describe them or apply them in an abstract way as a reading frame for other texts. Having chosen Cixous as my primary theoretical guide, I therefore developed a methodology that sought to inhabit the space between theory and creativity. The methodology, which is described below in more detail, required me to engage in a holistic process of writing, engaging the cognitive, emotional, and visceral aspects of my learning and increasingly requiring me to let go of conventional structures and to have faith that the process of writing itself could reveal the answers I sought. In doing so, each stage of the research elicited and demanded a different way of writing and thinking.

This way of working helped me to grapple with the increasing complexities that emerged as I became more deeply immersed in the questions surrounding resilient adult learning. Like Adrienne Rich's diver, such an approach submerges the researcher through layers of knowing and then unknowing, toward an understanding that is simultaneously confidently profound and completely honest about its situated partiality. I hope that readers who are wary of the jargon of deconstruction stay with me through the early chapters, which rely most heavily on literary theory, in order to get to the more liberated and immediate writing as I approach the wreck and its buried treasures. I want to demonstrate how this particular theoretical approach has allowed for deeper sea diving than comparable theoretical frameworks.

Ben Knights and Chris Thurgar-Dawson propose the use of transformational writing as a way of avoiding the "competitive intellectual aggrandizement too often associated with the transmission of theory as educational knowledge."[13] Here I adopt their approach and take the proposition even further. Transformative writing serves both a pedagogical and a research function in this book. It puts into practice the notion of the researcher as well as the learner as a "writing subject"[14] for whom the liberatory effects of theory are employed directly in the text. This book is a text that is therefore simultaneously an exercise in transformational learning, writing, and research. The transformation is enacted within the text itself, and the adult learning effects on the text are discernible as it progresses; the writing improves as the research gets deeper. In order to read resilience in ways that avoid the disguises and power games of the academy, though, this study has had to develop its own resilience. The text performs the same characteristics of resilience as those performed by the learners it depicts: it is elastic and prismatic; it is open to plural readings and it resists the imposition of single, closed readings; it takes on different academic clothes and at one point becomes "naked"; and it survives in the hinterland between two academic fields. This chapter, which provides a theoretical and methodological introduction to the study, is intended to introduce and begin to justify this refracted engagement with resilience and to provide an explanation for the approach that has been taken.

Jan Meyer and Ray Land[15] characterize the stages any learner goes through in a transformational learning event as portals, or conceptual thresholds. Each one is irreversible and destroys the security of the understandings that preceded it. The metaphor of the conceptual threshold is a useful image when illustrating the way that new knowledge is experienced as risky, exciting, and somewhat "troublesome."[16] Certainly, there has been a sense of moving on and rejecting earlier ontological and epistemological securities each time a threshold has been negotiated. The metaphor is not quite sharp enough for what I experienced in the course of this research project, though. The gateway metaphor, for all its mythological associations, still suggests that there is something deliberate, sensible, and restrained about the way that the learner approaches each doorway and hesitates before passing through. My experience of finding a theoretical framework has felt more visceral and atavistic than that; there has been something quite serpentine about my progress.

Enquiry as Ecdysis

In order to read resilient adult learning seriously, I took on and then shed two theoretical frameworks before arriving at one that served the study well. Before I set out what those frameworks were, I want to establish that the title for each one is used axiomatically, as shorthand for that framework, and specific works are cited to illustrate the usefulness and the limitations of each to the study. However, I fully acknowledge that this is a simplification of the vast, theoretically important, and complex output of each of the writers cited. The small sections of those bodies of work used here are what were taken on and subsequently shed. It is rather too cumbersome to explain that the first framework adopted and then discarded was "Bourdieu's theory of reproduction relating specifically to academic capital as a subset of cultural capital and with specific reference to the transfer from compulsory education to higher education." Instead, I refer to the framework as "Bourdieu" and go on to explain the specific aspects of his work used in the commentary. My understanding expanded with the application of each reading, but although I would argue that there is an intensifying linguistic and philosophical complexity with each one, the movement between them was not straightforward and linear but sidewinding and instinctive. Each new framework initially offered a new way of understanding resilient adult learning, but each time it became tight and dry, and I had to shed it in order to find a better one growing below it. Ecdysis—the term for a snake's molting—is a helpful metaphor here. Moving through the frameworks was necessary and important if I was to get as near to an understanding of resilient adult learning as possible. This peeling away of theories was helped by the inevitable friction I encountered while completing the study in the parched and precarious landscape that lies between disciplines.

This book challenges several fundamental claims of current mainstream research into learning and teaching, including the dominant "evidence-based" paradigm that prevails in Western education research and the monopoly of social scientific models as ways of thinking about higher education. Late in the process, though, I came to understand that this friction was necessary in order to slough off discarded frameworks. Indeed, it was just as necessary as the tender encouragement required for the new ones to grow in their place; I have needed the hard rocks as well as the soft sand to take me to the place of knowing/unknowing about resilient adult learning that is arrived at by the end of the book. With each skin that has been shed, not only have I have come closer and closer to understanding the "thing" itself (the performance of resilient adult learning), but I have also understood that the process of growing the new, fresh skin is part of that "thing." Each time, the membrane under the skin was growing, thickening, and breathing. The movement between skins is potentially infinite. There is no constant to which I aspire, no finality that I can attain—just more skins. Ecdysis suggests perpetual shedding, or in deconstructive terms, endless play, until death. It is not a perfect metaphor, but it can serve this first account well enough.

The struggle between the imaginative ambition of the project and the academic framework within which it has been produced also prevailed throughout the work. At the end of the study, I understood that it need not be resolved and that it could be the source of creative energy. This struggle—between two types of writing (which Cixous genders as feminine and masculine)—need not be settled on the side of one or the other; both can coexist in the study. In the same way, the work deliberately occupies the space between two disciplines—education and English. I realize that the very interdisciplinarity of the book puts it into a place of contestation, as Stephen Rowland[17] has argued. The work seeks to challenge the disciplinary field boundaries as well as their conceptual ceilings, and as such a deliberate theoretical eclecticism runs throughout the work.

The following account exploits the metaphor of ecdysis to illustrate my search for a theoretical framework that could adequately support the enquiry and that would give voice to the resilient adult learners in it. Represented like this, a smooth linearity is implied in the way that each framework was lived through and rejected. It also erroneously appears that this process was undertaken separately from the enquiry itself. Actually both processes—the enquiry and the search for a theoretical framework within which it could be analyzed—happened concurrently and symbiotically. The writing deliberately becomes theoretically radical and experimental as the work progresses. As my understanding became more nuanced and the subject matter became more elusive, it was necessary to find new ways of writing to cope with that. Before this is demonstrated in the chapters themselves, I will set out an overview of the ecdysis of three theoretical "skins": the work of Pierre Bourdieu, Jacques Derrida, and Hélène Cixous.

First Skin: Pierre Bourdieu

The first substantial theoretical framework to inform my thinking was the work of sociologist Pierre Bourdieu—in particular, his thinking on higher education and his argument that it reproduces existing patterns of disadvantage. Two striking images from the work of Bourdieu inform the study—death and the *miraculé*. Death functions literally and metaphorically throughout this book. It is symbolically present in the form of what Bourdieu and Jean-Claude Passeron call "the education mortality rate,"[18] as a way of describing the disastrous consequences of the unequal distribution of capital on students in higher education. Death is also present as a direct and literal reality in the lives of some learners whose accounts are included here. The second image is that of the "*miraculé*," or one on whom a miracle has been performed. The *miraculé* is Bourdieu's term for those people who are able to survive and thrive in the academic system and, as such, defy the gloomy prognoses that they will simply add to the "education mortality rate" with their failure or withdrawal. These two images are key elements in my own thinking about resilience throughout this work.

An important theme in this investigation into resilience is the way that certain learners are able to defy Bourdieu's pessimistic predictions of a "circumscribed trajectory"[19] in education, despite their undeniable lack of capital. Bourdieu and Passeron's argument in *Reproduction* is that "the educational mortality rate can only increase as one moves towards the classes most distant from scholarly language."[20] I am therefore interested in those learners who defy death or who, having died once in the educational system, are resurrected through adult education. I am also interested in how excluded and marginalized learners survive and maintain integrity in academic institutions that appear to demand compliance in return for inclusion. The focus of the study is the resilience of the adult learner who refuses to take part in the overall reproductive project, or who cannot conform due to preexisting disadvantage. Such learners will not collude with the predictions of failure, withdrawal, or expulsion on the basis of a lack of capital in terms of their reserves and their behavior.

Bourdieu's understanding of the transformational potential of education is always bounded and undermined by the relentless ability of the system to reproduce itself and to replicate the existing unfair distribution of capital beyond its walls. As Toril Moi has it, "According to Bourdieu there is an almost perfect homology between the class position of the individual pupil and their teachers' intellectual judgements of them."[21] She goes on to say, "For Bourdieu, then, the widespread democratic belief in education as a passport to freedom and success is no more than a myth: the myth of the *école libératrice* is the new 'opium of the people.'"[22] This is a depressing outlook that challenges any notion of education as a force for individual transformation or social reform. Capital is always linked to the drive for more capital, and those without it are forever doomed to be on the outside. Although most teachers working in higher education would recognize this description, they also know learners who have defied such predictions, and fiction has produced archetypes that serve to challenge the notion. Some readers will no doubt recognize themselves as *miraculés*. This book takes these exceptions seriously.

Moi identifies the loophole in Bourdieu's theory of education. It is his pessimistic view that the hierarchical organization of the education system serves the ideological purpose of making it "appear as if positions of leadership and power are distributed according to merit."[23] The most insidious device of such a system is to include a tiny number of "*des miraculés*— educationally highly successful members of disadvantaged groups,"[24] so as to present itself as accessible and based on a system of meritocracy and the fair recognition of natural talent.[25] Moi perceptively gets to the heart of contradiction in Bourdieu's writing in a footnote, because it "still leaves the problem of where the *miraculés* come from."[26] It is a good point. How is it that a learner with limited capital or one who has faced considerable difficulties in his or her life can remain resilient in circumstances in which that insufficiency should curtail the learning trajectory according to Bourdieu's theory? Bourdieu's term for these exceptions—*des miraculés*—reveals an uncharacteristically metaphysical turn for a materialist such as him. By attributing exceptional success to the inexplicable, he assigns it a peripheral and eccentric place in his schema.[27] I think it is more helpful to regard the puzzle of the *miraculé* as being central to an understanding of how subjects interact with educational structures.

Limitations of Bourdieu

Bourdieu seemed to have much to offer, but when I attempted to identify how the combinations of capital in the lives of the learners in the study had allowed them to achieve educational success, I ended up in a series of conclusive cul-de-sacs. The application of the model did not help me to understand what the mechanisms were that helped these people access the capital on offer to them. It suggested that anyone in the same situation would have behaved in the same way. Moi identifies this as a limitation of Bourdieu's argument and suggests the necessity for an autobiographical perspective to explain the continuing existence of the *miraculés*. Although there is an implicit acknowledgement in Bourdieu's use of the metaphor that capital accrues interest and so is always in a dynamic process of acquiring more power and capital to itself, there is no presentation of the subtle differences between individuals that allow more or less of the available capital to be used. As Richard Jenkins says of Bourdieu,

> His social universe ultimately remains one in which things happen to people, rather than a world in which they can intervene in their individual and collective destinies.[28]

This idea is central to my critique of the Bourdieusian analysis. It presents a problem for the educational researcher, because it renders the account of developing learner identity clinical and mechanistic. There is a tension in any work that appropriates a sociological theory that is built on the passive reception of social resources while at the same time adhering to a constructivist notion of learning as a process that is characterized as liberating and transformative. For Bourdieu, the limitation can be explained by viewing each individual success as the inevitable product of particular variables and sub-variables. He confidently asserts that

> If one sufficiently refined the analysis of that species of capital…or the analysis of the level, it would be possible to find all the cases empirically observed, in all their complexity but also in their quasi-infinite multiplicity.[29]

The quasi-infinite multiplicity becomes, then, a justification for, and an explanation of, individual success against the odds. It allows for openness but not complete infinity of meaning. His ideas, when taken in a diluted form are therefore too close to behaviorism on the one hand, and to passivity on the other, to sit entirely comfortably within either a constructivist theory of practice or a transformative philosophy of education.

I became uncomfortable, therefore, with an unaccompanied employment of Bourdieu's theory of capital to the stories of the learners in the study. This gave rise to another sense of restriction. Apart from the obvious point that Bourdieu was writing specifically about the French educational system in the latter part of the last century, there are two serious limitations to the pure application of his ideas to the study described in a book like this. First, as Moi points out, despite Bourdieu's long and prolific interest in the production of literary texts and the construction of literary theory, there is a fundamental problem with the application of his ideas to literary texts, because "they turn Bourdieu into just another furnisher of themes for close reading. What is lacking in such readings is the most distinctive and original aspect of Bourdieu's work, his sociological method."[30] I would not be as keen as Moi, though, to dismiss this thematic use of Bourdieu. It is certainly possible to read the life of a learner through a Bourdieusian lens in order to understand what kinds and quantities of capital they bring to a learning situation, and there is some educational return on such an exercise. The problematics of attempting to do this, however, are not a result of the *close* reading such an exercise produces but the *closed* nature of such a reading. The text is immediately closed down to a reading that either endorses Bourdieu's theory with a glib explanation of success that can be attributed to unexpected capital, or a rejection of Bourdieu's theory. On Moi's other point—about his traditional sociological method—I am less willing than she is to take a celebratory approach to Bourdieu's use of quantitative, empirical data in the first place, as my stance in the rest of this book will demonstrate.

The second limitation concerns Bourdieu's writing itself. His use of the term *miraculé* is either bemused or ironic. Bourdieu also alludes to the miraculous when he is writing about love. He explains the way in which couples are engaged in the matching of habitus (and the attendant social and cultural codes) when they think that they are falling in love. Couples, he tells us, experience love as "a happy accident: a co-incidence which mimics transcendent design ('made for each other') and intensifies the sense of the miraculous."[31] This seems to be something of an oversimplification of the experience of love that does not allow for the ineffable and the mysterious aspects of the experience.

Ultimately, Bourdieu can't account for the miracle that is worked on the *miraculé* within the sociological lexicon. The language of evidence-based sociology, such as Bourdieu's, cannot describe, and therefore cannot accommodate, the profound experiences of the adult learner. It either exiles words like love, death, resurrection, and hope, or it attempts to atomize those experiences. It is therefore ultimately limited to describing the prosaic and the political. Therein lies the real limitation of a pure application of Bourdieu's work to this study. The study needed to challenge its own boundaries in order to accommodate the miracle. The vocabulary needed to expand beyond the conventionally academic with its pretence of systematic order and logic that Bourdieu recognizes but escape.

Although I shed Bourdieu as a main framework, some of his key ideas remained influential and helpful. I implicitly draw on the notions of capital, habitus, and the field in particular in the interview with Jane in Chapter Six, and the overall impact of Bourdieu's writing has been to support my own decision to challenge the expectations of the norms of the academic field and the disciplinary habitus. His challenge to the way that the higher education system in France demanded obedience from its students and the way it replicated existing patterns of advantage and disadvantage is still powerful—cold anger underpins his detailed data analysis. As Claire Kramsch argues, "the contemptuous silences and condescending smiles, the compensatory effusions and forced invisibility, are all familiar to those on the receiving end of discrimination, whether it be race- or class-related."[32] The banal and everyday practices of discrimination, as they are experienced by students who do not or cannot conform to a narrowly defined notion of success in the university, are theorized and dismantled by Bourdieu in a way that no other academic has done before or since. For this I am grateful. Ultimately, though, I needed access to a framework that could help me articulate the meaning of those "silences" in a way that went beyond the sociological investment in the metaphysics of presence. The writer who seemed to have much to offer as well as an understanding of the power games of presence and absence, language and silence, was Jacques Derrida with his contribution to the practice known as deconstruction.

Second Skin: Jacques Derrida

Derrida's ideas[33] inform the notion of playfulness that runs throughout this book. His main challenge to the apparently unshakeable transcendence of the center[34] in philosophical terms opens up the possibility of conceiving of resilience in terms that challenge essentialist understandings. As a result, it is possible to adopt a reading practice that allows for multiplicity and the endless play of signification. The associated concept of *différance*, which has neither existence nor essence but is in constant motion, always undermining the categories of both being and absence, allows for an understanding of resilience to be developed that is understood in terms of its difference from its opposites, or binary oppositions. It also implies that meaning is constantly deferred; there is always *another* reading of resilience, because the mythical origin of resilience is permanently "obliterated."[35] This allowed the philosophical basis of the study to move away from the search for origins and the notion of *being* resilient toward more fluid understandings of how resilient adult learning is performed in a range of contexts.

Deconstruction—in its broadest and simplest sense[36]—had a liberating effect on the study because I knew that I wanted and needed to incorporate different types of texts into the enquiry if I was to read resilience as abundantly as possible. The work of Derrida provided me with an apparently satisfactory way of justifying my reasons for doing this. I have treated play scripts, poetry, and autobiographical writing as seriously as the interview data. The consequences of including literary works in an apparently social scientific text are profound, because their inclusion reframes the social scientific discourse as simply another narrative—one among many other possibilities. Laurel Richardson has written convincingly about the importance of including literary texts in her own work, which draws on post-structuralism. She makes the point that literature "violates a major pretension of science: the single unambiguous voice."[37] This is one of the desired effects of including literary texts in this book. The literary texts included are not secondary representations of truth; the literary texts and the "factual" data have equal claims to representing people's lives faithfully. Likewise, the interview texts are read creatively as texts which have a certain literary "functioning" and a literary "intentionality"[38] rather than as transparent and factual representations of learning trajectories. Deconstructive readings fundamentally challenge sociology's serious claim to *know* about reality on the basis of what it regards as evidence. By renouncing the truth claims of social scientific writing, I naturally also abandon the search for the center that such writing pretends to transparently reveal. So in the terms of the book, the pursuit of "the center"—the search for a real and stable thing that preexists its name, *resilient adult learning*, which can only be accessed by gaining evidence about it from real subjects—is abandoned from here on.

Fundamentally, then, adopting deconstruction as a possible primary framework contributed a series of broad understandings to the study. First, Derrida's notions of deferral and difference (in *différance*) allow for the inclusion of a range of types of texts in the study, which support the underpinning assumption that, while a single understanding of resilience is not able to be captured, deeper understandings may be gained through serious consideration of multiple readings. Secondly, working within a deconstructive framework has allowed me to challenge the authority and privilege of conventional academic writing and disciplinary boundaries, because they can be shown to emanate from what Derrida describes as a logocentric discourse.[39] This book is the result of a study that embraced rupture and that celebrates the joy of multiplicity and the resistance of authority that deconstruction offers. Literary writing performs an important function in the lead-up to this rupture, because it exists, to a certain extent, outside of the rules of the academic game.

Engagement with the ideas of deconstruction also allowed me to introduce apophatic readings of resilience into the text. David Mamet's play *Oleanna* is a useful representation of unresilient learning, which, when juxtaposed with Willy Russell's *Educating Rita*, produces a kind of deconstructive energy and allows for deeper understandings of resilient learning to emerge. Reading it closely seemed like an opportunity too good to miss, and Derrida's own emphasis on deconstruction as a kind of negative theology fundamentally supported the incorporation of texts that point to what resilience is *not* in addition to those that point to what it *is*. For this reason, the unresilient learning of Mamet's Carol in *Oleanna* and Leontes's refusal to learn in the first half of *The Winter's Tale* are taken as seriously as the clearly resilient behavior of Willy Russell's Rita in *Educating Rita* and the real learners in the study.

As I have said, the notion of play is an important one in this book. The work is playful in the Derridean sense because resilient adult learning is examined through a range of methods, none of which is sovereign, but all of which have something to offer to an open understanding of what resilience looks like. This book takes the playful world of the theater, fiction, and poetry seriously, as arenas in which deep understandings may be found. Disputing the serious and sovereign claim on truth that the academic, nonfiction text makes, I have looked to drama as a helpful discourse that blatantly declares itself as a sham. This final point is not, perhaps, actually Derridean. Nor is it true to say that the authors of such works of drama are necessarily consciously making such truth claims about their work. But I am arguing that adopting a broadly deconstructive approach allows me to hold up such fictional works as having claims to represent what is real that are as valid as those of "documentary" discourses and that this enriches the research in very significant ways. On this final point, the exercise of writing in a literary and creative way as part of the investigation performs a political and deeply functional role in the investigation. It challenges what Knights and Thurgar-Dawson (2006) describe as "the binary mindset which poses theory over (re)creativity."[40]

For all of the above reasons, the adoption of an approach that takes inspiration from Derrida's notion of deconstruction has liberated the book. At the end of the study, I find myself in a space of enriched unknowing regarding resilient adult learning in which multiple explanations can coexist. This is not a cold, philosophical assertion of the possibilities of textual plurality. Rather it is closer to John Keats's notion of negative capability[41] or, as St. John of the Cross put it in the sixteenth century, "I came into the unknown / and stayed there unknowing / rising beyond all science."[42]

Limitations of Deconstruction

The application of the work of Derrida, among others, to Anglo-American literary theory has had a somewhat problematic history. Since I come to this study from a background of English literature and education,[43] rather than philosophy, my own induction into deconstructive practice has been necessarily written through by this history, and this has an impact on the way that I read and respond to deconstructive literary theory. The interplay between the body of theoretical texts[44] that were imported in undiluted form into university teaching of English in the 1980s, the way that they were taught, and the consequent formation of student identities has been convincingly charted and critiqued by Ben Knights. It is Knights's contention that "bodies of knowledge and pedagogic practices are inextricably linked,"[45] and this has had an effect on me that I need to declare at this point in the study. Knights identifies that moment of theory in the 1980s as one in which the associated pedagogic practice involved "engaging in philosophy-style deconstruction" and in which the learner identity that was encouraged by such practice was one that embraced the "hermeneutics of suspicion."[46]

> To be successful, the learner had to tolerate contradiction, to refuse identification (with characters and authors), and refuse the seductions of aura whether that of text, the author, or the learning occasion itself.[47]

This aptly describes my own first encounter with what was broadly known as post-structuralism in my first degree in English literature in the late 1980s and early 1990s. Given the strong influence of the field of education on this book, I take the effects of this pedagogical induction into theory seriously. I was introduced to "post-structuralism"—as were many of my generation who studied English literature in the late twentieth century—in a way that was elitist, disdainful, and somewhat clinical. The effect of the introduction of continental philosophy into the English seminar room was "to create a classroom of competitive superiority and to foment its own specialist value by sectarian quarantine form a larger world of readers."[48] The unfortunate combination of apostolic applications of Derridean theory by literary theorists on both sides of the Atlantic, with the lack of training in philosophical reading and teaching techniques in university English departments has left me with a wariness of and discomfort regarding the adoption of deconstruction as a main theoretical framework. This is not to dismiss the vast, variegated, and important output of a writer such as Derrida per se. Rather, it is to argue that my own understanding and ability to apply those texts were circumscribed by a set of specific historical pedagogical circumstances that turned a movement that was radical and liberatory into "a model of exclusion."[49]

My other reservation was more utilitarian. My main stumbling block when considering whether to use Derrida's ideas came from the difficulty

I had with understanding his language and my own lack of knowledge of the philosophical canon. In his postscript to *Distinction*, Bourdieu critically reads Derrida's reading of Immanuel Kant. Bourdieu says of Derrida,

> Because he never withdraws from the philosophical game, whose conventions he respects, even in the ritual transgressions at which only traditionalists could be shocked, he can only philosophically tell the truth about the philosophical text and its philosophical reading which (apart from the silence of orthodoxy) is the best way of not telling it.[50]

It is perhaps unfair of Bourdieu to insinuate that Derrida was a game player, but the broader point about language is one to which I can relate. This is the problem I encountered when attempting to use Derrida's ideas in any sustained way in the work. I found that, without philosophical training, the exciting and sometimes very beautiful ideas of Derrida seemed inaccessible to me and that the limitations of my own readings of his work meant that I could not see in it the hope and the kindness that I required in order to serve the resilient adult learners whose accounts I wanted to include in the study. Engagement with his ideas liberated my thinking about the study considerably, but I needed a different kind of skin to take me into the more remote and hidden parts of the desert terrain.

Third Skin: Hélène Cixous

The basic contribution that Cixous's work makes in the book is introduced here, but I return to particular aspects of it and illuminate them in more detail in the subsequent chapters. I decided to use the work of Hélène Cixous as a theoretical framework because her writing allows for the openness and playfulness of deconstruction. At the same time, it is both literary and deeply personal; she seeks, and then demonstrates, a way of writing one's way out of oppression. Her writing is both passionate and compassionate. Academic writing, with its strict understanding of what is appropriate and inappropriate for inclusion in the text, limits a fully open reading of the *miraculé*, and his or her resistance of the *educational mortality rate*, to that which can be described within the academic text. I wanted to incorporate ways of writing that might be deemed inappropriate and excessive into the study, in order to understand resilient adult learning in new ways. The drive to question and upset constraining authoritarian structures is something that Cixous sees as a necessary function of a writing practice that she characterizes as feminine.[51] She argues that its adoption is essential if writing is to do something other than replicate the old oppressive hierarchies. She explores this idea in depth in her essay "Sorties: Out and Out: Attacks/Ways Out/Forays" (1975/1986, henceforth referred to as *Sorties*)—a text that is drawn on throughout the study as a theoretical framework and inspiration for my methodological approach.

The employment of Cixous's ideas as a conceptual framework liberated my thinking in three ways:

1. it provided me with an investigative tool with which to examine the texts;
2. it freed my own writing and enabled me to cross the boundaries between the personal, the creative, and the academic more fluidly;
3. it allowed me to apply her ideas about the sorts of resilient activities that are required of the feminine writer in defying the power of the masculine economy to the resilient learners in the study in order to understand how they are able to resist the brutal inequalities of the reproductive educational project.

The work of Hélène Cixous has provided me with a theoretical basis from which to challenge the central pessimism of Bourdieu's theory and the limitations of applying Derrida's philosophical language to real-life learners. It has also enabled me to think much more deeply about the connections between reading, writing, and survival. For Cixous, open reading and writing practices provide the necessary means for the reclamation of the feminine that is necessary to resist the oppressive reproductive project that is the work of the masculine economy. This reclamation occurs by disrupting the oppositions that lie at the base of Western philosophical thought, all of which she traces back to the basic opposition between masculine and feminine. She calls such a writing practice *l'écriture féminine*. The analysis that follows in the next nine chapters is an attempt to bring an understanding of the principle of *l'écriture féminine* to bear on texts about resilient learning that exist in a world beyond the philosophical-theoretical arena. *L'écriture féminine* posits writing as a form of enquiry—of writing one's way through knowledge to a state of unknowing insight. The very purpose of such writing is to depart from the familiar, logocentric understanding of the world and to find new ways of knowing. Writing as enquiry therefore forms a substantial part of the methodology of the book. This writing took me to new places throughout the work. This has been a risky business, because writing in the Cixousian sense means giving way to an entirely new way of knowing, through what Amy Hollywood calls "a disrupting and liberating mystical excess."[52] This transformational learning experience has been wild and profound and has called for a good deal of resilience to survive it.

For Cixous, the recognition of the destructive power of dualistic thinking is the basis for the overthrow of an oppressive system. She wants to alter the real, tangible consequences of the power structures that are brought about by such thinking in every aspect of people's lives. She urges her readers to terrorize the masculine economy by upsetting its hierarchies through writing. Her work has provided me with a way of examining texts as an arena for oppression and dissent, of domination and survival that neither subscribes to a restrictive view of language as transparent and closed, nor leads to the nihilistic and cerebral game playing of some applications of deconstruction to literary theory outlined above. In her work, deconstruction does not lead to nothing (albeit a nothingness that does not really exist beyond "stark oppositions"[53]) but to a new reality in which what cannot currently be said within the logocentric discourse cannot only be uttered but also celebrated in a new linguistic reality. Hollywood illustrates the distinction between Derrida and Cixous:

> Derrida's work tends to focus on loss, the absence that is inscribed within all language, and the destabilizing effects of that absence on meaning. Cixous, while attentive to those features of writing, particularly as they might endanger or be deployed towards liberatory ends, increasingly highlights the ways in which writing enables the dead to speak to us, creating a bridge between present, past and future.[54]

Finding a place in which the dead can speak is a central concern of this work. Hope underpins the writing of Cixous, and this makes it a helpful framework within which to think about resilience.

Cixous's insistence that the philosophical or academic discourse alone cannot liberate, because it is a product of the oppositional system she despises, helped me to feel more confident about inhabiting the space between the official, academic discourse and the personal, immediate autobiographical writing. As she says of the feminine writer,

> Her discourse, even when "theoretical" or political, is never simple or linear or "objectivized," universalized; she involves her story in history. [55]

This insistence that l'écriture féminine involves different kinds of writing beyond the "linear" and "objectivized" scope of academic texts allows for the inclusion of an exciting range of texts that deal with resilience. The crossing of generic boundaries is fundamental to Cixous's political and intellectual ambitions because, as Hollywood argues, her work is "vast, diverse, protean," and therefore it is "impossible to separate poetry and prose or literary texts ('those to be read') and critical essays ('readings')."[56] The texts included in this study range from direct biographical and autobiographical ("she involves her story in history") accounts of formal learning in higher education establishments to mythopoetical arenas in which adults learn in ways that are profound and transformative and in which the identities of teachers and learners are initially latent. A deliberate theoretical eclecticism runs throughout this work. Every text included here provides a representation of resilient adult learning in a way that illuminates the other texts and also intensifies and problematizes the emerging insights. The heterogeneity of the "data" included, is, therefore, reflective of the prismatic and elusive nature of resilience in that it resists capture and categorization, particularly by academic frameworks.

The book therefore performs what it seeks to convey. It is a deliberate attempt to occupy the epistemological space between English and education in order to understand something original about resilient adult learners. Cixous's use of the autobiographical mode to explore philosophical questions and the way that she employs poetic forms of writing in order to challenge sociocultural assumptions fundamentally supports the cross-disciplinary, cross-genre way in which this investigation works. Included in this work is writing traditionally associated with educational research, literary critique, analysis of interview data, and creative, autobiographical writing. This range represents a deliberate attempt to subvert the norms of writing in educational research and to attempt to demonstrate alternatives. In doing so, it draws on a body of writing that already exists which puts literary writing and literary theory to work in order to serve a range of enquiry purposes, including personal development,[57] ethnography,[58] and pedagogy.[59]

Finally, the approach taken here is an attempt to address the challenge that is sincerely and passionately articulated by the author of the nearest study I could find as a precedent for this book—Daniel Challener's book *Stories of Resilience in Childhood*. Defending his choice of a theoretical framework[60] for reading the various literary autobiographies, he rejects deconstruction entirely:

> Critics may have shown how deconstructive analysis could be used for political ends. But to suggest that critics or scholars or even the handful of policymakers and decision makers outside of the ivory tower who understand deconstruction have actually used deconstructive analysis to achieve change, have any impact, in the status of the lives of America's children is sheer nonsense. Deconstructive critics have spent their time on other things. I defy anyone to prove me otherwise.[61]

I cannot take him up on the specific point about America's children, but this is a sincere attempt to demonstrate a practical application of one version of deconstructive practice, as articulated in the work of Cixous, to a group of learners in higher education. In doing so, I hope to resist the power games and academic disguises that have perhaps beset the appropriation of deconstruction into literary theory in the past.

Outline of Chapters

There are contours in my relationship with the writing of Hélène Cixous. I have used her work as a practice, rather than an abstraction, throughout the book, and from the conceptualization stage onward the work resisted attempts to comply with a linear, rational, and objectivized way of proceeding. It never did conform to the model of research in which a question is formulated, relevant literature is read, data is gathered and analyzed, and conclusions are drawn. As soon as I appropriated the notion of *l'écriture féminine* as a methodological framework, any remaining plans I had for the work to conform to linear and logocentric expectations ruptured. My engagement with Cixous then became deeper and more driven, so that it moved from a theoretical engagement in the early chapters toward a more pedagogical influence in the analysis of empirical data in the middle section of the book. As such, she moved from philosopher to mentor. But when I started to write the autobiographical sections, her voice became more maternal, intimate, and confidential. As I moved toward the end of the study, my academic boundaries dissolved entirely, and I was astonished by how a deep engagement with her work allowed a transformation of the material to occur. As I wrote about my own life and resilience, the pain went through an alchemical process and became beautiful and blissful when it was transformed into feminine writing. These effects are discernible as the book progresses. Here, though, is a brief overview of how the book is structured.

Given the fundamental challenge that the work makes to the preeminence of mainstream social scientific approaches in educational research, no serious attempt is made here to have the work conform to such a model in retrospect. As has been stated, the work was not linear or tidy. Instead it begins from a center and radiates outwards. That center was originally no more than an idea that Willy Russell's 1981 play *Educating Rita* might have something helpful to offer to a study of resilient adult learners. An initial reading of that play led me to Rita's literary precedent—Eliza Doolittle in George Bernard Shaw's 1916[62] play *Pygmalion*. A corresponding reengagement with literary theory and the serious challenge it offered to the certainty and prevalence of social scientific explanations of education accompanied my extended reading of fictional texts relating to the subject. I was interested in how incorporating a character whom I considered to be Rita's opposite—Carol in Mamet's 1993 play *Oleanna*—could help me make still more sense of what resilient learning might mean. It became clear to me that Ovid's first-century (c. 8 A.D.) narrative poetic treatment of the Pygmalion myth in *Metamorphoses* links all three texts to each other. The first chapter considers the Pygmalion story from three perspectives: Ovid's c. 8 A.D. text; the opportunities for open readings of it afforded by Ted Hughes's translation of it in his 1997 book *Tales from Ovid*; and George Bernard Shaw's transposition of it onto the stage and his basic allegorical treatment of it as a story about teaching and adult learning. Taking my cue from Shaw, in Chapter Two I read all three versions of the Pygmalion story as an allegory of teaching and adult learning. From this analysis, I arrive at a model of five capabilities that seem to be significant in the way that resilient adult learners are able to negotiate their way through adult education. I consider the ways in which the Pygmalion story allows for resilience, and also the centrality of the notion of transformation in the texts. In Chapter Three, a reading of two contrasting texts—*Oleanna* (Mamet, 1993) and *Educating Rita*—is placed in the context of the developing understanding of transformational adult learning in the Ovidian sense. In that chapter, resilience is understood in relation to both its performance and its absence. There is a precedent for this sort of comparative textual work around resilience in the work of Challener, whose definition of resilience in child learners has already been mentioned. His literary analysis of resilience in childhood forms an approximate precedent for this work. His starting point is the juxtaposition between Toni Morrison's 1970 *The Bluest Eye* and Maya Angelou's 1969 *I Know Why the Caged Bird Sings*, as texts that represent clearly contrasting "unresilience" and resilience respectively. This understanding is deepened by the inclusion of Shakespeare's late play (it is estimated that the first performance was in 1610 or 1611) *The Winter's Tale* as another dramatic (and what Marina Warner calls an "inside out," [63]) reading of Ovid's version of the Pygmalion text in the statue scene at the end.

An initial set of capabilities that constitute resilient adult learning is distilled from the readings of the Pygmalion texts in Chapters Two and Three. The themes that arise from these readings are then applied to Shakespeare's *The Winter's Tale* in Chapter Four. The capabilities are applied in an attempt to understand how resilience is performed in this text, which much less obviously describes adult learning in a literal way but in which resilience itself is fundamental to the work.

Chapter Five begins the section of the study that is concerned with biographical interviews with real adult learners. The interview with Joe looks at the way that love and tenacity operate in tandem with each other in the experience of the resilient adult learner. The interview with Jane in Chapter Six represents the struggle of the resilient adult learner to remain on the margins of an academic system that expects conformity in return for its rewards. Resilience as a function of resistance is examined most explicitly in that chapter. In Chapter Seven, the interview with Sarah concerns the way that the learner is possessed by the learning to the extent that resilience is an act of passivity rather than an action. The chapter concludes with a consideration of what has been added to the study by the inclusion of the biographical material.

Chapter Eight introduces autobiographical material into the study. It is a reading of an interview that I conducted with my mother. It performs a double function in the book. On the one hand, it is a fourth biographical interview about the experience of resilient adult learning in spite of bereavement, and, on the other hand, it provided me with insights into my own resilience as an adult learner. This chapter combines literary, biographical, and autobiographical writing. Chapter Eight is written in the tradition of other academic texts that attempt to cross the divide between the study of literary texts and all their mythological allusions, and the application of that study to the autobiography of the writer. Texts in this tradition include Andrea Ashworth's 1998 *Once In A House On Fire*, Mark Doty's 2008 *Dog Years*, and Jeanette Winterson's 1985 *Oranges are Not the Only Fruit*.

In Chapter Nine, all previous academic frameworks are discarded. The chapter is written without any of the "authority moves"[64] of academic writing. To take one of the themes that emerges at the end of the literary analysis section of the book, the academic clothing is removed. The writing in Chapter Nine is an attempt at "walking naked," as W. B. Yeats put it in 1916, in order to get as close as possible to the experience of the resilient adult learner. It is a performance of vulnerability. Although no sources are explicitly cited in that chapter, in practice the writing was informed by three texts: Yeats's 1916 poem "A Coat," David Bowie's 1969 song "Space Oddity," and Margaret Atwood's 1988 evocation of childhood experience in *Cat's Eye*. What is offered in Chapter Nine, therefore, is a piece of fictional writing that is inspired by autobiographical experiences. Chapter Ten attempts to offer an alternative to the usual conclusions and summary ending of an academic book. Some reflections on the research approach are included, and the main aim of the chapter is to open a conversation about how this methodology might be of use to other researchers who are enquiring into other kinds of resilience.

It is worth stating here that this is not a book *about* Cixous. This work owes a significant debt to the erudite and sensitive readings of her work by a number of scholars,[65] and it does not attempt to compete with them. It is also true to say that my access to her work has been via English translations of it. I have responded to her writing personally and in the present tense. It has had a transformative learning effect on me and has also played a deeply utilitarian role for me as a researcher. It is this usefulness of her work in an educational context that interests me, rather than its "truth" or success in theoretical terms. This is a book written by a practicing teacher and researcher in the field of education who has used Cixous's work directly to help solve a methodological problem—how to understand and write about aspects of learning that are not fully explained by either sociology or psychology. This is therefore both an educational reading of Cixous's texts and a Cixousian reading of resilient learning. I aim to offer both an alternative model of research from the one that is usually associated with social science and a practical demonstration of what a genuine engagement with the notion of *l'écriture féminine* looks like in the terms of a research text. The book takes the work of this most boundary-crossing of writers and applies it directly to a field of the social sciences in which it is rarely used.

An attempt to imagine, accommodate, and write the experience of the resilient adult learner is what follows. I begin with an exploration of Ovid's poetic rendition of the Pygmalion myth in the next chapter.

CHAPTER 2

Pygmalion

In one episode in Ovid's *Metamorphoses*,[1] the sculptor Pygmalion creates a statue of a woman in order to compensate himself for the deficiencies of the real women around him. He subsequently becomes infatuated with his creation to such an extent that, with the support of the goddess Venus, it comes to life as a real woman (subsequently called Galatea[2]). Shaw's theatrical 1916 transposition of the mythical scene to the social and political arena of Edwardian London, in which the story is read as an allegory for teaching and learning, provides the rationale for a wider application of the text to the investigation into transformational adult learning in general and resilient adult learning within that context in particular. This chapter aims to

1. establish the link suggested by Shaw between the Pygmalion story and its allegorical use as a text about teaching and learning;
2. consider the possibilities for reading the text playfully, as suggested by two poetic interpretations of the myth;
3. read Shaw's text as a way of beginning to understand the actions of the (semi-)resilient learner;
4. draw on three versions of the Pygmalion story to suggest what they might offer the study in terms of understanding the way that resilient adult learners perform and are transformed by learning in different fictional contexts.

Ovid's text *Metamorphoses*, in which the story of Pygmalion can be found, is concerned with transformation—literally changing forms.[3] There is, therefore, a direct link between the story and the sorts of transformational learning processes that the resilient adult learners in this study go through. This book is informed by the assumption that adult learning can be transformational. A body of work already exists that considers and celebrates the nature of transformational learning.[4] Although this study acknowledges the value of such work, it is deliberately seeking a new way of reading transformational learning. Here, the notion of transformation draws on the poetic and the mythical rather than the psychological and social. What is being advanced, therefore, might be described as a tentative application of an Ovidian understanding of transformational learning. The main purpose of this chapter is to explore what such a notion entails and to consider how it might be helpful for the emerging understanding of resilient adult learning. If changing shape is the essence of transformational learning, then the challenge for the resilient learner is how to be transformed in a way that allows for the retention of autonomy while benefiting from the liberating effects of the transformation. In other words, the learner needs to resist being molded and owned by the academic system on the one hand, or of failing or withdrawing from the academic process on the other.

On first sight, read allegorically, Ovid's Pygmalion looks like an anti-hero. He imagines and then creates a passive, silent learner who is wholly dependent on him. He is creator and god; the source of all knowledge and power. He is the opposite of the celebrated teacher-facilitator deemed necessary for transformational learning within a constructivist framework.[5] How might a story that is, as Victor Stoichita[6] has it, "the first great story about simulacra in Western culture" have application to a study that takes for granted the notion of the autonomous, liberated learner as the result of transformational learning? Surely the teacher whose ambitions for learning go no further than the desire to reproduce himself in the body of another is manifestly antithetical to a transformative model of teaching and learning. But, as Dennis Feeney[7] emphasizes in his introduction to *Metamorphoses*, in relation to the whole poem, the text is highly receptive to multiple interpretations: "Throughout the poem Ovid continues to exploit the imaginative and moral possibilities of hybridism." This deep emphasis on multiformity means that the text can sustain plural, imaginative readings well.

Links to the Overall Theoretical Framework: Cixous

Despite Feeney's enthusiastic assertion of the text's potential openness to heterogeneity and what Roland Barthes would call "writerliness,"[8] the

Pygmalion story is undoubtedly open to simple readings, either as a misogynistic fantasy or a satirical critique of one. John Stokes recognizes the possible application of the story to pessimistic portrayals of the relationships between men and women:

> Ovid's archetypal story of the sculptor and idealized image seems to reflect a sexual impasse and a situation of gender inequality, as well as the power and limitations of the male imagination.[9]

Here, though, the recognition of the story as an allegorical account of the relationships between men and women is only a means to an end. Throughout this book, Cixous's ideas are drawn upon as a theoretical framework within which to link and to make analogous two metaphorical places: the point at which writing becomes free of the demands of the super ego and of its political manifestations in hierarchical systems and oppression of the other (in Cixous's words, *l'écriture féminine*), and the pedagogical space in which transformational adult learning occurs, that is to say, learning that has a life of its own and that has an energetic capacity to transform both the learner and the teacher. My interest in gender is therefore notional and metaphorical throughout the study. At some points in the book, there is a necessary and undeniable place for a consideration of gender in real terms, but mostly I am attempting to more broadly apply what Cixous has to say about women to marginalized adult learners—the *miraculés*, some of whom are men—in order to open up an understanding of their resilience.

This is a good point at which, however, to own up to, if not resolve, the considerable problematics of appropriating female as metaphor in a text about learning. Similarly, even in the context of a deconstructive reading experiment, the fact that all these texts were written by men needs to at least be acknowledged. The females in these texts occupy a liminal state. They are, in Elisabeth Bronfen's phrase, "metaphorically effaced"[10] rather than literally dead. Ambivalent figures, they do not attract quite the same cultural associations as the dead female body (comprehensively analyzed by Bronfen). Rather, they invite a different kind of masculine attention—one that acknowledges risk and in which the resurrecting swagger of the self-appointed miracle worker is always accompanied by the terror of what he might awaken. The Pygmalion gesture always, then, involves both feminine and masculine responses—the masculine desire to be god the mother[11] coupled with the feminine mode in which "the transgressive delight in risk and expenditure, inevitably appears as a form of animate mobility, despite its embrace of fatal risk."[12]

In *Sorties*,[13] Cixous juxtaposes and then conflates Ovid's tale of "Pygmalion" with Charles Perrault's *Sleeping Beauty* to explore the consequences of the historical fantasy of female passivity and silence as the object of male desire.

> Beauties slept in their woods, waiting for princes to come and wake them up. In their beds, in their glass coffins, in their childhood forests, like dead women. Beautiful, but passive; hence desirable: all mystery emanates from them. It is men who like to play dolls. As we have known since Pygmalion. Their old dream: to be god the mother. The best mother, the second mother, the one who gives the second birth.[14]

In this reading, Pygmalion is guilty of immense hubris; his aim is to awaken life unnaturally, as Frankenstein does. He is guilty of the ultimate narcissism—the fantasy of giving birth to something that is both himself and a projection of his own desire. Cixous therefore uses the Pygmalion story as the starting point for her exploration of how women should resist the part allotted to them in culture—passivity, silence, and death, or what she calls "the shadow she is."[15] She takes for granted that the story is an allegorical depiction of men and women's relationships and specifically applies it to the problem of why women do not write. For Cixous, the ideal of the passive, somnambulant woman is the foundation of patriarchal oppression. She draws attention to the notion of metamorphosis in the Pygmalion/Sleeping Beauty story and uses it metaphorically to examine the romance narrative:

> And, whereas he takes (after a fashion) the risk and responsibility of being an agent, a bit of the public scene where transformations are played out, she represents indifference or resistance to this active tempo.

Agency in the story is always located in the male in her terms, and, in my metaphorical terms (after Shaw), this translates as the teacher. This sort of transformation is no transformation at all, but merely the changes wrought on a mutable substance by an all-powerful sculptor. The remedy for this sort of oppression lies, for Cixous, in the agency that is evoked through writing and through the reclamation of the female body through sexual *jouissance*. Resistance, and therefore resilience, is alive in claiming agency and in waking oneself up; Pygmalion becomes redundant. I am not concerned here with whether this is a fair and accurate description of a particular type of male desire.[16] Rather, I am interested in the application of the tableau to the teachers and learners in three texts that allude directly or indirectly to "the Pygmalion myth": Mamet's *Oleanna*, Russell's *Educating Rita*, and Shakespeare's *The Winter's Tale*.

In her later work *The School of Roots* Cixous returns to *Metamorphoses* to consider more widely Ovid's concern with transformation. She says of it,

> There are metamorphoses of all kinds and genders here. Writing runs them through the other world, which is the world of writing.[17]

She makes the direct link between metamorphosis and writing. Stoichita's analysis of the impact of Ovid's text on the history of Western art emphasizes the way that linguistic transformation generates all the other levels of transformation in the poem from ivory to flesh, from sacrifice to divine reward, and from art to actuality.

> Of all these levels, the most secret is that which concerns the magical power of words, for it is neither Pygmalion nor even the gods who bring about the *trans/formation*, but the text alone.[18]

L'écriture féminine is fundamentally concerned with the transformational power of writing itself. Writing—real writing that has broken through the barriers of logocentrism and has gone beyond what Cixous calls "the wall"[19]—is never the passive creation of a controlling and self-controlled writer. Galatea, in her textual, rather than sculptural, form, can never be for Cixous what she is for Ovid's Pygmalion. When it is real ("feminine"), writing becomes more powerful than the writer and can have nothing less than a transformational effect on the writer. It is a daimonic force and is accompanied by dread as well as release. In order for this to happen, the writer needs to accept a certain passivity and to surrender to being written through. Therein lies the paradoxical opportunity presented by *l'écriture féminine*; one must be sufficiently active to resist the mechanisms of "the wall," but, once past it, one must accept complete passivity to writing itself. A theoretical commitment to Cixous's notion of transformational writing runs throughout this book. It would be ironic, therefore, if such a position was articulated but not performed. An attempt is made throughout the book to apply these principles to the writing. This becomes increasingly explicit as the work develops. Such a commitment has meant that a good deal of resilience has been required in order for this transformation to be effected within a text that must at some level conform to academic expectations. Resilient learning in this research context, then, has depended on having the confidence to surrender to the writing, rather than trying to control it. This goes against the dominant and prevailing understanding of the purpose of academic writing in the social sciences (the conventional style of writing that is still expected by the majority of research journals), which is based on the opposite notion of "writing up" something that is already known by the writer. This book therefore performs its own version of Galatea's awakening. The challenge has been to provide enough safeguards for it/her to wake up and live, without running away, setting fire to the library, or murdering me.

I will now explore the narrative of Pygmalion as it appears in three different texts. I am particularly interested in what each text has to say about the nature of transformation. By understanding the transformation of a resilient learner by means of education in mythic terms, I hope to understand something more about the notion of resilience. I am reading the sculptor/Pygmalion as teacher and the sculpture/Galatea as learner in all three versions.

Reading 1: Ovid—Orpheus' Song: Pygmalion[20]

In Ovid's interpretation of the story, the initial emphasis is on Pygmalion's sense of his own superiority and on his condemnation of the women around him. He observes, judges, and is disgusted by them. The emphasis is on his avoidance of what he despises and his deliberate choice to remain chaste. There is no sense that Pygmalion himself is in need of or capable of transformation, but, instead, it is the female world outside that is grossly imperfect. Pride and arrogance are woven through the description of him—this sculptor has nothing to learn, because he is already perfectly competent. He carves "successfully" and his work is "amazingly skilful."[21] When he falls in love with the statue, it is not with the object as an independent artifact; rather he falls in love with it because it is "his own creation." As Bonnie Roos points out, this love is no more than narcissism—his love for himself "embraces his own imaginative, artistic powers of creation."[22] This self-satisfied protagonist desires the statue, and that desire is primarily to address a physical need brought on by his long endurance of his self-imposed abstinence. His assumption that his feelings for the statue are requited sustains him—"He kissed it and thought it was kissing him too"[23]—and when he talks to it, it is not for the want of a two-way conversation, but rather for the benefit of hearing the sound of his own voice in his studio, uncontradicted. What he says to the statue is, after all, platitudinous nonsense: "He'd whisper sweet nothings."[24] His expectations of his statue's taste and aspirations are fixed very low from the start.

For Pygmalion, there is delight to be had in dressing his statue and then taking its clothes off, giving support to Cixous's claim that it is men who like to play with dolls.

Reversing conventional feminist rhetoric, Roos argues that this act of dressing the statue is one of disempowerment, because the voyeuristic male artist is "effectively cloaking its latent sexuality, and thereby denying the small claim to power it might have been said to possess." When he finally takes the statue from its pedestal and lays it down, he puts it on purple cushions that contrast with its white limbs, which themselves echo the snow-white necks of the heifers about to be slaughtered in sacrifice to Venus. This animation has a sense of death about it. At the point that Pygmalion asks Venus for help, he is nervous and cannot allow himself to directly ask for the statue to be made living, and so he settles for wishing for a real woman with the likeness of this statue—"a woman resembling my ivory maiden."[25] In this sense, he succumbs to the truth that his creation is inherently shameful and an offence against either the gods or nature, and he reluctantly settles for imperfection. After Venus grants him his wish, the moment of awakening is a second act of sculpture, of transforming one shape into another through the medium of sex:

> He pressed his lips to hers once again; and then he
> started
> to stroke her breasts. The ivory gradually lost its
> hardness,
> softening, sinking, yielding beneath his sensitive fingers.[26]

The sculptor carves new life from inanimate material—the agency is entirely his own. He has the backing of supernatural support, but the central action of giving life is his.

There is some sense that his own brittleness begins to yield—unlike his certainty at the beginning of the story, he is now "Astonished, in doubtful joy,"[27] and this doubt allows him, at last, to take on a more expansive attitude. He opens his heart in gratitude to Venus, and the union is indeed blessed by the goddess. Despite this, the Pygmalion we are left with at the end of the poem is pretty much the same as the Pygmalion with which we started. The only transformation that has occurred has been the transformation of ivory into flesh.

As an allegory of transformative teaching and learning, the story is somewhat depressing. Teaching is reduced to nothing more than alchemy, in which the base material of the uneducated learner is turned into an educated model that is entirely reflective of the teacher's desire and power, rather than of her own ability. The teacher/sculptor is privileged over the learner, and the success is due almost entirely to his skill, with the support of the supernatural power. The teacher is complete, superior, and knowledgeable from the very beginning. The learner is passive, mute, and subservient, and her only emotional investment is coyness and adulation at the moment of coming to consciousness and the consequent recognition of her creator.

The teacher is god/parent/lover and artist—everything, in fact, to the learner—and she can only be grateful. Transformation is complete but one-sided. It is a bleak and restrictive reading of teaching and learning, but this simple version of Ovid's story does make the task of understanding resilience in the face of it rather easy. There is no room for the development of resilience when the teacher is so certain of his own rightness and the learner is so dependent and passive. Resilience can only occur—in the ways that Shaw and Russell tease out (explored below and in Chapter Three)—when the learner resists the part allotted to him or her in the Pygmalion myth. Resilient learners, therefore, are distinguished by their ability to stay critical and to succeed without succumbing to obedient cloning.

This is a very simplistic and one-dimensional reading of the story. I now want to problematize it in order to think more deeply about its application to the investigation of resilience. Ted Hughes's interpretation of *Metamorphoses* in his 1997 work, *Tales from Ovid*, provides a much more complex and open reading of the story, which opens up the possibility of a different understanding of the experience of the resilient adult learner in the process of transformational learning.

Reading 2: Ted Hughes's "Pygmalion"[28]

Whereas in Ovid's text only the statue/learner changes shape, in Hughes's reading of Pygmalion both the sculptor and the sculpture—the teacher and the learner—go through the metamorphic event. Transformational learning is both bilateral and beyond the control of either player. This means that resilience on the part of the learner is far more elusive and nebulous than in the first version. Resilient learning in the story of Pygmalion becomes, in the hands of Hughes, something far more indefatigable, dangerous, and numinous. He takes the story out of the realm of the ordinary and into a supernatural space.

Hughes's Pygmalion has none of the arrogant certainty of the previous literal translation of Ovid's misogynist. This Pygmalion's terror of his nasty neighbors, the Propoetides, spills over to a fear of females in general. Hughes employs the language of madness to describe the all-consuming effects of this phobia; his Pygmalion is incarcerated in a paradox in which he loves women but is terrified of them. This is a long way from the self-satisfied, sneering isolate of the first text. In this version, the sculptor himself is in desperate need of transformation, because he is locked up within himself as well as within his studio. Trapped, he is left lonely and living a kind of death-in-life existence. The phobia would be bad enough, were it not for the accompanying adoration of females. He sleepwalks through life, disconnected to what is real and instead obsessed with the ideal of feminine perfection. His agony, though, provides the wide-open space of potentiality. His yearning, tortured subconscious is where transformation can take place. His dreams are not so much about the ideal of feminine perfection:

> As a spectre, sick of unbeing,
> That had taken possession of his body
> To find herself a life.[29]

In a brilliant move, which subverts the Ovidian story but draws on the legends that preceded it,[30] Hughes makes the spirit of the woman preexist her existence, both in ivory and in flesh. Pygmalion's dreams are the space into which the daimonic force of a female can enter, make herself at home, and take possession of him. Hughes takes the Pygmalion story into a new dynamic realm in which the specter searches for, and then occupies, the body and mind of an artist who is ready for transformation. The female spirit seeks out her sculptor, just as the resilient learner finds his or her teacher in the other texts. She is restless, homeless, and desperate for transformation, sick and tired of the life-in-death that she is experiencing and which mirrors his death-in-life. Her existence has been not dissimilar to the fate Venus decides upon for the reviled Propoetides, whose story starts the poem—she is almost banished, almost dead. Her task has been to find an artist who is ready to receive her. Pygmalion's readiness is constituted in his fear and his unconscious. He is the passive recipient of another being—a spirit who enters his dreams and then his body as a way of creating a sortie for herself. The female is never passive in this version of the myth—she gets inside him long before he enters her.

By introducing the notion of the daimonic into the scene, Hughes opens up the story to the possibility of profound, otherworldly transformation. Pygmalion becomes possessed by a spirit in search of an actualized life. The learner is much more powerful than the teacher, and the teacher has no choice but to give himself over to her. Once inside him, this spirit guides him to work at levels he has not been able to achieve before. Unlike the first Pygmalion, who is utterly convinced of his own talent, this Pygmalion is doubtful and amazed at what he seems to be achieving with a force that seems to come from outside himself.

He doesn't know what has got into him. He carves in ivory,[31] a material known for its beauty and purity and also its inability to shatter and shard, which, as Marina Warner says "has a closer affinity with animate life than mineral substances, stone or metal."[32] It is the precious material of danger and risk, the material of intimate devotional items—and there is a profound sense of the sacred in his practice. This sort of sculpture/teaching is a process of revelation, discovery, and liberation, both for the sculptor and for what is inside the ivory. And so he falls in love with this creation that he can't quite give himself credit for, and love for him is a process of waking up. Roles are reversed; he is awake, in love, astounded by what is happening, and he now has a real life in the place of what was previously no more than an excuse for a life. He is astounded by the rawness of his love, and he provides an invisible garment of modesty for the statue—his rather than hers—to protect him from what is so immediate and so perfect.

Pygmalion tries to dress the statue in order to help him come to terms with its power. With the devotional practice of a worshiper, he adds garments and decoration to the statue, as if its perfection is too much and he needs, somehow, to cover it up. But his artifice doesn't protect him. So he divests the statue and is dazzled by the sight of its naked body.

He takes it from the pedestal and lays it down in an attempt to get some perspective. When the time comes for him to ask Venus to give him his woman, language fails him. The phobic has finally faced his fear; he asks for a real woman in his life, and Venus, goddess of love, is listening to the gaps in the language.

Love overcomes fear in the moment of transformation, and when he gets back to the studio, his beloved statue has come alive. The final metamorphic scene is not achieved by his will or his art, as in the first text, but love has been there first, defying and defeating fear and transforming what was trapped in immobility into a being that is no longer art,

> But alive
> With the elastic of life.[33]

This being is flexible and resilient, not brittle and breakable. The awakening of the statue mirrors Pygmalion's earlier awakening due to her possession of him. The moment of transformation is one of surrender for both of them. For the sculptor, this is a moment of surrender to the power of love.

As an allegorical account of teaching and learning, this is a far more hopeful way of understanding transformation and resilience than that offered by the direct translation of Ovid's text. Here the resilient learner is one who understands, before she is conscious of it, the need to find a life, to take shape, and to transform into being. She brings resilience, with urgency to the learning situation, and the teacher merely facilitates her awakening.

As Hughes says in his introduction to *Tales from Ovid*, the transformative process sits at the heart of all the stories in *Metamorphoses*.

> Above all, Ovid was interested in passion. Or rather, in what a passion feels like to the one possessed by it. Not just a driving passion either, but

human passion *in extremis*—passion where it combusts or levitates, or mutates into an experience of the supernatural.[34]

Hughes's text opens up the possibilities of regarding resilient learning in terms that go beyond the prosaic and the ordinary. What Hughes brings to the study is a way of trying to understand the inexplicable in spiritual and mythical terms. His reading of the Pygmalion story can offer an understanding of how the resilient learner navigates this transcendental experience of learning. As Hughes goes on to say,

> Ovid locates and captures the peculiar frisson of that (metamorphic) event, where the all-too-human victim stumbles out into the mythic arena and is transformed.[35]

In the first reading of the Pygmalion story, the task for the resilient learner is simple—resist and break free from Pygmalion once you have got what you need out of him. Ted Hughes's reading of the Pygmalion story adds much more complexity. It demonstrates how driven and forceful resilient learners are—as Michelangelo is reputed to have said about his sculptures, "I saw the angel in the marble and set it free."[36] They are desperate for transformation, so if one teacher won't provide it, they'll attract another sculptor/teacher to themselves who can.

There is something relentless, and certainly daimonic, about resilient learning in Hughes's poem. Because it can't be controlled, prevented, or ignored, it seeks out its facilitator one way or another. There is an implication, perhaps, that there is also something of a cruelty to resilience on this scale; it batters down what's in its way and it discards teachers who won't or can't facilitate the learner's waking up. Viewed in this way, the effects of transformational education are so powerful and liberating that the endeavor would be terrifying for any teacher who really thought about it before taking on a student—the teacher would be overwhelmed and paralyzed by the significance and responsibility. This is where the resilient learner needs to come in—to force the teacher into action—just as the spirit frees Pygmalion.

Reading 3: George Bernard Shaw's Pygmalion[37]

George Bernard Shaw used the Pygmalion myth to explore the dynamics of adult teaching and learning in his dramatic rewriting of the story in his 1916 play *Pygmalion*. The myth serves as a framework within which he examines a transformational learning event—in his case, the metamorphosis of a working-class woman into an upper-class woman by means of education regarding her voice, vocabulary, and manners. The tension in the play rests on the struggle between the teacher's intentions to carve a new human being out of inanimate material, as if she were ivory, and the very animate woman's resistance to that process despite her own desire for transformation. Shaw's interest is in the act of transformation itself, and the final line of his commentary opens up the possibility of further enquiry into the nature of the resilient learner:

> Galatea never does quite like Pygmalion: his relation to her is too god-like.[38]

As such, he identifies the tension in the resilient learner between the kind of obedience necessary to fulfill the teacher's ambitions, and thus to achieve validated success, and the need to keep his or her own sense of self strong enough to resist those ambitions.

The associations between teaching and authority are set up in the play from the beginning. In the first scene, the Pygmalion figure (Professor Henry Higgins) is mistaken for a policeman by the Galatea character (Eliza Doolittle) when she sees him taking notes on her speech on a rain-soaked night in Covent Garden. From this point on, there is a clear association between authority and teaching. The play moves on the struggle between the learner and the teacher to gain control of the learner's voice. The resilience of the adult learner pivots on how robustly she can resist the control of her Pygmalion while still remaining alive and intact. There is some mileage, then, in reading Eliza as a resilient version of the adult learner. She is not fully resilient, though, and this is an important point. In Shaw's commentary at the end of the play, he explains that Eliza does not fulfill her defiant ambition of becoming a teacher. Instead, she opens a flower shop. Even here, though, Shaw will not allow the reader to indulge in any sentimentality. Rather, he announces that the shop "did not pay for a long time." Notably, what lets her down is her use of the written word. As he says, although she had

> acquired a certain familiarity with the language of Milton from her struggles to qualify herself for winning Higgins' bet, (she) could not write out a bill without utterly disgracing the establishment. [39]

Despite her practiced performance with the spoken word, it cannot mask her lack of education, which is made manifest in her writing.

There is a sense of deanimation in Shaw's reading of Pygmalion. As Roos has it, "the lively Eliza is ... transformed by Higgins into an immobile figure who must conform to society's expectations in a way that is almost more confining than freeing."[40] However, she can at least be read as an adult learner who moves toward resilience. Even in her semi-evolved state, she is very important as a dramatic prototype of an adult learner and is therefore included in this study.

Ovidian allusions are plentiful throughout the work. Higgins says to his mother,

> But you have no idea how frightfully interesting it is to take a human being and change her into a quite different human being by creating a new speech for her. It's filling up the deepest gulf that separates class from class and soul from soul.[41]

The text takes place in the space between the two previous readings of the Ovidian story. Eliza is not the passive, grateful, and obedient Galatea of the first text, but nor is she the forceful, transformational energy of Hughes's Galatea. Although she undoubtedly has the spirit of the second Galatea, she can never be truly resilient when her teacher is so resistant to transformation. She does, however, display some of the characteristics of resilience in her behavior. These are set out below.

1. She is willing to wear different clothes.

An important image in both the Ovidian and the Hughes versions of Pygmalion is of the sculptor dressing and undressing his creation. Shaw provides some indication of the resilience that is to come with his characterization of Eliza before the teaching begins. In his stage directions for her lodgings, her walls are lined with pictures of ladies' dresses "all wildly beyond the poor flower girl's means."[42] This flower girl has aspirations and hope, it is clear. There is also a dedication to dressing up, to performance, and this, perhaps, will allow her to develop some resilience. It means that she understands that the clothes she is currently wearing are not the only ones available. In fact, the clothes become the site at which the struggle for autonomy is played out. It is important to Higgins that she loses all her previous clothes before he can start work on her. He says to Mrs. Pearce, for example,

> Take all her clothes off and burn them. Ring up Whiteley or somebody for some new ones. Wrap her up in brown paper til they come.[43]

This concern with divestment is consistent with the Ovidian myth, in which Galatea's naked body is key to the transformation that takes place.

Obviously Shaw plays on the sexual implications of nudity and dressing up, but the device works pedagogically just as effectively. Eliza angrily (but futilely) resists Higgins's desire to undress her and to dress her up ("I can buy my own clothes"[44]).

Clothes occupy the site of both resilience and unresilience, though. The clothes stand for the kind of authorial/authoritative control of the artist that exists in the original myth—the ultimate power of metamorphosis lies in the hands of the sculptor, not the sculpted. As Mrs. Higgins says to her son, "She is a triumph of your art, and of her dressmakers."[45]

After she quarrels with him and tells him she is leaving, Eliza makes explicit the link between clothing and autonomy, directly to Higgins:

> *Liza*: Do my clothes belong to me or Colonel Pickering?
> *Higgins*: What the devil use would they be to Pickering?
> *Liza*: He might want them for the next girl you pick up to experiment on.[46]

It is significant that Shaw's stage directions for the scene in which Eliza leaves indicate that the contents of her bedroom have been "increased by a big wardrobe and a sumptuous dressing table."[47] In presuming to provide Eliza with an "education," in fact what Higgins has given her (or loaned to her) is a collection of new clothes. She articulates her position in exile in terms of the unfinished transformation that Higgins has left her with. "Why did you take my independence from me? Why did I give it up? I'm a slave now, for all my fine clothes."[48]

2. She initiates the teaching and learning experience and she won't be turned away.

There is certainly resilience in the way that Eliza seeks out her teacher and then insists that he teach her. She refuses to become a humorous anecdote for Higgins and Pickering; she insists on writing herself into the story. So she astounds the Higgins household when she turns up at the door asking for lessons. Like Hughes's Galatea, she initiates contact with the teacher—she actively wants to be transformed. Her touching pride in her own hard-earned economic capital ("Did you tell him I come in a taxi?" and "I'm ready to pay"[49]) indicates a strong sense of agency and autonomy from the very beginning. She "protests extremely" at Higgins's cruelty, for example, when he tells Pickering that he is tempted to take her on because, "She's so deliciously low—so horribly dirty."[50] She is undoubtedly tough; this Galatea is not of the delicate and passive Ovidian model. Although she keenly protests that her sexuality is not for sale ("I'm a good girl, I am"), she is clearly well aware of the pitfalls of being a single woman on the streets of London, and she takes care of herself accordingly—"I know what the likes of you are, I do,"[51] she says to Higgins and to Mrs. Pearce, "You got no right to touch me."[52] So although she initiates the transformational learning episode, she does so with a fierce sense of agency and self-sufficiency.

3. She withstands exile.

The language of Shaw's Pygmalion is brutal. Mrs. Pearce, the housekeeper, describes Eliza as "very common indeed,"[53] and Higgins boasts that he will "make a duchess of this draggletailed guttersnipe."[54] Eliza reacts with a mixture of aggression and acceptance. She is proud and resilient, and her desire for transformation supersedes her hurt. This tension is in place from the beginning, and, as stated previously, the insight Shaw provides into her life through his description of her lodgings steers the reader/audience away from sentimental assumptions about her original happiness as a member of the unrespectable working classes. It is important to remember this in order to see her subsequent exile in its social and political context. It suggests that Eliza had already developed the ability to be an outsider, long before she encountered Higgins. The sense of being outside does increase as Higgins's experiment progresses, though. She is painfully aware that she exists in uneasy exile and that she is distanced from her class but not acceptable in the new arena. Her position as an exile terrifies her. "I am a child in your country. I have forgotten my own language, and can speak nothing but yours."[55] She has a sense of dignity that both provides her with resilience and is the cause of her struggle. Her life, however, is made much more difficult because of her refusal to become the barely animate material that Higgins would prefer to work with.

4. She is open to using language without boundaries.

Spoken language is clearly a significant theme in the play, and it serves as the locus of struggle for control and transformation. There is a sense that Eliza adopts an innocent approach to language and that this makes her easier to teach. She is not oppressed by spurious moral coyness about "good" or "bad" language—to her it is all the same and it is all accessible.

I tentatively suggest, therefore, that the resilient learner has an open capacity for using language in plural ways and going beyond boundaries from the outset—it is all possible, and so this allows her to be open to different kinds of language. This capacity for learning is noted by the teacher as quintessential to her ability to learn. Higgins says,

She has a quick ear, and she has been easier to teach than my middle-class pupils because she's had to learn a complete new language.[56]

This "complete new language" allows her to take on words and cast them off in the way that others put on clothes. She then teaches the new language to others—like the dim but upper-class Eynesford-Hills, to comic effect.

5. She identifies other teachers.

Eliza is aware of Higgins's limitations, which he, ironically, celebrates—"I can't change my nature; and I don't intend to change my manners."[57] She knows that this is not a generous act of transformative teaching. Rather, it is the condescension of a bored and privileged professor as part of his social scientific experiment, and she knows this. Eliza demonstrates that, faced with the shortcomings of an inadequate teacher, the resilient learner seeks out others who can help her learn. She is not tied to pedagogical monogamy, because she understands the shortcomings of her official teacher, and she finds others. She credits the kindly Pickering rather than Higgins with her real education.

Unfortunately, though, Shaw can't make Eliza fully resilient. She remains an angry Galatea in the Ovidian sense, and she can never be transformed in the Hughes sense. She doesn't become a teacher after all. In Shaw's depressing notes that end the play, he states that she has been "disclassed" by her education.[58] He will not allow her to become a *miraculé*. He refuses to give his audience the happy resolution that they yearn for—his instincts are reformist, after all. As he says,

> The rest of the story need not be shewn in action, and indeed, would hardly need telling if our imaginations were not so enfeebled by their lazy dependence on the ready-mades and reach-me-downs of the ragshop in which Romance keeps it stock of "happy endings" to misfit all stories.[59]

As it is for Bourdieu, the existence of the *miraculé* is not a cause for celebration but a seductive deception about the extent and nature of inequality and oppression for Shaw. Bourdieu and Shaw understand our yearning for exceptions, but they will not give in to it or sentimentalize it. This is not the joyful imagining of the new type of Galatea that is later realized by Willy Russell. Rather, it is a depiction of a semi-resilient learner. An important finding from the analysis of this one play is that although the initial drive for transformational learning may be appropriated and instigated by a learner who yearns for transformation, that learner requires a teacher (in some form or other) in order to perform resilience in the fullest sense. A simple (but important) early finding, therefore, is that resilience does not reside *in* the learner. Instead, it exists in the spaces between her and her teacher and between both of them and the social and economic world that they inhabit. Eliza brings all the agency and burning desire for transformation that Hughes's Galatea does, but because she does not find a Pygmalion who is similarly yearning for profound transformation, she cannot achieve it herself and submits instead to unilateral metamorphosis. Resilience can therefore only be partial—because she cannot go through the full transformative event, she does not have the opportunity to develop and exercise full resilience in the face of it. As a semi-liberated, semi-resilient learner, Eliza opens the door for the analysis of her literary descendents in terms of their resilience. An analysis of two of those "descendents"[60]—Rita and Carol—follows in the next chapter.

CHAPTER 3

Educating Rita and *Oleanna*

Educating Rita[1] provides a kind of archetype of the resilient learner from which the rest of this book radiates. David Mamet's 1993 play *Oleanna*[2] features in this chapter because it represents the opposite—it offers a deferred reading of resilience through a negative image. *Oleanna* is an apophatic reading of resilience. Given the theoretical commitment of the study to deconstruction, it is necessary to examine both in order to understand how resilience is performed. This initial analysis is deliberately intended to be fairly straightforward. The point here is not to effect a sophisticated reading of the texts for sake of literary criticism. Rather, it is to explore the texts to see what they yield in terms of developing an early framework regarding the performance of resilience that might then be applied to the final literary text examined—Shakespeare's *The Winter's Tale*.

Oleanna explores the menace caused when a young adult student (Carol) falsely accuses her teacher (John) of sexual harassment and attempted rape. The play explores the nature of the sexual harassment discourse in particular and political correctness in general. Critics have tended to concentrate on what Mamet's work has to say about gender,[3] a more specific focus on sexual harassment in the academy,[4] wider notions of a cultural crisis,[5] and language and reading.[6] When critics have examined the play in terms of its university context, the struggle over truth and knowledge is regarded as central to Mamet's concern. Michael Billington, for example, in his review of the 2004 production at the Garrick Theatre in London, suggested that the play is "really a lament for the destruction of mutual trust and personal interaction that makes academic freedom possible." Some writers have considered the play directly in its pedagogical context. Richard Raymond, for example, considers Mamet's work in its "Platonic context" by juxtaposing the play with Plato's (c. 370/2005) *Phaedrus* in order to consider how both texts can support students' understandings of the workings of rhetoric.[7] In an exciting account of how the teaching of *Oleanna* transformed the pedagogical scene in an undergraduate English class, Stanton Garner argues that although the play harnesses "outrage to a gender politics that it does little to question," its *meta-pedagogical* impact on the classroom is to draw direct attention to the power exchanges between teachers and learners in a way that few other texts can do so directly.[8] He argues that, as opposed to the arenas of theater criticism or literary analysis, the classroom itself offers possibilities for open readings of the play in which its transformative potential can really be understood. As he says, "*Oleanna* in the classroom becomes a powerfully reflexive text, framing the student-teacher relationship and the larger institutional structures within which this relationship is articulated."[9] This final reading opens the way to an exploration of the text as one about the workings of resilient learning and of its opposite.

Academic freedom involves more than the simplistic assertion of the right to articulate unpopular points of view. It should also involve the entitlement to practice the various complex processes that are involved in learning and teaching without fear of sanction, prohibition, or humiliation. Learning intrinsically involves the shifting balance between the known and the unknown for both teachers and learners. The movement between autonomy and direction, and protection and exposure, is necessary if progress is to be made. Neither teaching nor learning is a simple process. The Western belief in separateness pretends that learning is somehow wholly internal, particular to the learner and disconnected from others, but, as Ben Knights argues, "human consciousness, human imagination, the ability to comprehend problems and invent solutions, to play and create, is inherently social."[10] Learning, therefore, cannot be regarded as the simple acquisition of skills and knowledge, and resilient learning cannot be understood as the uncomplicated demonstration of competences despite set-backs. Both teacher and learner need to be able to make mistakes in order to establish an effective pedagogic relationship with one another. *Oleanna* is an account of what happens when the pedagogic relationship collapses. Although it is framed in a specific ideological and historical context, it is a rich exploration of the experience of a weak, unsuccessful learner and a limited teacher. The specific sexual harassment discourse becomes not only a framework for Carol's failure; it also consolidates and nurtures her sense of isolation and misfortune. Her learning identity becomes that of an ideological victim of an oppressive system, rather than a pedagogic failure.

Willy Russell's earlier (1981/2000) play, *Educating Rita*, examines adult learning from the point of view of a successful, resilient learner. It offers much to the researcher who is interested in charting and illustrating the way a learning trajectory works (as Ray Land has done in relation to her pathway through various threshold concepts[11]), but it is also a beautiful and profound piece of writing. Rita is able to negotiate her way through the unknown rather better than her teacher, Frank, can, and the play provides suggestions about why this happens. I will read the plays alongside each other to see if any common themes emerge that might lead to a greater understanding of how resilience works.

Learner as Offspring

Both plays are dialogic. They use a conversation in the context of a tutorial as the site of learning. In both plays, the conversations are about texts. In *Educating Rita*, a range of literary texts are discussed, as are Rita's written responses to them. In *Oleanna*, only two texts are explicitly discussed—John's book and Carol's essay about it. A clear hierarchy—with the teacher in full control and in possession of the knowledge and the learner struggling to access it—is set up.

Ironically, as teachers, both Frank and John are very slow learners. Frank suffers because he cannot easily move from the omnipotent position that he has created for himself, and John is frustratingly dense in his inability to learn from the increasingly grave consequences of the mistakes he continues to make (inviting Carol to be alone with him and repeatedly interrupting their conversation by answering the telephone). Despite this, they both have a clear understanding of the way in which their professional identity as teacher is central to their understanding of themselves as people. John says,

> I want to tell you something. I'm a teacher. I am a teacher. Eh? It's my *name* on the door, and *I* teach the class, that's what I do.[12]

As such, his name (presumably his title is professor) does not just stand for an aspect of himself—it is his whole identity. The destruction of his professional status that Carol threatens, therefore, would also be the annihilation of his entire self, as he sees it. Ironically, for all of his liberal guilt about what he sees as the unequal power distribution between teacher and student, he is unable to apply it to his own behavior. In Act 1, he talks far more than Carol, constantly interrupting her and answering his telephone when she is speaking. As Garner puts it, "That John can and does interrupt Carol as frequently as he does underscores the politics of conversation and the unequal privileging of voice."[13] Thus the links between the domination of the conversational space and teaching are made very clear. Frank has a much clearer understanding of his limitations as a teacher than John does, right from the start, "I'm actually an appalling teacher."[14]

He sees the role of the teacher as a sort of intellectual alchemist:

> But don't you see, if you're going to write this sort of thing *(he indicates a pile of essays)*—to pass examinations, you're going to have to suppress, even abandon your uniqueness. I'm going to have to change you.[15]

But change itself is threatening, and both Frank and John remain closeted in their studies, with Frank insistent that the window should not be opened and resisting Rita's suggestions that they go outside, and John delegating to his wife all the messy business of house buying.

The notion of alchemy and creation through teaching pervades both plays. Frank makes the explicit link with Mary Shelley's *Frankenstein*, and he identifies himself with another gothic antihero ("Like Dracula, I have an aversion to sunlight"),[16] but the allusion is just as relevant to John. His interests are in the limitations of higher education and its disingenuous approach to the young, and his central argument seems to be that graduates are failed by the system because they leave without the ability to critique or to challenge. When Carol does develop her voice, and uses it to trap him and destroy his career, he attacks her, just as Victor Frankenstein kills his monster. The monster calls Frankenstein "creator," and the problematic aspects of Frank's work with Rita, as well as the deeply dysfunctional relationship between John and Carol, position the teacher in a parental relationship with the student. Despite his early protestation to Carol that "I'm not your father."[17] John goes on to start "talking to you as I'd talk to my son."[18] When Frank is angry with Rita, she identifies the same tendency in his behavior:

> What's up, Frank, don't y' like me now that the little girl's grown up, now that y' can no longer bounce me on daddy's knee an' watch me stare back in wide-eyed wonder at everything he has to say?[19]

So the parent/child model for learning in all three texts (*Educating Rita*, *Oleanna*, and *Frankenstein*) is portrayed as dangerous and doomed. Paradoxically, Victor Frankenstein gives an account of his own learning with his teacher—M. Waldman—which is serene and brilliant. M. Waldman referred to Frankenstein as his "disciple," and this seems to present a healthier antidote to the parent/child analogy that Frank and John indulge in. The picture of the learner as disciple is set up by Shelley as perfect—a kind of pedagogical heaven:

> In M. Waldman I found a true friend. His gentleness was never tinged by dogmatism; his instructions were given with an air of frankness and good nature that banished the idea of pedantry.[20]

Here we have a notion of equality and expansiveness that is not present between the protagonists in *Oleanna* at all and is present in *Educating Rita* only the very end. The absence of both dogma and pedantry suggests a freer way of being for both learner and teacher. But Victor chose not to replicate this state of pedagogical bliss with another. Instead, Pygmalion-like, he created the monster—dependent on him and yet repulsive because of that dependence. The contrast between Victor's experience of learning and the monster's experience of learning is evident when the monster explains that he learned from texts, reading each as "true history" and reacting especially strongly to *Paradise Lost*:

> Many times I considered Satan as the fitter emblem of my condition; for often, like him, when I viewed the bliss of my protectors, the bitter gall of envy rose within me.[21]

So learner as progeny, spawned from the hubris of the teacher, is portrayed by Shelley as immoral and demoniacal. Despite Frank's explicit reference to Mary Shelley, it is Carol for whom the allusion is more appropriate. Like the monster, she is uncontrolled and hurt, and when the teacher/creator cannot give her the protection that she seeks, she turns the tables on him, her speech eerily echoing the monster's:

> *Carol*: You asked me in here to explain something to me, as a child, that I did not understand. But I came to explain something to you. You Are Not God. You ask me why I came? I came here to instruct you.[22]

This sounds very much like what the monster says when he confronts Frankenstein:

> Slave, I before reasoned with you, but you have proved yourself unworthy of my condescension. Remember that I have power; you believe yourself miserable but I can make you so wretched that the light of the day will be hateful to you. You are my creator, but I am your master;—obey![23]

Both the monster and Carol claim the teacher's territory and power. The knowledge that they need to impart is an awful truth, and malevolence drives their teaching of it.

It is the teacher's worst nightmare—the creation that he has worked for has used what he has given it to turn on him and to destroy him.

Learner as Beloved

If the notions of parenting, creation and change are all hazardous in each play, are other, more optimistic, frameworks for the learner and teacher interchange in the texts? The links between longing and learning are embedded in fictional representations of the adult learner. Ardiss Mackie, reviewing Jo Kereos's study[24] of the links, points out that, in the literary and cinematic representations of teaching, "Eros may be sublimated or acted out in the pedagogic relationship, but regardless, it is central to narrative accounts of teaching."[25] It is certainly a feature of both texts examined here. The action in both texts takes place in the teacher's study between a young, female student and an older, more powerful male teacher. In both plays, the teacher's partner is silent and invisible—at the other end of the telephone. She is concerned with domestic realities and middle-class dilemmas, such as cooking and dinner parties (Julia in *Educating Rita*), and moving up the property ladder (Grace in *Oleanna*). Both Russell and Mamet play with the idea of desire within the romantic discourse, and both, like Shaw before them, subvert it. In each text, the ingredients for a romantic drama are set up—the younger woman, the older man with status, and the wife who is evident by her absence (but whom the man represents as tethering him with mundane domestic details which are an interruption to the really important relationship that is happening in the room—the conversation between him and the younger woman).

Romance works at a much more interesting level in the texts as well, though, because learning itself is portrayed as a type of romance. In *Educating Rita,* Frank actually makes the link between learning and romance somewhat wistfully:

> *Rita*: If y' were mine an' y' stopped out for days y' wouldn't get back in.
> *Frank*: Ah, but Rita, if I was yours would I stop out for days?[26]

On the one hand, Frank, for all his apparent understanding of narrative and characterization in the literary domain, seems to position himself naïvely and willingly within a highly romantic discourse in his relationship with Rita in a way that she, right from the beginning, resists, because of her more sophisticated understanding and experience of the world.

> *Frank*: Rita—why didn't you walk in here twenty years ago?
> *Rita*: Cos I don't think they would have accepted me at the age of six.
> *Frank*: You know what I mean.
> *Rita*: I know. But it's not twenty years ago, Frank. It's now. You're there an' I'm here.[27]

As such, he appears to literally fall in love with her—missing her and becoming jealous and possessive when she becomes more autonomous. But Frank's allusion is to a much more interesting connection between romance and learning that works on a second level. By suggesting that learning might be an affair of sorts, he is presenting us with a metaphor for what happens in transmission learning, in which the teacher regards the learner as an empty vessel to be "filled up" with knowledge—the model of teaching that both Frank and John adopt. The teacher becomes entranced with his own account of knowledge articulated by someone else. Despite his intellectual sophistication, Frank is callow and sentimental in his approach to both processes—falling in love and teaching—and this is why he suffers so much in the second half of the play.

The romantic discourse in *Oleanna* is surrendered much earlier on. Some interpretations have portrayed the idea of attraction more explicitly than others. Michael Billington[28] makes the point that what marked Pinter's 1993 production as different from subsequent productions was that it "restored the moral equilibrium by implying that the professor was physically attracted to his student: in his heart at least he was culpable." Frank's attraction to Rita is to her as a learner as well as to her as a woman. Given the previous analogy—between falling in love and teaching—it would seem plausible that the teacher would be attracted to a successful learner rather than an unsuccessful one. The attraction to an unsuccessful learner as a learner (rather than as a woman) seems to be contradictory, and this is borne out at the end of *Oleanna*, when John articulates his repulsion to Carol: "I wouldn't touch you with a ten- foot pole."[29]

Learner as Victim

The action in *Oleanna* centers on the build-up to Carol's false allegation of attempted rape. It is a frightening play, because the malicious accusation seems to come out of nowhere. It is possible to trace the inevitable descent into accusation and litigation in stages in the action, though. The first crucial moment is when John says,

> I don't know how to do it, other than to be *personal*,...but...

and Carol replies,

> Why would you want to be personal with me?[30]

Carol's narrow, rigid understanding of language function, featuring, as it does, this early in the play, suggests that she lacks empathy and is imprisoned by language. She does not connect. She is persecuted by language, while at the same time she uses it as an instrument of torture. She is terrified because she does not understand the words John uses, and she constantly works to whittle down his vocabulary in the same way that, later in the play, she wants to remove books from the library. Language for her is a rigid system with fixed meanings and moral codes, with linked punitive consequences for misuse—and not a human function with indeterminate meanings. Although John is the victim of her fundamentalist view of social language, he uses the same tricks over the house—resorting to calling in the lawyers when the conversation breaks down.

Carol is constantly interrupted by John, who keeps turning the conversation about her learning around to himself. He doesn't listen properly:

> *John*: Well I know what you're talking about.
> *Carol*: No. You don't.
> *John*: I think I do (*pause*).
> *Carol*: How can you?
> *John*: I'll tell you a story about myself.[31]

Carol accuses John of sexual harassment after he has put his hands on her shoulders, which she interprets as a sexual act, despite his protestations that it was devoid of sexual content. As a failing student, she has been unable to interpret his suggestion that if she retakes the course under his supervision that she will get an A as anything other than a sexual advance. She simply has too pessimistic a view of herself as a learner to envisage her work as ever meriting a grade of A. Through her lens of sexual harassment from then on, all references to herself and her teacher as people outside of those roles become suspect and dangerous. Garner notes the keenness of his own students to dissociate themselves from Carol, and he interprets this in sexual political terms, arguing that Carol embodies a type of feminist assertiveness and, as such, she is rejected: "Angered by the cold-bloodedness of her power play, many of my female students were clearly eager to dissociate from her."[32] I think that there is another dimension to his students' reactions to Carol, though. I think she has an effect on learners—most of whom surely hold some hope about their success and resilience—because she so starkly represents the opposite of resilience. No learner interested in success would want to associate themselves with such a character, and this transcends considerations of sexual politics.

Rita, by way of contrast, flirts with Frank from the beginning of the play. She is both completely unthreatened by his sexual references to her and in control of the sexual banter which, in fact, she introduces:

> *Rita*: That's a nice picture, isn't it?
> *Frank*: Erm—yes, I suppose it is—nice…

Rita: It's very erotic.

Frank: Actually I don't think I've looked at it for about ten years, but yes, I suppose it is.

Rita: There's no suppose about it. Look at those tits.[33]

Rita is free from middle-class constraints, and she is completely unthreatened by Frank, who makes it clear that he finds her attractive.

In both plays, the characters argue about what texts mean. Frank teaches Rita to avoid sentiment in her responses to the literary works and to consult the critics in order to make meaning of the canon. John tries to explain his own authorial intentions regarding his book and mocks Carol's attempts to write about it, quoting from her essay:

> "I think that the ideas contained in this work express the author's feelings in a way that he intended, based on his results." What can that mean? Do you see? What…[34]

The struggle for meaning is being contested by the receiver (or reader) of the action. But unlike Roland Barthes's utopian fantasy that meaning, once released from the author, liberates the reader into "a state of loss"[35] that is also blissful—the pleasure of surrendering oneself to limitless possible meanings, none of which is more valid than the others—there is still a dogmatic insistence that one meaning must be true and real. Given this, there is no space for either Carol or John to admit to the presence of misunderstanding.

Rita's resolve that hurt can be protective and educative means that she understands that her progress is linked to her mistakes. When Frank tells Rita that her essay will not pass, she says, movingly,

> If I do somethin' that's crap, I don't want pity, you just tell me, that's crap.[36]

By way of contrast, Carol's language in Act 1 is faltering and partial, and she tries to compensate for her lack of voice by adopting a passive role and privileging the written word—she takes notes. From her entrenched position of ignorance, conversational language cannot serve her in the way that is envisaged in constructivist models of learning. She is too frightened of language itself to use it as a scaffold: "I'm doing what I'm told. I bought your book. I read your…"[37]

Unlike Rita, who is able to play around with the teacher-pupil relationship, Carol clings to the passive, subordinate role of empty vessel. She points to language as her central problem: "I don't…lots of the language…"[38] Language is both the cause of and the site for the struggle between her and

John. His early comment is heavily ironic: "Let's take the mysticism out of it. Shall we? Carol?"[39] As a form of experience that is beyond language, mysticism would have served them both rather better than conversation.

For Carol, being at the university is not about learning but about attainment. Unlike Rita, who desperately wants to know, Carol just wants to graduate: "I *have* to pass this course,"[40] she says. She consistently demonstrates a disconcerting lack of ability to connect. She describes how she walks around with the one thought in her head—that she is stupid and unable to connect with others or to use them for support: "Nobody *tells* me anything. And I sit there…in the *corner*. In the *back*."[41]

Her positioning of herself as separate from the others suggests a person without the ability to relate. Even at the end of the play, when she is receiving support from the group, they are anonymous and sinister, certainly not her friends. She cannot understand the link between formal and informal learning on any level, and she seems to lack the ability to synthesize different events or points of view. When John is espousing his view of the shortcomings of higher education, she does not engage but simply replies that she wants to know about her grade, without engaging with his ideas at all. She has no understanding at all of the emotional domain of learning. When John asks if she is so hurt by what he is supposed to have done, she replies, "What I "feel" is irrelevant."[42] Unlike Rita, Carol has no desire to learn difficult things. The move to censorship at the end of the play is significant. By banning John's book, she will literally be removing the knowledge that is currently out of reach, thus relegating herself to the lower state of understanding, permanently. There are clear differences, then, in the two characters' approaches to learning.

Application of the Findings to the Emergent Understanding of Resilient Adult Learning

These readings, combined with the readings of the three versions of the Pygmalion myth in the previous chapter, suggest that five capabilities are performed by resilient learners. These capabilities are:

1. they engage in open readings, resisting closed meanings, and they take a playful approach to language;
2. they recognize, withstand, and negotiate the tension between inclusion and exclusion;
3. they show a willingness to divest themselves of their "clothing" (inherited ways of thinking and artificial concepts) and to try on new clothes;

4. they resist passivity by dealing actively with their teachers (for example, by finding alternative, unofficial teachers or by subverting the Pygmalion/Galatea relationship);

5. they can be read as *miraculés*; for example, they are open to a kind of resurrection.

Each is examined in turn with particular reference to Rita. Symbolic parallels are drawn between her and Hughes's Galatea (henceforth referred to simply as Galatea) and, when she shows particular resilience, to Eliza.

1. *They engage in open readings, resisting closed meanings, and they take a playful approach to language.*

The ability to read openly and to use language playfully emerges as a significant factor in the way that resilient adult learning is performed. Strong commitment to multiple readings seems to emerge as a key characteristic. The understanding that meanings may be multiple and resistance to fixed answers is central to Rita's way of dealing with the world from the outset. In fact, *Educating Rita* moves on the development of Rita as a reader. Clearly, Frank's struggle is how to maintain her ability to perform open readings while providing her with the tools that will allow her to carry out readings that are validated within the academic field.

Rita's ability to read in open and multiple ways is evident from the first scene, in relation to texts. In the exchange cited previously, she refuses to accept the apparent subject matter of a classical painting as the only way of reading it. By insisting that it works on multiple levels ("in those days they had to pretend it wasn't erotic so they made it religious, didn't they?"[43]), she refuses to accept the official or authoritative meaning as the only one. From the outset, this Galatea is as much teacher as learner. She refuses to accept Frank's vague distance from art as an appropriate reading, resisting his collusion with the diluted distance between reader and text that is insisted on by the academic world that Frank represents. Of course, her ability to read openly is the source of Frank's entrancement, as well as all his turmoil, with the actual process of educating Rita. Her passionate responses to E. M. Forster and Shakespeare astound him, but he is aware that he must operate within a system that validates only closed readings of officially circumscribed texts. His insistence that "you cannot interpret E. M. Forster from a Marxist viewpoint"[44] articulates a position that he wants to reject but cannot, because it sustains his own professional existence. Rita's insistence on reading openly and rejecting boundaries extends beyond texts and into the social space. Early on, she contests the precious academic definition of a word like *assonance* with as much vigor and confidence as she does the assumption made by her peer group that she ought to have a baby.

Rita's use of language is similarly unboundaried and open. Swearing performs a pedagogical as well as a dramatic (and comedic) function in both *Educating Rita* and Shaw's *Pygmalion*. On the one level, swearing is obviously emblematic of both Rita and Eliza's transgressive function in each play. It forces both Frank and Higgins to question their own assumptions about language, and it provides them with an outlet for their own dissatisfaction with restricted, middle- or upper-middle-class social mores. On another level, swearing draws attention to the rigid boundaries within which language is performed. Rita draws direct attention to the way that class and language interact, suggesting that education brings with it some sort of liberation from the oppressive effects of the rules governing appropriate and inappropriate language: "the educated classes know it's only words, don't they? It's only the masses who don't understand."[45] For both Frank and Higgins, the women's swearing has a liberating effect on their own language. It is worth noting here that this capability—the ability to engage in open readings and to resist closed meanings—is the single biggest contrast with the least resilient learner in the study, Carol. Her concern with dividing language into what is correct and what is incorrect, and with insisting on a single closed reading of an event (her teacher touching her) is what turns the play into the appalling tragedy it becomes. Rita and (to a lesser extent) Eliza use sexual language to empower themselves. For Carol, such language is corrupting, dangerous, and evil.

2. *They recognize, withstand, and negotiate the tension between inclusion and exclusion.*

The notion of exile emerges strongly as a theme that has an impact on resilience. Rita's darkest struggles are involved in her attempts to negotiate the empty space between her homeland (working-class hairdresser) and the new country to which she still has to gain access (middle-class academia). Frank's awareness of the agony of the struggle only heightens his misgivings about the teaching project. For Rita, the transition is resolved by the end of the play, but this is not the case for Eliza. In Shaw's *Pygmalion*, the struggle to survive exile is dark and isolating, and the outcome is far more depressing; Eliza remains in uneasy exile at the end of the play. Shaw's commentary is deliberately critical, and his instincts are reformist. Much of Shaw's political interest in the text is in what he calls the "disclassment" of Eliza. She survives it (in the sense that she is still alive at the end of the text), but she is dreadfully disempowered by the experience. Shaw's emphasis is much less on Eliza's personal ability to withstand exclusion and much more on the unfairness of the social structures and on what they do and do not allow.

A simple reading of both plays would suggest that the teaching and learning processes push Rita and Eliza into exile and that their resilience can be judged on their ability to withstand it. Reference to Hughes's Galatea may be helpful here. Galatea is "sick of unbeing," which suggests that what is protective for the adult learner in the state of exile is the passion for escape. Galatea has come from the position of exile in the first place—what she wants is to be accepted in the world of the living. She can no longer stand the exile from both the dead and the living world. Perhaps it could also be said, therefore, that Rita and Eliza are already exiles when they arrive at the doors of their teachers. They are also already "sick of unbeing" in their respective roles as hairdresser and flower girl. Rita says, for example, "I've been realizin' for ages that I was, y'know, slightly out of step."[46] They do not want complete acceptance into a new class as much as they want some sort of self-actualization. Rita romanticizes the middle and upper classes, but she is very clear about her motivation for embarking on education: she isn't ready to have a baby because she wants to discover herself first.[47] Although Eliza's motivation is more closely linked to social mobility ("I want to be a lady in a flower shop stead of selling at the corner of Tottenham Court Road. But they won't take me unless I can talk more genteel"),[48] it would also be wrong to suggest that she is happy in her initial situation. Shaw's stage directions for the first scene, in which we see Eliza make it very plain that we must not buy into a sentimental portrayal of the realities of working-class life, state plainly that "*She is not at all a romantic figure.*"[49] Shaw's angry reformist position is evident in his more detailed description of Eliza's lodgings in the stage directions—his instructions for details are typically symbolic, and images of a human being trapped in grinding poverty is clear; "*A bird cage hangs in the window; but its tenant died long ago: it remains as a memorial only. These are the only visible luxuries: the rest is the irreducible minimum of poverty's needs.*"[50]

Their rejection of where they have come from, therefore, represents a protective facility—it allows them to rebel and stand out and reject the norms of the peer group they are leaving. They have always been misfits. This would also suggest that they are able to take a similarly critical approach to the new land in which they enter. Although Rita is at first overwhelmed by the middle-class norms, she is also able to somehow understand exile as transition; but permanent exile seems to be the only long-term identity available to Eliza. Therein lies her inability to achieve full resilience—society and her teacher will not allow it. Rita becomes resilient because, ultimately, Frank allows her to—however reluctant he is to do this. Frank is closer to Hughes's *Pygmalion* than is Higgins. Higgins is utterly convinced of his own superiority at the beginning of the play and remains so at the end. Here the link between resilience and transformation is at its most obvious. As previously stated, Higgins freely admits that "I can't change my nature; and I don't intend to change my manners."[51] Therein lies the central inequality between teacher and learner, and it is what ultimately prevents Eliza from achieving full resilience. Like Ovid's "Pygmalion",[52] the metamorphosis is one-sided and hierarchical—the teacher never submits to transformation in the way that he expects the learner to.

Rita's ability to withstand her exile in the wilderness between the class she has left and the one she has yet to gain entry to is certainly painful, but she is supported, to a certain extent, by the institution and its context. The Open University is the framework for Rita's learning, and it is celebrated by Russell. The summer school is portrayed as a liberating and empowering experience, and it plays an important function in supporting Rita's social exile. By providing her with a community of learners, the institution protects Rita from the utter isolation and anguish faced by Eliza. The ability to survive exile therefore seems to be a capability of the resilient adult learner, but it should be noted that this should not be read as some "internal" ability or personality trait but a result of the interaction between learner, teacher, "institution," and the wider social context within which the learning takes place.

3. *They show a willingness to divest themselves of their "clothing" (inherited ways of thinking and artificial concepts) and to try on new clothes.*

As discussed in the previous sections, the dressing and undressing of the Galatea character is central to the symbolism in both poetic versions of the story examined. As Hughes tells it, when Pygmalion dresses the statue and adorns her with jewelry, it sends him over the edge of reason.

The spirit's first clothing is the body that she creates for herself, through the hands of Pygmalion. Once she gets into that body (and becomes a somebody), she can withstand taking on additional clothes. The garments provide Pygmalion with a new lens through which to view his beloved, and the result is almost too much for his mind to take in. When he takes the clothes off again, he is dazzled by the new sight of her naked body—he sees her anew. There is a cycle set up, then, which has as much to say about the way that the learner is read as it does about her own ability to withstand nudity as well as clothing.

The theme of clothing runs through both *Educating Rita* and Shaw's *Pygmalion*. Clothing metaphors are in strong evidence throughout *Educating Rita*. She uses the image directly to illustrate superficial identity change:

one day, y' own up to yourself an' y' say, is this it? Is this the absolute maximum I can expect from this livin' lark? An' that's the big moment that one, that's the point when y' have to decide whether it's gonna be another change of dress or a change in yourself.[53]

Frank returns to this theme later in the same scene when he attempts to instill discipline into Rita's approach to her work: "Then go back to what you do like and stop wasting my time. You go out and buy yourself a new dress and I'll go to the pub."[54] Although here the notion of changing clothes is being contrasted with deeper, "real" change, clothes are used to indicate shifts in identity at other points in the play. At the beginning of the second act, when Rita has come back from summer school, the stage directions describe how she bursts through the door *"dressed in new, second-hand clothes."*[55] At the end of the play, when Rita has been transformed by education and the reconciliation between her and Frank takes place, he celebrates her achievement by presenting her with a new dress.[56] So here the tension between clothing as metaphor for superficial change and a deeper notion of transformation is resolved.

I want to tentatively suggest that the resilient learner is able to resist being objectified in such a way and that she takes control of the dressing and undressing for herself. The resilient learner is also able to withstand nudity better than other sorts of learners. Perhaps the resilient learner also has more success seeing beneath the clothes of other people. This represents something of a dilemma, given the broadly post-structuralist framework of the book, because nudity suggests some essential or preexisting quality (what Derrida calls "the center"). This would equate to the notion of resilience as a preexisting innate quality in a learner. A post-structuralist approach would suggest that such a reading is naïve, though, and posit instead a situation in which resilience is simply the ability to switch between many different outfits—resilience itself being constituted in the alacrity and flexibility of changing clothes. This tension will remain in play for the rest of the book.

4. *They resist passivity by dealing actively with their teachers (for example, by finding alternative, unofficial teachers or by subverting the Pygmalion/Galatea relationship).*

If we accept that the Ovidian Galatea is subverted by Hughes and by Russell, a vital component of resilient learning would seem to be a basic rejection of passivity, obedience, and silence. The agency of the spirit that gets into the sculpture has to preexist the learning experience. The sense of actively seeking out the teacher is most alive in Rita, but it is also evident in Eliza. Both of them are extremely persistent and will not be turned away, despite great insults on the part of the would-be teachers. Rita most clearly identifies her Pygmalion in the ways that the spirit does in Hughes's text. She recognizes him a long time before he recognizes her. He has much in common with Hughes's Pygmalion—he is in an unhappy, liminal space himself, which makes him open to transformation. He romanticizes Rita's class, her sexuality, and her youth—seeing all three as a refreshing distraction from his moribund lifestyle. Like that Pygmalion, Frank has his problems: he is an alcoholic and bored with his job and his life. Just as the spirit is "sick of unbeing," and so she searches for, identifies, and possesses Pygmalion in Hughes's version, so Rita seeks out Frank and possesses him, refusing to let go, despite his attempts to get away: "Listen: I'm on this course, you are my teacher—an' you're gonna bleedin' well teach me,"[57] she says. Eliza, Rita, and Hughes's Galatea initiate the learning situations, but, as has been stated, only Rita and Galatea are transformed, and this is because Frank and Pygmalion allow them to be by being transformed themselves. But it is clearly the case that there are plenty of resilient learners in the real world whose experiences with poor teachers and unsupportive institutions demonstrate that this is not the case for everyone. What such learners suggest, therefore, is that they subvert the system—they will not be molded. It is also true that the resilient learner is able to seek out alternative teachers. Eliza learns from both Pickering and Mrs. Higgins, and Rita gains much from her teachers at the summer school as well as from her peer group.

5. *They can be read as* miraculés; *for example, they experience a kind of resurrection.*

Finally, the basic motif of the Pygmalion scene—that of what has been inanimate coming to life—has important symbolic implications for the study. The notion of resurrection—although not technically correct (Galatea has never been dead as such, merely inanimate and previously disembodied)—is a useful additional image. The learners have been educationally dead (with reference to Bourdieu and Passeron's "educational mortality rate" set out in Chapter One). They have a history as far as education is concerned; they are not blank slates. By definition, they have either failed at school or they have had truncated academic trajectories. Animation is therefore an important idea. The resilient learners have a clear sense of their end goals and their reasons for learning, and there is a very clear sense that they want to be transformed. Learning certainly is a transformation for Rita and for Galatea. The central motif of the *miraculé*, initiated by Bourdieu but amplified by the theologican Jeffrey John's more open reading of the Gospel miracles, as texts of "systematic, subversive, highly risky inclusivism,"[58] informs the study. The way that the *miraculé*—both in its educational sense and in its Biblical manifestation—finally resists atomization and analysis is a central idea that informs the notion of resilient adult learning.

These five capabilities have emerged from the initial readings of the texts. They serve two purposes in this study. On the one hand, they offer an early understanding of emerging commonalities among resilient adult learners. On the other hand, they provide a useful analytical tool with which to interrogate other texts in the study. In the next chapter, an application of the five-capabilities model opens a highly contrasting literary text to a reading of resilient adult learning. *The Winter's Tale* links to the other three plays in this section through the Pygmalion myth. Its themes of death and resurrection, banishment, survival, and repentance and second chances resonate profoundly with my thinking about resilience. Adopting the model as a reading frame allows for an original reading of a Jacobean play in the context of this interdisciplinary, mixed-genre study. The highly mythopoetical nature of the text takes my thinking outside naturalistic representations of resilient adult learning in helpful ways: its very contrast is what renders new insights in the next chapter. The play's difference allows for a clearer appraisal of the appropriateness of the model.

CHAPTER 4

The Winter's Tale

Shakespeare plays an important role in the writing of Hélène Cixous. She identifies him not only as a supremely feminine writer but also as a hero. She says of him, "of course my hero is Shakespeare. I adore him. I know I share that opinion with the whole world. I don't think anyone has gone further than Shakespeare, because he's not only an artist in writing, he's a painter, a sculptor, a musician, a psychoanalyst—he's everything, really."[1] Critics draw attention to the way that elements of her dramatic writing are "strongly reminiscent of Shakespeare."[2] In this chapter, I take my lead from Cixous's reading of *Antony and Cleopatra*, in the final section of *Sorties*, to openly read his late play *The Winter's Tale*[3] as a text that has much to offer us in terms of understanding resilient adult learning. As I will demonstrate, all five indicators of resilience set out in the previous chapter are performed in the text. Resilience is a dispersed and shifting presence in the play; the capabilities are played out by different characters, at different times, in different situations.

Cixous's essay *Sorties*[4] provides the theoretical framework for this reading, as it does for the other texts in the book. In this chapter, I take one aspect of *Sorties*—Cixous's use of the economic metaphor—and apply it to *The Winter's Tale* in order to see if it will reveal the deconstructive energy in Shakespeare's play that might, in turn, reveal some insights into resilient learning. Cixous's use of the economic metaphor provides the missing link between the following elements of the study, which have previously existed disparately: my use, and then rejection, of Pierre Bourdieu's capital metaphor[5] in the early stages of this work as a way of trying to understand resilience;[6] Bourdieu and Jean-Claude Passeron's dismissal of unusually resilient learners as "*miraculés*";[7] my own adoption of the miracle motif as a way of understanding the resilient learner; the symbolic application of the miracle of resurrection as a way of thinking about resilient adult learners; and the particular text examined in this chapter, *The Winter's Tale*.

The play is noted for its prevalent use of financial vocabulary. Patricia Parker[8] links the range of critical literature that draws attention to the proliferation of economic references in the play and the corpus of work that concentrates on the number of images of the female body, and particularly pregnancy (such as Carol Thomas Neely[9]), in literal, metaphorical, and even homophonic senses—the latter being evident in Margreta De Grazia's playful interpretation of the significance of "bearing" in the text. She argues that the play grafts "a new lexicon of commercial and legal terms onto its romance plot of separation and return."[10] Return, in both senses of the word, is central to the play because of the spectacle of the final scene, in which the miracle of coming back from the dead and of being given a second chance is presented as a hopeful alternative to the destruction and misery caused by the purely economic understanding of the word as it is played out in the actions of the first half of the play. Resurrection in this sense is also the experience of the resilient adult learner, who *returns* to education and who is "reborn" into successful learning in a way that writes off previous failures and underachievement. Shakespeare's text therefore lends itself to a Cixousian reading as a way into thinking about resilient learners for both reasons. This chapter forms a junction between the two theoretical viewpoints through which I am looking at resilient adult learning—Bourdieu's notion of capital and Cixous's utopian vision of emancipation through the feminine economy in *Sorties*. By reading *The Winter's Tale* through her lens, I hope to open up some new understandings of resilience.

The play opens into a kingdom that dramatizes the worst excesses (as if such a system was capable of excess) of the masculine economy that Cixous describes in her introductory section of *Sorties*. Leontes's court is a world of stark oppositions. Property and patrimony underpin all relationships because of the collusion between phallocentric and logocentric power, and Leontes, as Cixous predicts, suffers for it. By the end of the play, the action has moved into another place, beyond the geographical boundaries of both Bohemia and Sicilia, which I will argue is close to Cixous's imagining of the Realm of the Gift. This is a different sort of kingdom, in which bestowal, charity, and peace offerings replace the calling in of debts and mounting of capital. The whole text is concerned with this movement from one economic arena, in which all is regulated and there are winners and losers, to another, in which generosity and ambiguity reign. The two geographical locations—Sicilia and Bohemia—are not simple sites for the two economies, though. Although Sicilia is in many ways a dramatic representation of

Cixous's description of the masculine economy, it still has enough capacity to have produced a Paulina. And although the pastoral scene in Bohemia is a more open place than its neighbor, it is still a place in which legitimacy and hierarchy are enough of a threat for Perdita and Florizel to flee for their love and their lives, and in which Autolycus flourishes as "a versatile economic opportunist."[11] Before I apply my model of resilience to the play, I want to explore Cixous's masculine/feminine economic metaphor in a little more depth and consider what the implications of that might be for learning in general and for adult learning in particular.

Cixous's Fiscal Metaphor

Cixous draws on the fiscal metaphor throughout *Sorties* to advance her vision for a new world (dis)order. "Savings,"[12] "return," and "revenue"[13] are key concepts that she uses to make the fundamental link between the "political economy and the libidinal economy."[14] The difference between society as it has been since "Ancient History"[15] and the utopia she envisages is the difference between two financial systems—the masculine economy and the economy of the feminine. As with the numerous other extended metaphors in *Sorties* (the earthquake, the volcano, the sea, and flight, for example), the metaphor is both thematic and polymorphic, appearing in numerous different guises in ways that recast its original use. Although at some points it is clear that she really is calling for a new economic reality as a necessary element to the sexual revolution (because how could it be otherwise if what is intended by her description of utopia is to "transform the functioning of all society"[16]), mostly it operates figuratively as a way of inscribing a difference between what has been and what could be. The metaphor is at its most mercurial when it appears to be functioning literally. She embeds a specific reference to the international financial realities that formed the context in which she was writing (the early 1970s), for example, in a point about the limitations of masculine sexuality as the basis for a political system: "Masculine energy, with its limited oil reserves questions itself,"[17] whereas in the imagined future when the masculine economy has been overthrown, "without gold or black dollars, our naphtha will spread values over the world in quoted values that will change the rules of the old game."[18] She posits an alternative; in the feminine economy, subjects will be made richer by what they give away. This is not pure speculation, she says. There is evidence that, historically, the fractures in the system have allowed the subversives (those "uncertain poetic persons" of both sexes[19]) to get through the dominant repressive system because they have been able to resist the official economic machinery with their texts and their bodies, by "accepting the other sex as a component." They have been made "much richer"[20] as a result.

In a world in which the notion of return as basis for an economy is disputed, capital becomes part of the problem, rather than a neutral way of describing what is accrued. Capital is as suspect as profit and ownership for Cixous—it is evidence of the old world with its parsimonious concerns for recovering what it gives away. Bourdieu's notion of capital is, by implication, gendered, and it is rejected by Cixous, who imagines (she can only imagine, but, as she says, citing William Blake, "whatever is thinkable is real"[21]) another way of being that extends beyond the political/economic sphere to all aspects of human experience—including learning. Capital itself is contaminated, because it emanates philosophically from a system of loss and finite resources—what is gained by one must always be paid for by the other. Whereas capital for Bourdieu is always "at stake in the field," as Richard Jenkins puts it,[22] Cixous seeks to imagine a world in which capital becomes redundant to the superior possibilities set out by the gift. For the gift to be a real possibility, Cixous has to challenge the whole libidinal economy and its societal ramifications. The impossibility of the gift existing within a masculine economy (because it is always given with the expectation of some return) is the origin of all inequality, she argues:

> All the difference determining history's movement as property's movement is articulated between two economies that are defined in relation to the problematic of the gift.[23]

The genuine gift is admissible in the feminine economy because of the ability of women to accept and accommodate the other, libidinally and reproductively, without violence. This could be the basis for a different way of being, of developing an economy that celebrates life and hope, rather than one that colludes with "the old story of death."[24]

The central understanding of the economy of the feminine, then, is in relation to the gift—to giving without return. As Jeff Massey[25] points out, "Cixous's feminine giver seeks not for a direct return or profit, but to establish (social) relations through the act of the gift." In this way, the basic assumption that property is the basis of all interchange—in whatever sense—of loving, living, dying, and in this case, of learning, would be overthrown, and in its place would be a new understanding that all those functions were not tied to the individual but are expansive, boundless, and created in the spaces between individuals rather than belonging to either party.

The application of Cixous's ideas to learners is not without basis. Teaching and learning are central to how she sees her work—"Wherever I go, I say I am a teacher,"[26] she says—and others have made the link between her thinking about sexual politics and transformative education agendas.[27] Cixous herself anticipates pedagogical applications of her ideas by making the link between knowledge and the feminine economy as a way of imagining another way of being:

> There would have to be a recognition of each other, and this grateful acknowledgement would come about thanks to the intense and passionate work of knowing.[28]

According to this plan, learning is not the acquisition of knowledge as a commodity but a passionate act of co-construction. This would seem to lead the way to a more equal and generous exchange between the learner and the teacher than what is conventionally understood by that relationship. The masculine economy prevails, though, and learning happens within it all the time. This book is an examination of how successful adult learners are able to maintain resilience within the traditional pedagogical system that marginalizes them. The masculine learning economy—with its emphasis on knowledge as property, hierarchical relations between teachers and learners (see Chapter Six), and anxiety-ridden regulatory academic management (see Chapter Nine)—is the conventional version of adult learning in higher education. Apart from what gets through the gaps (the academic versions of the "uncertain, poetic people" on both sides, teachers and learners), it is all we have. There is another story, though. There is a space in which resilient learners survive and thrive beyond the margins of the system and, in so doing, undermine it. I am interested in what this space looks like and how it affords learners and potential learners the capacity to develop those qualities that they will need in order to be resilient.

It is in this light that I will read *The Winter's Tale*, with sequential reference to the five hypothetical capabilities to perform resilience that were developed in the previous chapter.

'Resilient Learning and *The Winter's Tale*'

1. *They engage in open readings, resisting closed meanings, and they take a playful approach to language.*

Leontes's court is a claustrophobic, tense, and serious place in which everyone watches their wallets and the clock. Time is money, and gratitude is counted in terms of "debt."[29] When Polixenes and Leontes express their friendship for each other, they do so in financial terms because, as Michael Bristol points out,[30] in a traditional gift economy (to be distinguished from Cixous's version—see note 33) the host and the guest are very aware that in order for the equilibrium to be maintained, they must repay the other what has been offered in friendship so that "the imbalances that come to exist between giver and recipient, between host and guest, may be redressed." These two kings have been in each other's pockets for the better part of a year, and even before Leontes crystallizes his anxiety into violent jealousy, the atmosphere is edgy. This is not a place in which resilience can easily be developed, governed, as it is, by rigid man-made systems such as a punitive legal framework and an overwhelming hierarchy in which everyone—husbands and wives, courtiers and servants, and children and adults—knows their place. The law of property governs the way everything is perceived—time, nature, love, children, and friendship. Cixous draws attention to the philosophical foundations of "masculine" societies like Sicilia in *Sorties*, in which[31]

> the opposition appropriate/inappropriate, proper/improper, clean/unclean, mine/not mine (the valorization of the selfsame), organizes the opposition identity/difference.

The list of oppositions aptly describes Leontes's organization of the world and his own place in it. He is committed to dividing everything—people, places, and concepts—into mutually exclusive oppositions, and his chief anxiety is based on the central binary "mine/not mine." Polixenes's presence upsets the hierarchy—two kings in one place for so long was always going to be a problem—and his wife Hermione's pregnancy is disturbing evidence of the way that the natural world can't be controlled and regulated like everything else in his kingdom. Her body is a constant, visible affront to Leontes's world of property and propriety, because it brings into the scene a version of encompassing the other without oppression.

Sicilia's economy is tightly controlled, and it is being upset in two ways: the presence of another king (albeit a friend) upsets the hierarchy, and an individual who "doubles her market value"[32] without making the requisite loss has the potential to send the whole system into chaos. Once he has begun to think of the possibility of Hermione's infidelity with Polixenes, Leontes can't see her body in terms other than those that emanate from property and ownership, and the context in which he is placed supports his emotional expression of economic meltdown. As Bristol has it, his "jealousy is a type of spatiotemporal derangement of the ethos of the gift, hospitality, and expenditure."[33] His jealousy drives him even further away from a tolerant and resilient position. Leontes cannot bear ambiguity. Instead, he seeks the comfort of a dreadful truth. His search for evidence of Hermione's infidelity with Polixenes destroys his trust in his wife, his advisors, and the Oracle, but he sticks to the rules of the masculine economy nonetheless, because he has to—he is the king and this environment provides him with no other possible way of being.

The ability to tolerate and cherish multiple readings and to resist fixed meanings is an important factor that emerges from this section as a key commonality among resilient learners as they are represented in the range of texts examined in Chapters Two and Three. Leontes personifies its opposite. He says, for example,

> Too hot, too hot:
> To mingle friendship far, is mingling bloods.
> I have *tremor cordis* on me: my heart dances,
> But not for joy, not joy.[34]

To take friendship between a man and woman this far (to a point where they go beyond formal courtesy and royal protocol), he implies, can only result in one thing—the exchange of bodily fluids ("mingling bloods"). His vocabulary is staccato and aggressive; his very syntax prevents the fluidity about which he expresses his disgust. Mingling is terrifying and repugnant; relationships must be one thing or another, marriage or single-sex friendships. Mingling is an anathema to him, because he cannot believe that a friendship between a man and a woman can exist without infidelity, or theft as he sees it. All things must be kept separate and compartmentalized, or the body will revolt in dangerous ways—straight through the heart. The more he attempts to disjoin, the more vulnerable he is to uncontrollable forces. He instructs his son, for example, "We must be neat—not neat, but cleanly, captain."[35] Language is to be organized, and what it represents is to be divided up and fixed in space and time. The last thing Leontes wants is slippage and deferral. He asks Camillo in horror, has he not seen, heard, or thought that "My wife is slippery?"[36] As such, the thought of her sexuality is conflated with her dishonesty, and both are evidence of her worst crime of all—the resistance of fixture and the center. Slippage, fluidity, and plurality horrify Leontes, because in his world everything must mean something and nothing else. There is no capacity to read any of what is happening in multiple ways; the answer—the truth—must be found out and pinned down. To admit slippage would mean letting in anxiety. Instead, he attempts to master anxiety by adopting what Derrida calls "a fundamental immobility and a reassuring certitude,"[37] in which Polixenes and Hermione's relationship must be categorized as either completely innocent or entirely adulterous. He cannot contend that their affection means nothing. "Is whispering nothing?" he asks Camillo, denying the possibility that it could mean anything other than adultery and plotting.

Here Leontes begins to sound like the other spectacularly unresilient learner in the study, Carol, in David Mamet's *Oleanna*.[38] I suggested in Chapter Three that Carol represents a kind of archetypal unresilient learner; she is experience to Rita's innocence. A consideration of the opposite of resilience is inextricable from an exploration of resilience "itself" because, as Blake has it, without contraries there is no progression.[39] Moreover, if this book is to have application for teachers and learners, then it ultimately needs to imagine a type of adult learning that exists beyond the binary system—that "universal battlefield"[40] in which genuine transformation can be allowed to take place. Reflecting on Carol provides a useful lens through which to examine Leontes, who performs in similar ways. Carol's accusations—first of sexual harassment and then of attempted rape—are tragic single readings of a single text. When Carol's teacher puts his hand on her shoulder, she must pin it down to a fixed sexual meaning, no matter how dire the consequences. Like Carol, Leontes's investment in boundaries makes him both highly vulnerable and extremely dangerous.

Carol's terrified anger directed at her professor is based on his accommodation of the possibility of nothing: "YOU BELIEVE IN NOTHING. YOU BELIEVE IN NOTHING AT ALL,"[41] she screams at him. For Leontes, too, *nothing* must be angrily resisted, the existence of the black hole denied:

Why then the world and all that's in't is nothing,
The covering sky is nothing, Bohemia nothing,
My wife is nothing, nor nothing have these nothings,
If this be nothing.[42]

Nothing is indeed the cause of all Leontes's woes. Unlike Othello, who at least has *something*—a handkerchief—on which to pin his jealousy, Leontes has nothing. He believes that everything must have its center and, he asks, what is the likelihood that the center "would unseen be wicked?"[43] Camillo warns Leontes that his drive to fix meanings to some wicked center is risky and "most dangerous" and that this way of thinking gives rise to "diseased opinion," but Leontes will not be warned, and he remains imprisoned in his logocentric cynicism: "All's true that is mistrusted."[44] He is unable to release himself from the conviction that truth must surely reside in one place, even though that place is so painful.

There are direct parallels between the plots of these two very different plays. One of the charges that Carol brings against her professor is what she describes as "flirting,"[45] for which she cites the evidence in her notes, including his casual remarks to female students, for example, "Have a good day, dear."[46] Indeed, it is her conviction that the professor's apparently friendly

gesture (his offer of extra tuition to help her pass the course) was in fact a flirtatious advance that fuels her campaign against him, despite his protestations
that the act was devoid of sexual content. To admit that such an encounter
might mean nothing and everything would risk annihilation. A restricted
reading of *Oleanna* might concentrate on it as a play about sexual politics,
as if the audience is being asked to judge whether or not the professor did
harass his student. In fact, Mamet is far more subtle and educative in his text.
Directors and readers are similarly given little to go on in terms of imagining
the nature of Hermione's behavior in *The Winter's Tale*. The only relevant
stage direction states, "she gives her hand to Polixenes" in Act 1, Scene 2. As
with *Oleanna*, just one gesture—the placing of a hand on another—becomes
the site of and the catalyst for chaotic dissolution. Leontes is transfixed by
Polixenes's and Hermione's body language from then on, observing that their
"paddling palms" and "practised smiles"[47] can only be evidence of deliberate
sexual assertion. In the same way, Carol's evidence of her teacher's misde-
meanors is provided as if there is only the same possible interpretation.

Despite its frivolous nature and apparently peripheral relationship to
the serious business of teaching and learning, flirtation (or whatever it is
that exists in the gaps in the language that describes regulated and official relationships between people) is theoretically important. Flirtation is a
playful, ambiguous space that defies the power of the appropriate/inappro-
priate binary and upsets reductive readings of courtship and friendship by
accommodating both. It frustrates the "sex cops"[48]—who take the form of
the enforcers of patriarchal power in the case of Leontes and of puritanical
American feminism in the case of Carol—because it represents a thriving
black market outside of the masculine economy. Bourdieu's cynical assertion that romance is simply a "sign reading operation"[49] becomes more pertinent and interesting in the case of the ambiguous space between romance
and friendship (i.e., flirting). In the flirtatious relationship, signs must be
continually written and read in plural ways; as soon as meaning is captured,
playfulness terminates. As Murray Schwartz puts it in relation to the playfulness that is intrinsic to the pastoral life in Bohemia, "such a capacity
to play depends on tolerating the separateness of self and the other at the
very moment that separateness is denied in fantasy."[50] For both Leontes and
Carol, flirtation is a place of torment, because it involves everything that
is challenging to their world view; signs run riot in an arena in which "the
domain or play of signification henceforth has no limit."[51] Terrified as they
are by the absence of apparently transparent signification, both of these characters (whom I read as unresilient learners) attempt to nail meaning down
to simple sexual transgression. Therein lies the terror for Carol and Leontes
when they witness flirtation in others. All the rules around the appropriate/

inappropriate binary are exploded in a performance of play in which the old rules of fixed roles and stated intentions are suspended or ignored. It is significant that what Carol particularly hates about the professor is his propensity to "transgress"[52] or to disregard the rules. To debate whether or not the accused characters are "innocent" or "guilty" of flirtation is to miss the point. It is their accusers' inability to tolerate the ambiguity of playfulness that is the real crime in both plays. Both Leontes and Carol personify the opposite of resilience, because they are so wedded to single readings.

Leontes's world is one of brutal binaries—wife/whore, friend/enemy, and legitimate heir/bastard. The center cannot be denied even though the consequences of believing in it are so calamitous; there can be no margin of error, no possibility of plural readings. When Hermione tells him he has made a mistake, Leontes retorts,

> No: If I mistake
> In those foundations which I build upon,
> The centre is not big enough to bear
> A school-boy's top.[53]

The center protects Leontes from the inevitable anxiety of admitting that there may be no center, but, as Derrida points out, "the center also closes off the play which it opens up and makes possible."[54] For Leontes, this means a downward spiral into belief in betrayal and disloyalty. At the center is the truth, and the truth, he believes, will bring with it restful justice and closure, no matter how painful. Hermione's ability to exercise sexual preference leaves Leontes in a terrible, ambivalent place, in which he projects onto her his own violent fantasies:

> Affection! Thy intention stabs the centre.[55]

Here, as Neeley[56] argues, in historical linguistic terms the center has plural meanings: "'Center' can be the center of man in a sexual sense, the heart or soul of man, or the center of the universe." Shakespeare opens up the play on the word that its own meaning closes down.

In an attempt to put an end to the center's terrifying ability to slide around, and to settle Hermione's guilt once and for all, Leontes refers to the ultimate bringer of truth (or he thinks that is what it is until it gives him the wrong answer)—the Oracle—to confirm that he is correct, not for his own sake but to prove the truth to the others:

> Though I am satisfied, and need no more
> Than what I know, yet shall the Oracle

Give rest to th' minds of others; such as he
Whose ignorant credulity will not
Come up to th' truth.[57]

Like Carol, then, Leontes is stuck in a painful devotion to a fixed concept of truth, unable to read in plural ways the possibilities of what each encounter might mean. He would rather lose everything in pursuit of a fixed meaning than live with the intolerable ambiguity borne out of the doubt that Hermione might have slept with his best friend. He is also contemptuous of others who are open to alternative readings, sneering at their "ignorant credulity." He is tyrannical and dogmatic in his slavish worship of truth and material evidence. He is not open but already convinced that he has all the knowledge he needs—"I am satisfied"—and he is in no need of transformation in his own mind. Truth is not truthful, though, but merely fixed meaning. His jealousy is the natural consequence of the collusion between phallocentrism and logocentrism that Cixous describes; it is where the masculine economy over which he presides leaves him. Even the death of his little boy, Mamillius, does not make him stumble or change course from his suicidal mission to find the center. This death is inevitable, because the lad occupies a dangerous space between the masculine and feminine economies, or, as Susan Snyder has it, "In a world that ruthlessly polarizes male and female, Mamillius can't survive. Unable to be an ally, he can only be a victim."[58]

By the time he comes to put Hermione on trial, Leontes uses language that has become so poisoned that it is no longer recognizable to her, "Sir, / You speak a language that I understand not," she says.[59] He informs her that her daughter has been banished, punished because she cannot be his property without doubt: "Thy brat hath been cast out, like to itself, / No father owning it."[60] The property of the child unproven, he must send it away from this kingdom in which property is everything. Hermione rejects his property-based reading of life: "To me can life be no commodity."[61] His language becomes reduced to instructions; he tells Cleomenes and Dion to "Break up the seals, and read."[62] Reading has become an act of the simple revelation of the truth. The seals must be broken—the codes deciphered, playfulness denied. He is shaken further when the meaning that is revealed is not the truth that he wanted to hear. "Hast thou read truth?"[63] he barks in angry disbelief, and when the truth is not the one he wanted to hear, he denounces that truth, rather than revoking his own belief in the search for it:

There is no truth at all i' th' Oracle:
The sessions shall proceed: this is mere falsehood.[64]

Leontes crashes out of reason at this point, clutching desperately to his belief in the center but rejecting the center with which he is presented; he sacrifices all he has loved to preserve his frame of reference. He is horrified and fascinated by the binary between legitimacy and illegitimacy. The anxiety that he may never know the final truth about the legitimacy of his daughter drives him to want to destroy her in the most violent way possible:

> The bastard brains with these my proper hands
> Shall I dash out.[65]

An illegitimate other in his court would be an intolerable affront, but if it had brains as well, it might well destroy his world. Knowledge of this child must be reduced to an assertion of his ownership of it, and because that is ambiguous, it must be destroyed. Like Herod,[66] Leontes knows that there is something significant about this child, and it must be destroyed at all costs. Illegitimacy threatens the whole system, and it need only exist as an idea to cause havoc; what is illegitimate must be marginalized, stigmatized, and banished. But the illegitimate do survive, on the margins, as *miraculés*, in the desert and on the borderland between the certainties of the masculine economies and the dangers of the wilderness. It is in one such remote and deserted place that the real resilient learner of the play is found.

2. *They recognize, withstand, and negotiate the tension between inclusion and exclusion.*

In *The Winter's Tale*, resilience is performed by the text itself, and the capabilities are played out in different ways by different characters. The text not only contains characters who inhabit the roles of less or more resilient learners, but the text itself also takes on a pedagogical purpose, coaxing the audience/readers into a more resilient, open position by the time the final scene is reached. Perdita displays many of the features of resilient learners; she is the closest the text gets to providing a single character who can be read as a resilient learner in a way that corresponds to the other learners in this study. She is certainly a *miraculé* who has survived the following events:

1. her birth in prison;
2. the death of her brother;
3. her father's rejection of her and its violent expression;
4. her father's psychotic behavior toward her mother;
5. abduction from her mother before she is weaned (and her mother's subsequent disappearance);

6. abandonment as a baby in a dangerous place;
7. the death of her first guardian in a gruesome attack by a wild animal;
8. exile from her family, her nation, and her class.

This is not an auspicious start to life. For anyone to survive at all in these circumstances would be remarkable, but the miracle of Perdita is that she retains and develops the capacity for faith[67] and playfulness,[68] the ability to inspire[69] and to feel profound love,[70] and the courage to resist oppression.[71] She has been born into the excesses of opprobrium and tyranny, and although she has not yet acquired language, she can, with Paulina, "see what death is doing."[72] Death precedes language. Imprisonment and then deportation are realities before she finds a safe home. Survival is, from the very beginning, inextricably bound up with Perdita's identity. When she is left by Antigonus to live or die in the wilderness in "some remote and desert place,"[73] it is on specific instructions from her father that she be left with only her own resilience as a guard. He tells Antigonus to leave her, "Without more mercy, to it own protection."[74]

Her homeland is a place in which patriarchy has gone mad, gone murderous, and in order to survive, the little girl must be taken to another world, in which she can have the necessary space and enough love to develop resilience. In the "deserts of Bohemia,"[75] she is left to the mercy of wild and predatory nature. Hermione understands how serious her daughter's expulsion is—she is in no doubt that the baby has been "haled out to murder."[76] In his Winnicottian reading of the play, Brooke Hopkins (2005) argues that Leontes's violation of the sacred space between the mother and the newborn child is the outrage that Hermione feels most keenly (of those she lists in her speech in the trial scene), because she understands its significance. Hermione is so devastated because she has not had the time to provide the parenting that the little girl needs in order for her to develop resilience. Instead, the baby

> is from my breast
> The most innocent milk in its most innocent mouth
> Haled out to murder.[77]

The destruction of that space threatens the child's ability to love and trust in what she cannot know because of "faith's ultimate grounding in the potential space between mother and child."[78] Instead of love and security, Perdita witnesses exclusion, abandonment, and death.

Antigonus is the link between the economy of death and the economy of life into which she is saved. Heartbroken about leaving the "Poor babe,"[79] he pauses, surrounded by natural phenomena as violent as the human actions he has left behind, to speak with Perdita in his arms. As Schwartz points out,[80] not only is this the longest speech in the play, but it is also a speech within a speech. Hermione had reappeared as a ghost in Antigonus's dream, and his account of what she said indicates that the mother understands the seriousness of her daughter's situation. Antigonus prepares the audience for a magical understanding of this woman who

> Appear'd to me last night, for ne'er was dream
> So like waking.[81]

Perdita hears her mother's words spoken by a ghost that is not a ghost, in a dream that is more than a dream, reported by a carer who is about to die. Resilience is born in that dream. Perdita hears, before she understands it, an account of her mother's voice, and she is from then on protected by it. Hermione, refusing to lie down dead/not dead, is resurrected initially in the arena of dreams, appearing in the imaginary world of the dream, crossing over from the binaries of day to night and waking to sleep in the same way that, later in the play, she will inhabit the space between the binaries of life and death. Hermione, "barred" as she is, as a real presence, has to find a way of getting back to her daughter and providing her with what she will need to develop resilience. Antigonus is called on to awaken his belief in the same way that the audience is also asked to dissolve fixed oppositions from this point on. We believe, as Leontes does, that Hermione is dead, and so this is her first resurrection in verse. As an audience, we are being asked to begin to question our own investment in the binaries between waking and sleep, and between life and death, in order to believe in the space occupied by this apparition of Hermione. Shakespeare asks us to begin to demonstrate and develop resilience.

Hermione's voice provides the baby with love. As Cixous (1975/1986) has it,

> The Voice sings from a time before law, before the Symbolic took one's breath away and reappropriated it into language under its authority of separation. The deepest, the oldest, the loveliest Visitation. Within each woman the first, nameless love is singing.[82]

For Cixous, women are always in exile in a hostile land (the Symbolic) where language orders and subjects them because language is overwhelmingly patriarchal, but most women forget they are in exile, because their subjection to the Symbolic is almost complete. The dream provides a way of ensuring that Perdita will not forget her homeland while she is in exile.

Hermione gives instructions for her daughter's naming. Perdita, meaning "lost," is the name given because, for her mother, as she says in the dream, the little girl "is counted lost for ever."[83] As such, Perdita's entry into language is supported by a dream ghost of her mother who provides her with the first word, which signifies loss and which is a reminder of the blissful state they have lost together. From then on, language, for Perdita, is always deconstructing itself, always reminding her of what came before it. The Real will never be lost for Perdita, because she has the memory—the prelanguage memory—of something that existed before death took over and to which she will return; it is embedded in her name.

Perdita is lost, then found, in the most Cixousian of locations—the coast. The coast is always changing. Land and sea meet at a point that is never constant but subject to tides, erosion, and deposition. As Schwartz points out, the coast is a place "that demarcates fluidity and solidity, change and fixity, and also brings them into interplay."[84] This sets the tone for her identity from then on. Perdita is constantly changing, adapting, and moving. Like the sea, she is nomadic, in perpetual transit. Later, Florizel is to see it in her and to love her capacity to "change in continuity, not loss,"[85] reflecting her fluidity in the beautiful lines he addresses to her:

> When you do dance, I wish you
> A wave o' th' sea, that you might ever do
> Nothing but that: move still, still so,
> And own no other function.[86]

Her fluidity and her ability to change are the only things that are fixed about her. She is bisexual in Cixous's sense of the word—of truly allowing for masculinity and femininity to coexist in a way that depends on a profound commitment to the "non exclusion of difference."[87] When she arrives in Sicilia, for example, the servant says of her,

> Women will love her that she is a woman
> More worth than any man; men, that she is
> The rarest of all women.[88]

This ability to change and act in fluid ways allows Perdita to resist the consequences of internalizing exclusion at all levels. Shakespeare subverts the female stereotype robustly throughout the text, through the three strong female characters, but it is in Perdita that he realizes the capacity for multiplicity and liberation most extremely. Schwartz argues that "Perdita encompasses sexual differences (virginal *and* erotic), social differences (shepherdess *and* "queen"), mythic differences (Flora *and* Persephone), and in imagistic terms, differences in the substances of life itself (earth *and* water)."[89] This capacity to exist across the boundaries and to resist categorization is highly protective and characteristic of other resilient learners in this study. Her capacity to embrace difference and to resist the distinction between self and other allows her to survive and thrive in exile.

In the natural world of Bohemia, which is so different from the place of her birth, she is brought up by gentle men—a clown and a shepherd—father and son, who have no understanding of the masculine economy: "I should be rich by the fairies,"[90] says the shepherd. In this alternative, pastoral, feminine world, these men know how to bring up a baby and are able to give her the good-enough love she needs in order to develop resilience. Here she can flourish and survive and develop resilience; she has been left in an environment that can foster resilience in her. Perdita is exiled from her family and from her social class. The pagan, feminine world in which she is raised provides her with more resilience than she could possibly have been allowed to develop at home. It is not a sentimentally produced idyll, though, nor is it the full realization of Cixous's economy of the feminine. As Susan Snyder and Deborah Curren-Aquino note, it is the most complex and diverse pastoral environment of Shakespeare's works.[91] The pastoral must be disturbed, though. The masculine economy has to make a reappearance, in the shape of Polixenes and Camillo, come to claim back Florizel from this "witch." As with all resilient learners, the time for playing on the outside can't last forever. The center will assert itself eventually. Kings have to be appeased; the academic management system must be addressed in the end, and the resilient learner needs to find a way of getting back inside far enough to be validated while never being swallowed up by "home."

This tension between gaining enough symbolic capital in Bourdieu's terms to be validated by the system and resisting it enough to survive is central to the resilient learner's struggle. When Perdita runs from Bohemia to Sicilia, she does so to avoid the wrath of an angry king whose concern for maintaining the patrilineage exactly mirrors her migration in the opposite direction in the first part of the play. She leaves under cover; however, she is not going home, but to Elsewhere. The resilient learner's dream of Elsewhere is not some sentimental whimsy; it is the fundamental basis of her survival, as Cixous explains in her own autobiographical account of her own resilience as a fatherless Jewish girl growing up in occupied Algeria:

> There has to be somewhere else, I tell myself. And everyone knows that to go somewhere else there are routes, signs, "maps"—for an exploration, a trip—That's what books are.[92]

Perdita must escape again once she has been exposed by the king as an impostor who dares to allow his son to fall in love with her. She is, again, in real danger of death, and her resilience resides in her ability to take on a disguise.

3. *They show a willingness to divest themselves of their "clothing" and to try on new clothes.*

When the shepherd finds Perdita, she is just a "bundle in a box" wearing "a bearing cloth for a squire's child,"[93] but thereafter she is always wearing somebody else's clothes. After she is a baby in a box, she is a shepherdess,[94] then a shepherdess dressed as Flora,[95] the queen of the sheep-shearing festival,[96] then she escapes from Polixenes in disguise, only to be recast by Florizel as the daughter of Smalus, the king of Libya,[97] before being revealed as she "really" is, the daughter of a king. A traditional reading of the play might suggest that her "real" identity as a princess is what has protected her all along, providing as it does her innate intelligence, beauty, confidence, and eloquence. The reading of the play as a text that can support a performative understanding of resilience falters at this point. If resilience is already "in" resilient learners in the way that this reading would suggest that royal blood is in Perdita all along, then this investigation has limited applications to real university practice. But Shakespeare is more playful than that. Perdita does not dismiss her identity as princess as false, but she presents it as yet another set of clothes—a point that is supported by her foster father and brother's simultaneous acquisition of the clothes of gentlemen.[98] Throughout these transformations, she is aware of what is going on, and she finds it ridiculous: "and me, a lowly maid, / Most goddess-like pranked up."[99] Perdita understands what is subversive and incendiary about so freely taking on and putting off different costumes, and she anticipates the subsequent arrival of Polixenes and worries about what she will do, disguised as she is:

> Or how
> Should I, in these my borrowed flaunts, behold
> The sternness of his presence?[100]

She knows that those in power disapprove of dressing up because they believe so firmly in their own clothes.[101] There is something very threatening to rulers about those who can see through the sham. The little boy who points out that the emperor is naked has the potential to rock an empire to its foundations. Perdita can see through her own disguises, and she does not see the "borrowed flaunts" as fixed elements of her identity, unlike the two

kings, who are trapped in their roles/clothes. Resilience is therefore constituted in the conscious knowledge that one is dressing up/undressing and the
knowledge—the revolutionary knowledge—that if these clothes don't fit it
is easy enough to find some more. She knows the meaning of choosing to
wear particular costumes:

> sure this robe of mine
> Does change my disposition.[102]

So there is no preexisting worldly disposition that is stronger than the clothes
it wears. With this knowledge comes courage.

Perdita's language is playful and highly eloquent (like her mother's), to
the extent that Camillo doubts his own belief in her outward appearance:

> She lacks instructions, for she seems a mistress
> To most that teach.[103]

Likewise, other resilient learners are able to take a playful approach to teaching and learning, resisting the stricture of teacher and learner, and adopting
different roles at different points. Her resilience allows her to see through
other people's clothes in a way that is remarkable for a Jacobean woman. She
says of the angry and arrogant Polixenes,

> The selfsame sun that shines upon his court
> Hides not his visage from our cottage, but
> Looks on alike.[104]

She has a sense of her equal value and will not accept the categorization
that is afforded her. But it also makes her vulnerable. The link between
self-survival and divestment is spelled out to Perdita by Camillo, who tells
her to

> Dismantle you, and as you can, disliken
> The truth of your own seeming.[105]

Exiled as she is, she can only operate subversively if she is to survive. Polixenes
understands that Perdita is a threat, and so the lovers must escape from his
power. In true Cixousian style ("To fly/steal is woman's gesture, to steal into
language to make it fly..."[106]) she flies away with her lover, wearing the
clothes of a thief.

The links between clothing, language, and power are explored by Bourdieu and Passeron:

> The traditional professor may have abandoned his ermine and his gown, he may even choose to descend from this dais and mingle with the crowd, but he cannot abdicate his ultimate protection, the professorial use of a professorial language.[107]

This means that for the resilient learner, who understands that the language is just clothing and that there are other clothes to wear (and even, most dangerously of all, that it is possible to walk naked), is very threatening to academic management systems and limited teachers. The Polixenes(es) of higher education have as much power as the Polixenes of Bohemia in the play. Like him, they have it in their power to delay, to interrupt, and to undermine those subjects who will not wear the clothes that are provided for them. Ultimately, they can fail and expel Perdita if she refuses her costume or if she insists on seeing through the ermine and the gown. Although resilience is borne in the ability to understand the significance of taking on and casting off academic frameworks, so is danger. As soon as the learner sees the sham and resists it, s/he puts herself/himself in jeopardy. Perdita survives that jeopardy by finding a community that will help her; by using the sustaining power of love (first of her mother, secondly of her adoptive family, and thirdly of Florizel) to resist oppression; by putting on new clothes and by refusing to believe in the clothes of others; and by means of the help of two individuals who are able to exist beyond the hierarchies of the masculine economy. The first is an outsider in the masculine economy, a thief, Autolycus, who, despite himself, engineers her acceptance in Sicilia. The second is an insider in the masculine economy, the teacher Paulina, whose moral authority and insight raises her above those who would seek to control her. Both allow the learner to find a subversive position of survival that can still be validated by the system. They do so by subverting the teaching and learning scene.

4. *They resist passivity by dealing actively with their teachers (for example, by finding alternative, unofficial teachers or by subverting the Pygmalion/ Galatea relationship).*

A conservative reading of the Pygmalion myth treats the learner (the sculpture, Galatea) as passive and as a victim to the teacher's (the sculptor's, Pygmalion's) egotistical molding of her. A radical and transformational reading, such as that provided by Ted Hughes,[108] though, affords agency to the learner, who is able to select and then animate the teacher in a way that will allow something deeper than academic metamorphosis (what I call transformation) of both of them to take place. I am interested in the ways that transformation differs from metamorphosis. I suspect that the resilient learner resists simple metamorphosis and drives toward a transformational experience. This allows for a reading of the story in terms of Paulo Freire's binary of dialogue/anti-dialogue in teaching and learning relationships. In the transformational learning event (such as that presented by Hughes), teacher and learner are "engaged in a joint search," and their relationship is "loving, humble, hopeful, trusting (and) critical."[109] A less than transformational learning event (which I will call metamorphic, after Ovid's "Pygmalion") is "loveless, arrogant, hopeless, mistrustful (and) acritical."[110] It is feasible to suggest that the former might be more easily fostered in a learning environment that is closer to Cixous's economy of the feminine than in a masculine economy.

Ovid's Pygmalion[111] is a kind of antihero to the sorts of resilient learners already featured in this book. Two of the five themes I have explored in this chapter—the ability to engage in open readings and the willingness to divest themselves of received wisdom and instead to "walk naked"—as commonalities among resilient learners, require them to be critical and to robustly reject what is controlling and authoritarian. These attitudes would seem to be an anathema to the passivity and silence required of a Galatea in the Ovidian sense. The teacher whose ambitions for learning go no further than the desire to reproduce himself in the body of another (like Mary Shelley's *Frankenstein*—see previous chapter) is manifestly antithetical to a transformative model of teaching and learning. Hughes's subversion of Ovid's text has parallels in Shakespeare's much earlier subversion of it in *The Winter's Tale*, which is, as Snyder and Curren-Aquino point out, "perhaps the most Ovidian of Shakespeare's plays."[112]

In the final scene of the play,[113] Shakespeare reworks the Pygmalion story by importing its key elements (the statue of a woman that comes to life, a man who is dumbstruck by the spectacle, and the presence of love as a metaphysical force throughout the scene), but he radically changes each element. Shakespeare's final scene is very different from both the tragic spectacle of death in his source text—Robert Greene's *Pandosto*[114]—and the erotically charged union in Ovid's *Metamorphoses*. He disrupts the exclusive dynamic between sculptor and sculpture by introducing a third figure, Paulina, who is not a sculptor in the literal sense (although it is clear from the outset that the whole thing is her work of art) but a facilitator of the metamorphic event. Here the learner is not the statue but Leontes himself, with Paulina as his teacher, assisted by both Hermione (the sculpture) and Perdita (the "looker-on").

Although she attributes the sculpting to somebody else, Paulina presents herself as part of the artistic team from the outset; Leontes refers to the space where they stand as "Your gallery,"[115] and Paulina is very clearly the curator/owner. She says of the statue, for example, "therefore I keep it / Lonely, apart,"[116] but she is more than this as well. When she draws the curtain, it is clear that wonder and awe are the only appropriate reactions from the audience; "I like your silence: it the more shows off / Your wonder,"[117] she says. Leontes is in awe: "Chide me, dear stone,"[118] he says, deferring to both Paulina's expertise and her wisdom as teacher as well as to the moral and emotional superiority of the stone itself. He is able to connect this stone with his own stone-heartedness of previous times: "Does not the stone rebuke me / for being more stone than it?"[119] When Paulina brings "the statue" to life, it is Leontes who changes from a living death to a fuller way of living. The stone is rolled away; life takes over.

In this scene, it is not the sculptor who invokes the help of the gods through prayer, but Perdita, "a looker-on,"[120] who asks the statue itself to bless her. Perdita, reared to mistrust the binaries, disregards them and treats the statue as if it is real from the outset. The statue is so real that it frightens Leontes, who feels "mocked with art."[121] He is moved beyond his fixed meaning and immobility by the statue, exclaiming,

No settled senses of the world can match
The pleasure of that madness.[122]

Paulina wakes Hermione up with the help of music while Leontes looks on. The gifted teacher brings the reluctant learner to a point at which he can begin to perform resilience. Perdita, the resilient learner, is able to believe in the transformation so readily because she has experienced it so many times already. In Shakespeare's scene, the teacher is able to hijack the reproductive scene and changes an event that would otherwise be merely metamorphic into one that is transformative instead. The application of this theme is therefore thematically interesting but not entirely successful, because the changes to the teacher/learner (sculptor/sculpture) narrative are so profound. A reading of the Galatea/Pygmalion scene suggests that the teacher Paulina brings a "learner" to life who is already alive and part of the plan. The teacher and learner are both teachers. The resilient learner, Perdita, watches the spectacle and finds what she has lost. Learning, for her, is therefore an act of remembering in the Platonic sense rather than shape changing in the Ovidian sense. For the previously unresilient leaner, Leontes, the transformation from lifeless statue to real woman crystallizes what he has spent 16 years learning. By the end of the play, Paulina has taken him to a place in which he can begin to develop the capacities required of a resilient learner.

5. *They can be read as miraculés, for example, they experience a kind of resurrection.*

When Paulina takes charge in the final scene of the play, she is insistent that both audiences—the one on the stage and the one in the theater—make themselves ready for the resurrection they are about to witness. They should do that, she tells them, by finding their capacity to believe:

It is required
You do awake your faith. Then all stand still.[123]

Until the statue is revealed, the theater audience has believed, like Leontes, that Hermione is dead. The revelation of her resurrection moves the audience to a new space; a miracle is performed in front of us. The awakening of the statue transcends the division of death and life and of art and reality. In order to understand what Paulina intends to teach us, we are asked to read the miracle scene playfully in a way that goes beyond both literalism (she has set the whole thing up by hiding Hermione for 16 years) and symbolism (she is keen to emphasize that this is not a magic trick). Like the depiction of the resurrection as a pedagogical act in the Gospel of Luke ("Then opened he their understanding" Luke, 24:45), this awakening is presented as a lesson. Jeffrey John's[124] argument that open and playful readings of the miracles as radical acts of inclusion is applicable to Shakespeare's rewriting of the final miracle in *The Winter's Tale*. The learning point is not in the magical spectacle but in the existence of love that allows it to happen. Although Paulina does much to protect herself from charges of witchcraft, she has to resort to the language of magic in order to prepare them for what is about to happen: "my spell is lawful."[125] She then takes the same approach with both audiences as she did with Leontes earlier in the play. She distinguishes between those who have the imaginative capacity to read in free and open ways (i.e., resilient learners) and those whose poverty of imagination makes them dangerous. Her wisdom lies in her understanding of the nature of transformation as well as its limitations. She is able to protect the learners who are capable of it from the dangerous actions of those who are not:

On! Those that think it is unlawful business
I am about, let them depart.[126]

The statue is pre-linguistic; it is a performance of innocence and direct communication beyond the endless chain of representation and deferred meaning. It exists outside of the masculine economy and outside the binaries. Paulina insists on "silence" and that her audience is "still" before they can apprehend the miracle. Despite the joyful shock of resurrection and the gift of life, the scene is also a serious meditation on death. Antigonus and Mamillius are conspicuous absences in the final tableau. This resurrection is not a sentimental fantasy, because Paulina presents it as both completely illusory but also completely real. The difference between death and life is love, which is a power that is stronger than both states and which reveals both as constructions. What has been lost is found through a pedagogical miracle. The miracle is love. Hermione has been, as Polixenes has it, "stol'n from the dead."[127] On the one hand, death is robbed of its victim by the transformative power of love and forgiveness; but on the other, death has served a pedagogical purpose. The final scene provides hope in the face of death, but it also teaches us not to be afraid of death, because it is what allows learning to begin. As Cixous puts it, "In the beginning, there is an end. Don't be afraid: it's your death that is dying. Then: all the beginnings."[128] The play ends with Leontes articulating his emerging understanding of that. The actors on stage and the members of the audience are invited to reflect on what has happened in the intervening 16 years since they were first "dissevered."[129]

Who is the *miraculé* in this play? Hermione is not a Lazarus—she is complicit in the miracle. Rather the learners, Leontes, Paulina's audience on stage, and Shakespeare's audience in the theater, are the ones who benefit from the miracle. This final scene presents us with an act of generosity that can only fall outside the masculine economy—there is no expectation of return or exchange for this resurrection. It is an act of love, and therefore it can't be accounted for in terms of capital. The resurrection staged by Paulina is the ultimate gift—it is a "feminine" act—that undermines the masculine economy.[130] Resurrection happens in the Realm of the Gift. Return (economic) is displaced by return (coming back). As Cixous states, "Love can't be exchanged for social adaptation, its life signs have no market equivalents."[131]

My reservations about Bourdieu's capital model are borne out by this reading of *The Winter's Tale* as a text that has something to offer this study of resilient learning for two reasons. First, love is not accounted for in the Bourdieusian model, other than in highly reductive, cynical terms.[132] The absence of any engagement with love compromises a serious attempt to understand the ontological nature of returning for the resilient adult learner. Resilience itself becomes a vacuous concept in Bourdieu's schema. Cixous's concern that death and love are the components of writing, and therefore learning, is much more hopeful. Resilience is what breaks the chain of endless reproduction in an education system that rewards the rich with ever more capital. For resilience to be fostered and for outsiders to thrive in such a system, learners need to be open to the miracle of transformation, and teachers need to give up their endless desire for reproduction. In the feminine learning economy in which resilience would be encouraged, both teachers and learners would want to be transformed by learning that is stronger than both of them. They would have the capacity to take part in the transformation and not try to control it. It would have to be a system based on love rather than property. In the end, the gift is what provides resilience—this is what Paulina the teacher teaches us.

Cixous's bemused reflection on those who refuse to give of themselves suggests that a learning economy based around an uncomplicated notion of giving would have resilience built into it: "Mystery of the gift: the poison-gift: if you give, you receive. What you don't give, the anti-gift, turns back against you and rots you. The more you give, the more you take pleasure. How could it be that they don't know that?"[133]

As such, Cixous's notion of the anti-gift mirrors Freire's notion of the anti-dialogue between teacher and learner. Both take place in and constitute the masculine economy which ceaselessly reproduces itself by rewarding those insiders who already have power and capital with more of the same. What Shakespeare does at the end of *The Winter's Tale* is to provide an example of a teacher who takes the gift seriously and who uses love to defy the old story and to create a space for the *miraculé* to survive.

The Pygmalion story has allowed me to read the resilient learner allegorically, and this has opened up the reading of literary texts in ways that have offered insights that are useful for the entire study. The story strikes primordial chords. It raises questions about the power and place of art in an apparently clinical and ordered factual text. Art here (literary texts), once incorporated into the text, has an incendiary, disordering effect. Shakespeare's and Hughes's radical readings of the Pygmalion myth allow for reconsiderations of the relationship between truth and art to be opened. Paulina might be read, not just as a kind of teacher, but as a personification of an instinct for enquiry. Marina Warner calls Paulina "an embodiment of unswerving good heart and truthfulness, (she) uses the deception of art to make manifest Hermione's virtue."[134] The deception of a particular form of art—literature—is used in this study to unmask a truth that apparently transparent social scientific texts conceal. Art will not behave itself, though. It will not be used merely as an accessory, for the provision of ethnographic data or even as a more humanistic reading of the social scene, in the way that some sociologists suggest. Ultimately Galatea wakes up and, in doing so, inevitably causes a rupture to take place.

At the end of this section, Galatea has taken on a three-fold allegorical function in relation to the book:

1. she represents the resilient learner in relation to her teacher (represented by Pygmalion);
2. she represents artifacts—literary texts and the dynamic relationship they have on an apparently docile and clean social scientific piece of writing;
3. she represents writing itself—the writing that is gaining life as the book progresses.

The use of the five-capabilities model tentatively suggested as a result of reading the Pygmalion texts in Chapters Two and Three has opened up the analysis of *The Winter's Tale* considerably. It has certainly served its analytic purpose. The capabilities themselves also stand up as appropriate readings of the way that resilience is performed.

So far, though, the study has only encompassed literary texts. It is relatively easy to get a literary text to open itself up to a particular reading if the reading is carried out in a sufficiently open manner and if plurality is allowed for. A real person is about to enter this text. The presence of a real person in a text brings with it other more pressing concerns that have some impact on the ethics of carrying out such a reading. An account of a real person's life is not so easy to represent in a clever, thematic way. In the next section, I apply some of the findings from this section to the transcripts that have come out of my work with real resilient adult learners. I begin with an application of the five-point capabilities model to the first of those interviews in Chapter Five—an interview with Joe. My methodological question at the beginning of this next section is therefore twofold. First, is the substantial content of the five capabilities applicable to real learners, and secondly, is the analytical approach afforded by applying the five capabilities thematically to an interview text a helpful way of proceeding in terms of allowing us to get closer to the real, lived experience of resilience?

CHAPTER 5

Joe

In Chapter Four, I suggested that the Realm of the Gift presented possibilities for escaping the relentless demolition work of the masculine economy and that it provided a looser and more generous environment within which resilience might be fostered. *The Winter's Tale*[1] presents possibilities for the resistance of the predictable progress of history. The seemingly endless destructive movement of history—with its emphasis on property ownership, revenge, and violence—is halted by love, the miracle, and the work of the gift. Outside of Act V of *The Winter's Tale*, though, the battlefields, genocide, and famines of history proliferate everywhere with terrible predictability. In the same way, Pierre Bourdieu's bleak vision of endless reproduction is an accurate description of the social effects of education.[2] Capital is rewarded with more capital. Within this apparent black hole of inequality, how does the survivor survive? How can the resilient learner resist the script that is historically imposed on him or her?[3] The central challenge for the resilient learner must be how to find a way to resist the script that history has written for him or her as an educational failure and, instead, to find ways in which the system allows for slippage. If the economy of the gift provides a hopeful way of fostering resilience, it is pertinent to ask how love might support the resilient learner in ways that allow him or her to renounce and defy history's reproductive project. This chapter considers the function of love, among other things, in the life history of a resilient adult learner, Joe. Here I take the same approach as I did in my analysis of *The Winter's Tale*, to see if the five capabilities of resilience will similarly open up my interview with him.

History features strongly as a theme in Hélène Cixous's *Sorties*. Without resistance, it is always reproductive, a depressing account of "*two* races—the masters and the slaves,"[4] in which the particular contextual identities of the oppressed may change, but "the other" is ruled, named, and defined by those who rule. History positions the subject either inside its protective "dialectical circle,"[5] or it excludes and silences him or her. Cixous's affinity is with history's others—excluded, colonized, and silenced as they have been. As always, her intellectual responses are instinctive and passionate; she places the story of her own childhood in Algeria in the context of global events. The personal is always part of the wider historical account, and survival (and therefore resilience) is framed in the language of political resistance.

> I had fits of rage that made History difficult. I didn't give a damn for hierarchy, for command...[6]

Although at times, superficially, Cixous's account of history would appear to echo Marxist accounts of the same (she writes that there is "no property without exclusion," for example[7]), her understanding is at once more poetic and more personal than an economic account of oppression. She evokes legend and myth, rather than factual accounts of wide-scale industrial and social change, to illustrate the ancestral roots of modern problems. Similarly, although the assertion that oppression is "what masters do: they have their slaves made to order. Line for line,"[8] the line is not necessarily a production line in a factory or a line of unpaid agricultural workers, as it might be for a Marxist historian; rather, it is the line in a text or a line of verse. The othering nature of History, therefore, is certainly systematic, but it goes far deeper than its manifestation in the economic system. Its "annihilating dialectical magic"[9] has its roots in language itself. It speaks with a poisonous tongue.

Understanding the way the machine works is only half the story. Recognizing "the mechanism of the death struggle"[10] is not enough to set us free. We need to first know whether or not there is real potential for liberation and for a happier existence as an ahistorical subject. The central question for Cixous, then, is "Is the system flawless? Impossible to bypass?"[11] If there are faults in the machine, then there is hope that it can be escaped or even overturned. The rebel must refuse victimhood, therefore, and turn contraband. This is never simple: the tension between agency and reproduction is always in play.[12]

Books represent an escape route—they are "anti-land" in which possible other ways of being can be imagined and lived through. Readers can give the machine the slip by going on an exploration through a literary wormhole beyond which other worlds exist in which other ways of living are possible. So reading sets the scene—it raises the possibility of another for the other. And in the texts can be found other rebels—those who have conscientiously objected to the "infernal repetition" of history.[13] They are the heroes on whom we can begin to rely for inspiration, because they have demonstrated how it is possible to have strength without authority and to use it to challenge the masters. They are recognizable because they are History's others, "isolated, eccentric, the intruders: great, undaunted, sturdy beings, who were at odds with the law."[14] For Cixous, resistance and rebellion are born in the combination of three activities—reading, writing, and the action of the gift (i.e., love). I have already established the link between *l'écriture féminine* and adult learning. Cixous's concern with the emancipatory effects of writing serves at least two important functions in this study. It literally drives the methodological approach, and it serves as an analogy for learning as an analytical tool. Her assertion that writing is a place in which history can be avoided is therefore important for both frameworks. As she says,

> Everyone knows that a place exists which is not economically or politically indebted to all the vileness and compromise. That is writing. If there is somewhere else that can escape the infernal repetition, it lies in that direction."[15]

Only through writing and the search for a new way of loving the other without recourse to oppression or property can the hitherto victims of the hierarchical course of History begin to resist their place in it. There is a potential for what Liliana Alexandrescu calls the "miracle of reincarnation,"[16] with reference to Cixous's historical writing for the stage.[17] In the same way, the resilient learner is able to write his or her own resilience in the text—to find himself or herself through adult education, as Polixenes puts it, "stol'n from the dead."[18] This chapter concerns the first interview of this section of the book. It provides important insights into the interaction between love and learning as a form of resistance to history's reproductive project, and therefore of resilience. The interviewee is also a historian, and he reads his own autobiography through that lens. His understanding of the historical subject (in both senses) is sophisticated. The way that he negotiates the tension between understanding—with remarkable clarity and a lack of attachment—his own individual life as part of the vast social and economic sweep of history, while at the same using his own life to resist the historical script, is a fundamental component of his resilience.

Explicit Themes

Joe is a successful graduate of Kingsley College.[19] I arranged to meet him at an art gallery. We had lunch together in the gallery restaurant, and then

I interviewed him over coffee. After the interview, Joe took me on a tour of the local area in his car. He was very knowledgeable and passionate about the history of the place. I learned a lot from being with him, and I enjoyed his company.

Joe's resilience as an adult learner is obvious throughout the text; his is a remarkable and inspiring story that he summarizes as follows:

> I left school in 1957, done nothing 'til 1995, and then four years later it was, I had a diploma in history and historical theme from Kingsley, a certificate of higher education through Kingsley…and a second class history degree. In four years. With honours.[20]

Resilience is demonstrated in ways much stronger than simply completing the program and graduating, though. It emerges in particular regarding his account of three things:

1. his insistence that his disability, caused by a serious spinal injury that left him unemployed, should not prevent him from learning and achieving (he gains an honors degree in history from a redbrick university[21]);
2. his refusal to allow the low expectations about his academic achievement that were a feature of his early life to limit his achievement as an adult;
3. his return to college and the completion of the year at Kingsley, despite having a heart attack over Christmas.

After a secondary modern education[22] in the 1950s, in which it was commonplace to just be turned out as "factory product," Joe worked in an industry that involved "lifting, climbing, heavy work," until a severe spinal injury impaired his ability to carry on. After the first operation, he returned to work, but then the condition reoccurred, and this time it was much worse. The injury rendered him unemployed and unemployable in his previous industry. The economic conditions (early 1990s in a northern UK city) were not conducive to finding alternative work.

> At the time unemployment was fairly high and the chances of someone who was partly disabled finding employment was pretty rare.

So he joined the ranks of the long-term unemployed with little hope for what the future might bring. One day, when he was signing on as usual, he saw an advertisement in the window of the job center (*labor exchange*) for a year of study at Kingsley College, which is situated in a city far removed from his home town.

> I never had a pen, so I went back in the job centre, borrowed a pen and paper, wrote it all down, sent it off to Kingsley.

He applied and was interviewed, and after that,

> I got a letter about ten days later saying that I had been accepted. That's when the fear set in.

He fought the fear, though, and with the support of his wife, at the age of 54, he left his home and family in the north and moved to Kingsley for a year to complete a course in history at Kingsley College. Despite having a heart attack on Christmas Day, he went back to college and successfully gained the qualification. He subsequently went to a prestigious UK university, where he successfully completed an honors degree in history.

Resilience is performed by Joe in relation to these events by a series of actions:

1. he goes back into the job center to get a pen to write down the address of Kingsley College;
2. although he is fearful about the interview at Kingsley, he still goes;
3. he leaves his family to live in the city where Kingsley is situated for a year;
4. he throws himself into writing his essays, despite the fact that he has not written anything for a number of years;
5. he goes back to college after the heart attack;
6. he enrolls at a redbrick university as a mature student;
7. he overcomes significant physical discomfort in order to study—going to the reading room at the national archives library, for example;
8. he continues to learn after gaining the degree—presenting papers at the conference at Kingsley, despite being fearful.

Joe's story is a compelling account of how it is possible to refuse to be part of history's reproductive project. He uses education to resist becoming what Cixous calls "History's condemned,"[23] choosing instead to *read* history and using the historical perspective to read his own history differently and to write himself differently by learning about it.

Joe's explicit account of resilience centers on his insistence that self-determination is the key to success and on his gratefulness to his wife for her support. He uses a variation of "you've got to want it/work at it" 14 times in the interview. Commitment to study is pitched against "just wasting," "dossing,"[24] and "being itinerant." Those people who lack drive irritate him because they waste places that could go to other people who are more deserving. He also cites "the prize" (the degree) as an incentive, but he acknowledges that the experience of studying itself is also part of the prize. He implicitly acknowledges the importance of good teaching, high expectations, and the institution. He supports Kingsley College and is grateful for the opportunities it provided for him: "I believe in the college and I believe in Janet,[25] what she does, and what she tries to do." He "couldn't be more pleased and proud" of his acceptance into the university. The alternative to education is also cited by him as an incentive—the alternative to study was "despair, not having anything to do, being unemployed." Finally, and perhaps most importantly, Joe cites the love of his wife as a source of immense resilience. Her love for him is set out in detail as being a key feature of his recovery from the spinal injury and subsequent surgery. She also encourages him to go for the interview, to take the place at Kingsley, to return after the heart attack, and to go on to the degree at the university. He makes it clear that all of this was done at considerable cost to herself. Her love for Joe is the foundation for all the other considerations of resilience in the text. Throughout the interview, there is a tension for Joe between being pleased and proud of his overall achievements, which are considerable, and disappointment with his specific achievements—for example, he returns to the fact that he gained a respectable, rather than a very good grade, several times during the interview. Underlying all of this, though, is the philosophical understanding that the learning is part of a wider reality—"that's life"—in which agency is always mediated by circumstance and perfection is therefore unrealistic.

Implicit Themes

In order to open the text more fully, I have applied the same set of capabilities that were applied to *The Winter's Tale* to the interview with Joe. Each will be taken in turn as a way of reading the interview.

> 1. *They engage in open readings, resisting closed meanings, and they take a playful approach to language.*

In the interview with Joe, reading features as both a literal activity and a way of understanding life. His education provides him with the means with which to read as a historian. Joe told me that he had always enjoyed "English literature," reading books like "*Swiss Family Robinson, Black Beauty*, and *Robinson Crusoe*." As a child, he loved to read about heroes and explorers of other lands. As such, Joe is familiar with this access to other worlds. As an adult learner, reading happens in a series of enclosed spaces to which Joe has access. These are the Ashenden Library,[26] Sir Stephen's Library,[27] a thrift store, the Quaker Reading Room, and the national records archive.[28] Some of these places would be otherwise restricted, but Joe has been given "the keys" (through adult learning) that permit him to enter. He has been taught how to read in ways that make the texts, as well as the places in which they are kept, accessible. His higher education teachers have given him "the keys that open the tool box."

The places where reading happens are secret, sacred, and deeply exciting. In Sir Stephen's Library, for example, the books are "in presses, they're all chained." Joe can unlock the chains because his teachers have given him the means to do so. His literal account works symbolically as well—it is as if a light has been shone on all those texts: "It's dark and you press a light and all the ceiling is lit up—it's fabulous." For Joe, there is a sense of exclusivity and secret joy in these places. Everything is deeply exciting. And in the Ashenden Library, the whole system is designed to support study—you take your books to the desk and they keep them for the next day, with your name and topic on them. You can then pick up where you left off, "So if you want them for a week and you're in there for a week and you can go on there for a week."

Sometimes reading just a fragment has taken Joe off in completely new directions. He based his undergraduate dissertation on an investigation into the life of an anti-slavery campaigner on the basis of "a letter, a little booklet" that was given to him by his tutor. A whole life was there waiting to be documented and with it a story about resistance to the slave trade. In the same way, just finding "six lines" in the thrift store about a female veterinary surgeon who was arrested and sent to prison for failure to register and to enlist in the Second World War allowed him to do an entire study on female conscientious objectors.

Joe studies history and then applies a historical reading to his own life, placing events in the social and economic circumstances within which they took place. He reads historically. The history of class, politics, and economics intermingle with his personal account of resilient learning all the way through the interview. Social history—the opposite of "kings and queens"—provides Joe with a way of reading that helps him deconstruct not only his own past but also that of others:

> Being social history, it helps you look back on your past more, and see how things were weighed against people.

In this sense, Joe's resilience is partly constituted in his ability to read as a historian. He rereads his own compulsory education in its historical and economic context. There is a notable lack of bitterness in Joe's account. He does not lament missed opportunities, but merely wonders about how his life would have been different if he had benefited from them. He is happy, fulfilled, and engaged in reading the past and the present accurately and unsentimentally. Running throughout his account is the understanding that one need not forever be a passive historical subject—it is possible to resist the reproductive project. Reading is a constituent of resilience throughout the interview. His success as an adult learner proves that it is possible to find a space that allows him to resist the reproductive project. He does so by appropriating the historian's clothes and language and using them for good. Language is not doomed. Joe finds a way through it by choosing to write the "underwritten" stories of history.

Writing itself is the process through which transformation can happen. He applies to Kingsley for a place, and in return he is invited for an interview. His account of this success echoes that of an earlier time in his life, when he was 10 or 11; he submitted an essay about the [English] explorer Martin Frobisher to a competition and unexpectedly won.

> And I got a load of stuff back, I couldn't believe it...All posters and booklets, it was all addressed to me because I'd won this competition.

He also remembers writing for the school magazine:

> I wrote a little article and that was published in this as well. So I've always been that way inclined, to write and express myself.

As such, writing is linked to achievement for him from early on in his life. Writing is not just a way of expressing oneself but also of telling a truth. He is concerned, for example, that women's history is "underwritten." There is a sense that writing can have a political dimension, because it allows him to bear witness. He can use it to rewrite the history of others, including his schoolmates who left school at 15 without being able to read or write. He realizes now that they might have been dyslexic. When he thinks about his learning at school now, as a successful adult learner, he reads non-reading differently and understands the dire political and personal consequences of illiteracy:

> We used to make fun of them because they couldn't read or write. Even at 15 they left school without being able to read, write. When you think

about it now and you know a lot more, and you think, "crikey, they could have been dyslexic."

2. *They recognize, withstand, and negotiate the tension between inclusion and exclusion.*

Many of the situations that Joe describes are characterized by being partly inside and partly outside inner circles, establishments, and institutions. He grew up just outside the big city and attended the local secondary modern school as a result of the education system that "separated you" from the students who were destined to go to university "and onwards." He says very little about what happened between the time he left compulsory education in 1957 and his return to adult education in 1995, other than that he worked in jobs that involved "heavy, lifting work" in an industry to which he could not return after he sustained two serious back injuries. He found himself on the outside, "unemployed." But he refused to accept this state as a permanent one, so he applied for social security funding and when he did so, he saw the advertisement for Kingsley College.

> When I rang up to Kingsley and asked for more details, she said that "you realize, it's not part of the actual college, don't you?" And I said, "well, I really don't know that." She said, "No, it's not part of the actual college, but there are certain benefits attached to coming to Kingsley, which the full-time university students enjoy."

Joe turns this to his advantage, though. He enjoys the pedagogical environment of Kingsley, which combines very high expectations with a high level of support for those who choose to access it. He depicts attending Kingsley as an excellent experience and one that stood him in good stead for his degree at the redbrick university. While there were limitations at Kingsley (they only have a small library, for example), he makes up for them by accessing the capital-rich establishments associated with the university based in the same city, with which the college has links. He throws himself into the experience of life in this university city.

> You get a card which allows you to go to any of the lectures, in any of the colleges, any time.

As such, learning is something to be enjoyed and devoured. He goes to the lectures and he joins the debating society[29] ("I'm lucky, I've got a lifetime membership"), but most of all he enjoys the libraries—working in the Ashenden and Sir Stephen's libraries is glamorous and exciting. At no point does Joe show any rancor about what his tutor wanted to warn him about— that he is not a full member of the university. On the contrary, Joe portrays the dual membership as utterly fortuitous and key to his success. Kingsley is depicted as the best possible version of pedagogical input: "At Kingsley University they teach you to think and argue and ask."

He sees Kingsley as the answer to the problem that would now be called widening participation:

> If they made places like Kingsley for younger people to give them confidence, there would be a lot more working-class people going to university. You know, making something of themselves.

Here the outsider status of Kingsley (not being part of the whole university) is depicted in an entirely advantageous way.

All the time that Joe was away in his new academic home, he was away from his real home in the north; "My wife stayed here. At home, with two children, and I went to (the new city)."

And although there is a real sense that he misses them, and he is keen not to waste the opportunity at Kingsley because of that, he consistently portrays the arrangement as his wife's sacrifice rather than his own. This sense of wasted opportunities counterbalances what Joe presents as the opposite to resilient learning. It is the sort of thing that he condemns the less resilient adult learners for:

> There's no good just going there, just wasting...because people like that went there for a few months, then disappeared.

The unresilient learners become the disappeared. Unlike Joe, they are unable to understand the experience as transitory and preparation for something else. They are literally and figuratively homeless. "I think probably a lot of them were pretty itinerant. A lot of them didn't really have any real home, or home base." The Kingsley experience for them, then, is just another nomadic episode, and one that they can't sustain. In a way that contrasts sharply with all his benevolence and his historian's view of everything else in his past, Joe is angry with and contemptuous of these unresilient learners. His explicit account for this anger is that they are squandering a place that could have gone to somebody else who better deserved it. Perhaps the disappeared also represent the dangerous supplements to Joe's resilience (for the same reasons, as I argued in Chapter Three, that Carol received a hostile reaction from Garner's students). They are the confirmation of Bourdieu and Passeron's theory about the inevitability of the educational mortality rate: "Someone would say, 'Oh where's so and so gone?' Just gone."

They have been unable to sustain their existence in temporary exile, even an exile which provided a seat in the Ashenden Library and membership of the debating society. For such people, exile has been too much. They have either returned to their homes or to their homeless state that is home, even though the college went to extraordinary lengths to retain them:

> When they packed up for Christmas, obviously a lot of people went home. Those that didn't have any home, the college rented rooms for them in the YMCA, to spend Christmas in.

Joe regards those people who merely see the year as an opportunity to find a home as lazy and undisciplined. The fact that they are searching for another home in a way condemns them:

> There's no good point in going there, if you're just going there to spend a year [here with a] roof over your head, as a guest dossing in someone else's front room [living room]. You've got to want to go. You've got to really want to go.

In this way, resilience is constituted in the acceptance that time will be spent in exile—in a homeless state—and that although learning itself is a kind of home, it must be understood as such. He did not see the experience at Kingsley and then at the redbrick university as something to automatically gain more capital—"I had no real expectations of working. It was the satisfaction of achieving something."

> 3. *They show a willingness to divest themselves of their "clothing" and to try on new clothes.*

Joe's identity shifts throughout the interview as he takes on different clothes and then removes them. His experience of adult education has provided him with a secure identity as a historian and "bona fide researcher." He also speaks like a historian—giving precise dates for events ("In 1996, I was 54 and going to university"), putting time lapses in their historical context ("But since 1957 I've done no higher education"). He also puts those events into the social and economic contexts that gave rise to them; he was educated in the 1950s, for example, when working-class people were "more servile" and "more resigned to their place in life," and he became unemployed in the early 1990s when "unemployment was fairly high and the chances of someone who was partly disabled finding employment was pretty rare." With reference to his compulsory education in a secondary modern school, he stated, "the rest of you were factory product. That was the system." When he was interviewed for the place at Kingsley, he understood from the start what kind of history he would be studying:

> They [the interviewers] said, "what sort of history do you like?" I said, "Well, I'm not into history of kings and queens in general," and she said, "Good."

He uses the capital provided to him as a Kingsley student to gain access to the places in which he can pursue his knowledge—the Quaker reading rooms, for which

> you've got to send a letter from someone who vouches for you that you are a bona fide researcher.

The national archive library research room and the libraries also feature strongly in the account. None of these places is indiscriminately accessible to the public, so Joe's identity as a researcher gives him access. He is sufficiently inside the system to benefit from the privileges it provides.

What education has given him, he explains to me, is the confidence to wear different clothes and to not be intimidated by the clothes that others wear:

> I think you have to talk to anybody at a social group. I mean, it shouldn't be that way, but it does help you.

When he graduates from university with his honors degree in history, he wears the clothes of a historian—a tie depicting the Bayeaux Tapestry. History is literally written on him. The prize—the qualification—also allows him to rewrite his own educational history and those of others.

> I bought a suit. I haven't worn a suit for years. I bought a suit and a nice tie. Bought one from Past Times.[30] It was a pattern of 1066.

The graduation ceremony is part of the "prize" and a celebration of all that he has achieved. Dressing up is part of that ("they lend you all the robes"), but the learning is bigger than what it represents ("A bit of paper with a ribbon around it"). However, this should not detract from the importance of the event ("So I've got that photograph that I had taken indoors").

There is a sense that he thinks that the dressing up is a secondary and frivolous activity, but he still sees it as part of the overall importance of what learning has provided him:

> Dressing up wasn't the incentive. It was the fact. That bit of paper, you've done it. You've been there, you've done it. You've done your job, not your job, you've done your major. You've worked and you've done it. There it is.

The dressing up at the graduation ceremony contrasts sharply with an earlier episode, in which he had to get undressed as far as possible. His spinal injuries resulted in him being removed from the job in which he worked (interestingly, he never told me what this job was, suggesting that the clothes he used to wear are now so far in the past that they are not worth mentioning), and he had to undergo a series of major operations. The operations gave him access to a view of himself that was not just naked, it was beyond flesh:

> [I have had] what they call a spinal fusion. They open you up, right around there. I know I'm being a bit gory; they take your stomach out. What he's (the surgeon) doing, he's not looking at your body, he's look-ing at the screen above. You've got a camera in your back, in your body. And he's looking up there what he's doing. And they took the disk out, because it was damaged. Took the disk out, shaved a piece of my thigh, and they fused that into the vertebrae. Put everything back, stitched you up, and about three weeks before I went for the operation I had to go to one of these prosthetic companies. They made a plastic cast from the waist to the neck. Made out of plastic. Like a suit of armour. You put that on with Velcro. When I had the operation I had to wear that all the time for six months except when I got into bed.

Joe has had the rare experience of seeing himself from the inside. It is an inside that was damaged and has since been mended. He knows he has guts, because he has had them taken out, and all of it has been played on a screen above him. A prosthetic spine and rib cage has taken the place of his real one, and he knows that what appears can be replaced, can be synthesized and redressed. Joe portrays this as emancipatory knowledge rather than a tragedy, and it is therefore important to his understanding of his resilience.

4. *They resist passivity by dealing actively with their teachers (for example, by finding alternative, unofficial teachers or by subverting the Pygmalion/Galatea relationship).*

Joe says very little directly about the pedagogical processes at Kingsley and the redbrick university, and there is no sense at all that he has struggled against the academic management system at either institution or found either of them wanting. Teachers are presented affectionately and, in the case of Janet, with enormous loyalty and support. There is, therefore, no negativity in the way that there is with some of the other resilient learners in the study. Joe loves learning, he loves history, and he loves higher education. This is not to say that he has become commodified by the system; he is energetic and opinionated, and he argues, but he uses the knowledge to provide critiques of the society in which he lives, both in the past and the present. Joe constitutes himself as a resilient learner through reading and writing. Writing emerges as a form of resilience. Joe's story as an adult learner begins when he goes into the job center as usual to sign on. When I ask him what led him to make such a dramatic change in his life he says, "I think it was despair, not having anything to do, being unemployed." He was in a state, therefore, in which he was ready and willing to respond to the advertisement for Kingsley College in the window of the job center. His resilience is constituted in writing from the very start:

> I never had a pen so I went back in the job centre, borrowed a pen and paper, wrote it all down, sent it off to Kingsley. I got a reply and they asked me to write a few short essays, which I hadn't done since I left school in 1957. I wrote a few short essays, and Janet, my tutor there, she looked at them and sent back comments.

As previously stated, this echoes an earlier episode in his life in which the act of writing and sending his work out into the world brought forth rewards, when, as a schoolboy, he entered a competition by writing a essay about Frobisher, the explorer and, much to his surprise, he won. He sees prizes as attainable and the pursuit as worthwhile: "the fact that there was a prize at the end—university...I didn't want to blow that, so I went back."

So Joe throws himself into his learning, taking advice from his tutors about what to do.

"My first tutorial was rough..." He met his tutor, who gave him his feedback on his first essay:

> He said, "very good Joe, for a first essay. Can I see the notes?" I said, "I've thrown them away." He went, "Joe, you've done the first great sin. You've thrown away your notes. You've committed the first big sin. You've

thrown away your notes!" So ever since then I've never thrown anything away. I've got a filing cabinet indoors, full of papers.

As such, great credence is given to developmental writing. Writing itself is understood as way of learning, rather than simply an expression of what is learned elsewhere. And good support is provided.

> Obviously it got easier as you went on. You know what you had to do. You knew the discipline and you knew what the keys were. You had the keys.

He is provided with the keys that unlock previously prohibited learning spaces.

> The tools. They give you the keys (to) unlock the tool box—this is what you do and this how you do it. Now you've got to learn from that and do it every week. It became easier and easier. In the end, like, they said, "you have to do a 10,000 word dissertation." Oh—that's okay.

He is immensely grateful to his teachers: "God love Kingsley, they're for the underdog, the little people."

5. *They can be read as miraculés; for example, they experience a kind of resurrection.*

Joe's specific historical concerns are with unwritten histories—with the absences and the silent spaces and the stories of those people who have objected to dominant historical trends—less-well-known anti-slavery campaigners and female conscientious objectors—resilient people, in fact. His studies have included people like the planation farmer, who opposed slavery and who set up sugar plantations in India with paid workers as an alternative to the slave-trade-dependent industry in the West Indies. Joe was interested in telling this man's story because, "he was a man who isn't mentioned in history a lot at all." Through historical reading and writing, Joe is able to undo the spell of shackles and silence. Likewise, he is interested in women's history because "women's history is underwritten, it isn't extensive as it should be." The idea that something that is underwritten can be written, and therefore restored to life, is close to the notion of resurrection that underpins the thinking about the nature of transformative adult learning in this work. Writing can refuse to collude with death, as Cixous says in her essay "School of the Dead,"[31] and we can choose to resurrect the dead and forgotten through the generous act of writing about them. So Joe resurrects the people he writes about. In so doing, Joe's own resurrection through education is effected.

Joe's interest in history, developed from an early interest in the lives of adventurers such as Frobisher, is given focus and taken on as an adult learner. Joe's learning itself represents a kind of adventure. He has traveled a long way from his roots, but as a historian he goes back to those roots:

> Only a couple of years ago I managed to get hold of some friends from Friends Reunited from my own school. None of them went to university and when I told then I had been to university since, they couldn't believe it.

He revisits his own history as a learner—he was someone who "had a good voice," who could sing in the choir, who wrote for the school magazine, and who won essay-writing competitions, but all of that went unused for nearly four decades. History is understood realistically throughout all of this. There is a tension all the way through the interview between an understanding of history as something over which the subject can exert agency and a resignation that events and circumstances limit that agency—you can only do so much.

> I just wish I'd worked a bit harder in university. That shows my expectations have gone up in those few years. Whereas before, I got as far as an interview at Kingsley, but there I am, worried, disappointed, that I didn't get a [top grade] at university. That's life.

Agency is therefore always dynamic—always changing in response to historical circumstances but also always with the potential of shaping history as well. You can conscientiously object—to war, to slavery, or to lack of educational opportunities—and you can do something about it by trying to create an alternative that is better and fairer; but you are always constrained by your own historical context. What transcends the historical context and the potential of the individual subject to have agency within it is love and its potential to enable the resurrection.

Love emerges as a significant force of resilience in several guises in the interview. It is the miracle that allows for the resurrection through adult learning. Joe's passion for learning and achievement is, first and foremost, the reason he provides for his own resilience. He recognizes a fundamental difference between those people like himself, who want success and completion, and those who don't. Central to his account of resilience is his description of his very serious back injury. He returns to it late in the interview. Earlier he had simply told me, "I've got a bad back." Only late on in the interview did I understand the extent of what he had been through. His wife's support of him through the time when he was wearing "a suit of armour" and when he had his whole stomach taken out is central to his account of resilience. He ends the interview with her story. As such, he enacts what he described earlier about the underwritten nature of women's history. He brings his wife to the center of this story of resilience, and her love for him becomes the narrative of resilience. She emerges from the sidelines and moves to the center. She is "wife, lover, friend, everything," and her multiple identities place her at the center of this account.

He portrays her many times as "a rock." It is his wife who insists that he take the place at Kingsley: "I've got my wife to thank for that." And the resurrection of Joe from a state of despair to the status of historian becomes what Sebastian in *The Tempest* calls "A most high miracle."[32]

Joe's wife is the instigator for his survival and resilience. Even before he returned to adult learning, it was she who kept the family together while he was in the hospital.

> She was working part-time, two young children to bring up, take to school, cook, etc. She used to work in the evenings, because I'd come home and she'd work in the evenings. She changed her hours to work in the day, so she could bring the children right up to (the city). We never had a car, 10 mile trip from (where I lived) to (the city) with two young children. To see me in the neurosurgical unit. She's done that twice...so I felt I owed her something.

Her support and strength was key to his decision to accept the place at Kingsley. His initial response after he was offered the place was a feeling of fear, but his wife insisted that he take up his place, even though it must have made her own life very difficult. "That's when the fear set in, and I said I'm not going and she said, 'You are you're going.'" She overrides his fear and enables him to rise again through learning. So he goes to Kingsley and studies for his certificate. And when he has the heart attack at Christmas, his wife is there to support him and to insist that he finish the course:

> And she said to me "you go," and I thought, I've got to finish it. Because my wife supported me while I've been at college as well.

And still she supports him, accompanying him for the weekends when Joe presents at the public history conference; "she spends her money" while Joe presents his papers on the unwritten histories. His story of resilience is, therefore, in itself a writing of the unwritten history. He, finally, refuses to accept credit for his own resilience, passing it instead to his wife and her love for him.

Here the application of the five capabilities has allowed for a systematic analysis of the interview text in the way that it allowed for good analytic work in Chapter Four. The capabilities also stand up, by and large, as articulating some sense of commonality among resilient adult learners. There is a sense here, though, that Joe's interview has become somewhat compartmentalized and fragmented as a result. The capabilities model opened up the reading of *The Winter's Tale* considerably. Here, although the model has been a helpful analytical tool, there is some sense that it has closed the text down. The fluidity in the analysis has been lost, and Joe himself is less embodied than he might be. Despite the theoretical framework set out at the beginning, this analysis remains a logocentric, social scientific analysis of an interview. In the next chapter, I provide an alternative way of reading the interview data. I will temporarily shed the capabilities model in order to find a more open way of reading and writing about the resilient learners. The interview with Jane in Chapter Six, then, is the first attempt at a more purely Cixousian reading of an interview with a resilient learner. This is developed in Chapter Seven with regard to the interview with Sarah. In both accounts, I begin to take a more playful approach to my own writing in order to let the subjects live through the spaces in the text. Metaphor is deliberately developed in both chapters as a way of teasing out the currents and undercurrents in the interview texts while at the same time trying to evoke the theoretical tensions in my analytic technique.

CHAPTER 6

Jane

Hélène Cixous's writing in *Sorties*[1] is rich in images that evoke the morphological processes of planet Earth. Land and sea are mighty, moving entities. Female *jouissance* "reaches, covers over, washes a shoreline, flows embracing the cliff's undulation."[2] Inside the woman writer is a "white depth, a core" that is "covered by an infinite number of strata, layers, sheets of paper."[3] There is a sense of oneness between the writer and all things in *l'écriture féminine* but, warns Cixous, "this does not mean that she is undifferentiated magma";[4] such writing is always stratified and complex. The spaces between the pen and the paper and the reader and the text have their own topographies and contours. Pamela Shurmur-Smith[5] draws attention to the frequency and intensity of physical, geographical images in Cixous's writing. She notes the centrality of these metaphors to Cixous's expression of her aspirations for reading and writing in general and of Derridean deconstruction in particular, citing Cixous's description in her own notebooks of what Derrida represents:

> [H]e is situated at the point of contact between two slopes, versants, inclines, sides—at the reversal point of climb and descent, of desire into mourning, of mourning into burst of life, of you into me, of he into she.[6]

The location of reading and writing in a place—a place that is always dynamic and always reflecting and resisting the illusion of stability—allows this version of deconstructive practice to escape reduction to the arid application of abstract ideas that characterizes some versions of post-structuralist theory. Pierre Bourdieu's sincere concern about the dangers of this tendency in his observation that Derrida plays a "supremely intellectual game"[7] can be countered by pointing to Cixous's imagining of open ways of reading and writing (in her own and Derrida's work) as being linked to bodies—the body of the reader, the body of the writer, and the body of the planet—all of which, like James Lovelock's Earth,[8] are part of the same, complex, interacting system.

A powerful and recurrent image in Cixous's work is that of the volcano. In her 2004 interview with Susan Sellers about her own writing practice, she uses the volcanic simile to illustrate the force of writing and the necessary passivity of the writer in the face of it, "as if it were a volcano spitting lava, and the shape of it, the appearance of the matter, the way it is disposed on the page, is decided by the spirit of it, which is something I don't calculate."[9] This links to her earlier work in which the as yet undemonstrated power of feminine writing is heralded as an almost inevitable event that will, at some point, tear out and overwhelm the apparently safe and stable constraints of the earth's crust: "at the end of the Age of the Phallus, women will have been either wiped out or heated to the highest, most violent white hot fire."[10] There will be an eruption: "Voice, unfastening, fracas. Fire!" Then, she prophesizes, the tectonic fires will be liberated: "An outpouring that can be agonizing, since she may fear, and make the other fear, endless aberration and madness in her release."[11]

I am seeking to make analogous and to build a bridge between two places—the place in which profound and transformational adult learning happens and the place in which writing becomes stronger than both the writer and the hierarchical constraints within which she operates—in Cixous's terms, feminine. Cixous's description of writing as "a place of intransigence and of passion. A place of lucidity where no one takes what is a pretence of existence for life,"[12] resonates with the rare experience of deep adult learning that emerges from various texts in the study and which is transformational in the Freirean sense, because "it frees the educator no less than the educatees from the twin thraldom of silence and monologue."[13] I am interested in the ways that Cixous's revelations about the liberating nature of writing might be transferable to, or at least provide ways to think about, the processes adopted by resilient adult learners. It may be that the struggles needed in order to resist superficial, logocentric ways of writing might involve the same sorts of practices that are necessary to avoid being swallowed up by hostile academic and external environments.

This chapter concentrates on an interview with a real resilient adult learner, Jane. I am interested in the way that the application of Cixous's central volcanic metaphor opens up the reading of the transcript to reveal the deconstructive energy within it. On the surface, the interview text is an apparently safe (in the sense that it is seemingly nonthreatening, like a dormant volcano) liberation narrative[14] about learning as a function of the recovery from a marriage breakdown and the dissolution of a previous identity as wife and mother. Below that is a much more interesting and darkly energetic story in which Jane gives voice to her anger about the system that has liberated her; she exposes and reviles the oppressive and controlling nature of her saviour. Hers is an active text in which constant, intrusive, tectonic activity threatens to detonate and fracture its brittle crust. By the end of the transcript, she reaches a Cixousian place in which the illusion of stability is revealed as such.

Extrusive Resilience

The explicit resilience story that structures Jane's narrative centers on learning as a survival strategy in the aftermath of the breakdown of her marriage. It is a familiar but powerful liberation narrative in which she draws on the feminist understanding of self-discovery to explain how the motivation to learn supported her recovery from abandonment. These are the first words of her interview:

> Like lots of women going back into learning, it was the breakdown of a relationship. I was married when I was 19, I was married for 29 years. Basically my old man ran off with another woman...I was stuck at 48 wondering what the hell I was going to do for the next, however many years.

She tells her story as her own, but she positions it firmly within a tradition of other narratives ("Like lots of women"). Hers is a story of the creation or recovery of self that has something in common with Nicole Ward Jouve's[15] insistence that the feminist autobiography needs to allow for the creation of a self in the traditional sense before it can safely be deconstructed. This surface account of resilience needs to be in place before Jane can allow herself to deconstruct it. A set of straightforward binaries underpin the account—unhappy marriage versus happy independence, unfulfilled wife and mother versus emancipated academic and, later, Kingsley versus the university.[16] Jane tells me that she had been "defined in my relationships with other people. I had been his wife and their mother."

As such, she recounts the progress from powerlessness to success. Jane's is a logical and linear narrative—she uses the temporal circumstances of her divorce to punctuate her spoken account and to integrate an understanding of the part that learning played in that account. Milestones are set out as the framework for the recovery. The calendar year serves as a plot—time is framed simply and sequentially:

> So he left on Boxing Day and I put in for Kingsley at the Easter. By the September I was at Kingsley.

And,

> So actually, he left on the Boxing Day, we were divorced in the July of that year, and almost a year to the day, I was accepted at (university).

And later,

> A year to the day I was divorced, almost to the day, I was accepted at the university.

The liberation narrative of the adult learner (which is explored in depth by Willy Russell in *Educating Rita*[17] and is analyzed in the light of this study in Chapter Three) is combined with a mainstream feminist reading of recovery from a marriage breakdown. Rejection from the marriage is positioned against acceptance by the university in a simple binary. Learning, firstly at Kingsley and then during her degree, is characterized throughout the interview as an alternative activity to abandonment. She frequently uses the image of nothingness to describe what she was "running away" from. Jane was left with "a big vacuum" in her life, and into it came learning. The vacuum is full of nothing but exhilarating potential, like the hollow craters below the earth's surface that are so dangerous because that is where volcanic activity is born. She resisted the deficient identity that she was presented with because it was "the pits" and left her "down on the floor." There is a clear trajectory from the abyss, nothingness, and victimhood toward emancipation.

"I had been seen as deserted wives tend to be, as rather a victim. I'm not really a victim mentality," she says, echoing Cixous's autobiographical assertion that "I cannot inhabit a victim, . . . I resist: detest a certain passivity, it promises death for me."[18] She is deserted/desert-ed—left to fend for herself in the desert. "People who write go into the night, into the desert," says Cixous,[19] and Jane ventures out as a learner into the open space and finds herself in it, writing off her marriage as she speaks a different story. Like writing, deep learning must be preceded by risk, by time spent in the desert under the night sky. Learning provides a something as an alternative to the nothing—it fills up the hours and it gives her a purpose. The fact that she had "reached the pits, really," forced her to do something that would be "instrumental for digging myself out." Risk and security are in balance—learning is "a safe way of running away," and the fact that she was granted a three-year career break helped her enormously, because "if I hadn't had that safety net, I don't know if I would have taken the risk." There is spadework involved in the escape plan—just what Jane needs—but she digs upward, not downward, and on the way she realizes that the circumstances that preceded the journey to the desert were restrictive and diminishing.

> I was Mrs. Cereal Packet Family. I'd stayed at home to look after the kids for 15 years, doing all the crappy part-time jobs.

Fifteen years of reading the back of cereal boxes is presented by her as intrinsic to the desert, the pits, and the floor—not its idyllic opposite. For her, going to Kingsley is not just an alternative to abandonment, it is an alternative to the restrictive circumstances that gave rise to it.

> It was the first time since I was 19 that I had been defined in my own right, and I found that awe-inspiring.

So, after Jane's husband leaves her for another woman, she goes to Kingsley College for a year, where she excels, and from there to a full-time degree program at an elite university. She graduates goes on to have a successful career. It is a remarkable account of the way that successful adult learning can transform a life from a dependent, unfulfilled position of a middle-aged, middle-class wife and mother to a position of intellectual and professional self-efficacy and financial independence.

Jane believes in the liberating function of adult learning, and she does a good deal of "outreach work," talking to "women at conferences" about the benefits that come from it. She is honest about the security that was afforded to her by being part of a community at Kingsley and through the all-female university residence system in the university—she stresses the importance of the social and emotional aspects of learning, as well as the academic, telling me that

> I joke with people that I came to university to avoid cooking my own meal, but there was an element of truth in that.

As with other interviewees in this study, there is a symbiosis between agency and fate in the account of the journey that leads to the learning, and it is in contrast to her account of the marriage breakdown, in which she bestows herself little agency. She talks about fate taking a hand but also about the importance of having "a strategy" and the fact that she was "focused" in the pursuit of her goals (which were presumably to survive and to avoid victim-hood). This is a hygienic and becoming account of the adult learner's story—it is unlikely to upset teachers, learners, or funders, but it is also not fully evolved. This is not to suggest in any way that Jane herself was disingenuous but rather that the accepted adult learning narrative, while being a powerful account of one version of resilience, is by its very nature a simple and partial version of the trajectory, because the process of change necessarily involves agency and activity. This safe, logocentric discourse as an explanation of resilience (there was nothing to go back to) is a very important one. The tremors that lie beneath it, though, represent a far more interesting account of the real, lived experience of the adult learner's progress. There is another account of resilient learning that concerns the struggle of the adult learner to achieve and to maintain mature autonomy within an academic system that insists on obedience, and which infantilizes her in order to achieve it. It is the struggle of the adult learner who recognizes the sham but who is dependent on it to succeed. Both versions of the resilience narrative are in constant play, and they move against each other throughout the transcript.

Intrusive Resilience

There is a running fault line in Jane's account between her endorsement of the educational capital (which, as Pierre Bourdieu argues, is the "certified form" of economic and cultural capital[20]) that is provided to her as a university student and graduate on the one hand, and her challenge of what she regards as the "façade" of the system on the other. A pedagogical binary is set up between Kingsley and the university. Kingsley represents sympathy with the adult learner and genuine engagement with the learning (process), and the university represents an exclusive performance of academic skill (outcome). Even early on in the interview, when the resilience narrative is smooth, she explicitly states, "I enjoyed Kingsley academically a bit more than I enjoyed [the university] to be honest."

There is an unresolved tension that lurks beneath a lot of what Jane says about her time at the university. It operates at word as well as sentence level. Two semantic fields are identifiable in the transcript: one that clusters around the notion of excellence (cream/prime/best everywhere), and another that evokes its shameful underbelly (credentialism/exams are there to scare you/failing at Medicine was getting only an average grade/he wasn't plagiarizing (but) he got the highest grade). Throughout the interview, Jane oscillates between endorsing a hierarchical understanding of higher education institutions as being representative of the natural order and endorsing, and also challenging, the corresponding assumption that innate ability, rather than privilege, is what defines the student population at the university. She sets up the university as the academic ideal and those who study there as a natural elite:

> You are obviously being judged with the *prime* of the kids in the country.

And

> We're talking about the *cream* of the bunch. These kids have been the best everywhere. [my emphases]

This smooth-surface discourse is undercut and mirrored by another semantic field that is opened up by adopting Cixous's interest in homonyms and rhyme.[21] The first version of resilient learning concentrates on the prime/cream discourse, but this is constantly subducted by a second, in which the sins of the system are revealed. The students who are the "cream" and "prime" of the kids in the country cannot be separated from the *crimes* of the system that *preens* itself and parades its successes on the basis of the subordination of whom and what it excludes. Jane is aware of the necessary spectral presence of failure, which ensures that the cream and the prime can exist and be validated. Bourdieu offers a sociological explanation of the same phenomenon:

> The specific contradiction of the scholastic mode of reproduction lies in the opposition between the interests of the class which the educational system serves statistically and the interests of those class members whom it sacrifices, that is, the "failures" who are threatened with *déclassement* for lack of the qualifications formally required for rightful membership.[22]

The ritual sacrifice of those inside the learning academy must be constantly reenacted in order for the successes to be legitimated. Jane's support for the hierarchy is constantly under threat of being overwhelmed by the disruption of it, partly because of the symbolic capital she invests in the dominant groups there. So it is precisely because, for example, "you are being judged with the prime of the kids in the country" that "(it) is not guaranteed to raise your self-esteem." As such, the capital provided by the university has currency outside of the institution, but this is undermined by the allotment of capital inside.

Just as another resilient adult learner, Jane Eyre, is disturbed by but dependent on her other upstairs, in Sandra Gilbert and Susan Gubar's depiction of the madwoman in the attic as a central figure in the (sub)consciousness of the nineteenth-century woman writer,[23] this Jane's account of the liberating effect of university is dependent on, but constantly at risk from, attack by another version of the same institution—one that is controlling, anti-intellectual, and immoral. At the signifier level, the practiced, narrative account of resilient adult learning that is presented to the "women at conferences" is always under threat. Jane's words are constantly at risk of setting fire to themselves. She resists her own approving discourse throughout the interview. So unlike Kingsley, which remains a celebrated signifier throughout the discourse, the university is always mutable. To return to Ward Jouve's point about the necessity of the construction of a stable self before women can risk deconstruction,[24] Jane's autobiography as a learner must first be cultivated within the confines of an uncomplicated account of a protective institutional space before she can allow herself to begin to break it down somewhere else.

The university is used as an emblem of her triumph over adversity. She celebrates the first version and the way that it maintains its high standards and celebrates excellence as follows:

> Some universities accept it [a qualification from Kingsley] as being the first year undergraduate... You certainly couldn't do it [use the qualification as an equivalent of the first year of study] at [this university].

And

> That's one of the joys of [this place]; you don't just mix with your subject. You know, you're sitting around a table... and you've got experts in every subject.

Undercutting this discourse is a much stronger one that critiques the emphasis on performance and façade and the lack of depth of learning and that draws attention to the damage that it does. The two versions are mediated by a third place in which resilience can be nurtured—the matriarchal space of the all female residence.[25] To some, this exclusively female space would be restrictive, even oppressive; but to Jane it plays a fundamental role in the account of her survival. She deliberately chose to live on campus "so that I was part of a community." It is a community that can offer support for the lone adult learner and that prevents her from being—as she was after the divorce—"left alone in the big house."

She celebrates her hall of residence because it provides a less hierarchical, more playful space: "It's not like some of the other colleges, it's very inclusive. We don't have a high table." So the women's college is able to provide a female environment that houses a different kind of table, but even there people can't stop long for breakfast, because the academic pressure is so intense. It is a long way from the breakfast table of her previous life, in which she was Mrs. Cereal Packet. Here the community provides support, encouraging resilience in each other. One of the things that led her to the university was the promise of a free lunch: "I'm into free lunches."

Despite her insistence that the student population represents "the cream," she disputes that genetic/innate ability has a bearing on the nature of learning once in the system: "They're training for the civil service. It has nothing to do with intelligence."

As a former civil servant, she can recognize the process and can remember/imagine its consequences. Despite her cream/prime explanation, she disputes the part that genuine intelligence plays: "I got here and I was totally unprepared. Some of the girls had prepared for years," she says.

She presents a picture of a hierarchical, conformist structure that falls short of its own rhetoric in terms of scholarly ambitions. Her way of coping with it has been to develop resilience through other means: "What I did was, I diversified. I became president of the college."

The female world of the college is not entirely the playful, equitable place that Cixous envisages beyond the "sublatable, dialectical"[26] nature of phallocentrism. Formal power still exists, but Jane uses the hierarchical privilege to reach out to others: "I did a lot of access work."

The paradox is that the attractiveness of the elitist system also makes it quintessentially forbidding to the nontraditional, adult learner. I was interested to hear about her degree dissertation. It was an investigation into the experience of young, white women who married into traditional Muslim families. Many of them were "wild" (something that made her feel "quite envious"), and they had come from unstable backgrounds and had experienced "rocky childhoods." She takes an implicit feminist stance to her data,[27] expressing unease with the fact that her subjects had given her something for little in return and reflecting on her own life experiences in light of her findings. She returns to her earlier autobiographical theme of the isolating nature of motherhood in her reflections on the women she interviewed:

> They were often quite socially isolated, not because they were Muslims but because they had small children. And I've been there, I know what that was like.

Her conclusion about the women in her study seems to resonate with her own situation at the university:

> They were doing something because they thought it was permanent, and that it was traditional...[but they were]...doing things that normally

wouldn't have been accepted. That, in itself, was changing the culture they were joining, their presence, just their presence, was changing it.

In this way, the essence of the experience of the adult, nontraditional student is encapsulated. It is the same dilemma that Rita in *Educating Rita* faces for much of the play—she is driven to want to be like the other students, but her own presence means that the system needs to adapt in order to accommodate her. Rita wants to become one of what she calls "the proper students"[28] (a phrase that is also used by Jane about her time at Kingsley), but in order for her to do that, Frank, both as an individual teacher and as the representative of the university, has to be changed in order for her to be admitted and accepted. The resilient learner is therefore a catalyst, a change agent, and both resilience and resistance are necessary to withstand the norms of the environment she enters. The conflation of privilege and academic achievement is fully understood by Jane, but she also recognizes the undisputable advantages of the symbolic, educational capital[29] that is conferred by the institution. The tension lies in her dismay about the former and the attraction to the latter. She can't ever take pure pride in the rewards of the system, therefore, because the system itself contaminates and interferes in the whole-hearted celebration of the capital it bestows. She is trapped, because she can't overthrow the system that has condescended to admit her unless she steps outside of it, but the value granted to her as an insider performs a liberating function from which she cannot/will not return.

Jane is angry about the substantial experience of learning at the university. She had enjoyed Kingsley, where she was "flying" because "it was so liberating." Her description of learning there shares many common features with other learners in this study; for example, "It was like a door opening, it was so exciting." The door is a central image in the accounts of adult learning featured in this work. Jane says she initially chose to study sociology because "I wanted to open it up," but when she gets there, she finds that it is not just the door to the discipline that she wants to open but also the discipline itself. Previously she found the validation of identity that learning brings to be "awe-inspiring." The academic processes that are part of the university experience are, by contrast, presented negatively. The tension between the two universities—the one that liberates and the one that controls—remains unresolved throughout the interview. Significantly, the strong teachers (she mentions "the good ones" as the opposite of those who treat her like a child), who provide valuable guidance for her dissertation and who help her to remain resilient, are invisible and silent throughout the text. In order to problematize Jane's presentation of her education there, I will examine the account according to three fundamental pedagogical concerns: teaching, learning, and assessment.

1. Teaching

Jane's age, in addition to setting her apart from the norm, is the source of both her resilience and her conflict with the system. She deliberately chose to go to an institution that catered for her as a mature student, and this, she feels, was the right decision, because she did not feel isolated in her college at the university. She also used her age to inform her decision about her choice of subject: "I wanted to do something where I felt my great age was an advantage, rather than a disadvantage." Her maturity is a constant source of difficulty for her, though. She distinguishes between the good teachers, who were not threatened by her, and those who were. Not only did she present tutors with pedagogical challenges, but also her own sense of identity was challenged by the system.

> One of them actually said to me, "you must remember, I am the teacher." It is very difficult if they take that stance. You go back to being a child again.

The child is a recurrent theme in many of the texts in this study. For Jane, the pressure to become "a child again" in order to make her teachers feel secure inhibits her development and diminishes her faith in the pedagogical process. She strenuously resists the characterization—the laziness of its construction contrasts sharply with her own forging of a complex learning identity in the earlier part of the interview.

One circumscribed version of teaching and learning positions the adult learner as progeny. In Chapter Three, I noted the way that Frankenstein's monster serves as a motif for a pedagogical dystopia in which the teacher attempts to reproduce himself/herself in the person of the learner. The references to the positioning of the adult learner as a child are plentiful in the fictional and nonfictional accounts of adult learning. In *Educating Rita*, Frank explicitly links teaching to the activities of Dr. Frankenstein—"I shall insist on being known as Mary. Mary Shelley"[30]—and Rita resists it by telling him "I can do without you,"[31] thus opening the way for his painful metamorphosis into an excellent teacher and the corresponding apotheosis of Rita as the archetypal resilient adult learner. The hopeless teacher says to the hopeless learner in David Mamet's *Oleanna*, "I'll talk to you as if you were my son,"[32] but their tragedy is that neither of them has the resilience to move beyond this position, resulting in the learner turning, like Frankenstein's monster, from pathetic dependence to rage and attempted patricide. Like the professor in *Oleanna*, the poor teachers who position Jane as a child are depicted as morally corrupt and corrupting. In contrast, those who "are really confident love teaching mature students." The good teacher, by definition, is not attracted to the creepy Frankenstein version of pedagogy, because the nature of learning is understood quite differently. The adult learner, then, is the conductor as well as the gauge for good and generous teaching.

2. Learning

There is, though, a more radical position available for the figure of the child in the adult learning scene than the one that Jane rejects. In Hans Christian Anderson's story of *The Emperor's New Clothes*, the emperor's subjects are told that only the innocent can see the fine clothes worn by the emperor. Only a little boy can tell the emperor the truth—that he is naked. The sham is revealed. The figure of the child in the story starkly illustrates the bounden duty of the truly innocent—to look intently and to speak freely. Jane's problem is that, like the little boy, she perceives and can articulate the sham but, unlike the little boy, her innocence is not protected. She is in the tortuous position of serving the sham while at the same time seeing it for what it is, as the following quotation illustrates:

> It seemed to me that a lot of academia is a façade. I don't know how you can go through the [elite university] system, if you have any intelligence at all, and not question it.

The façade is vigorously upheld by those it serves but also by those it doesn't, just as the citizens in Anderson's story all buy into the fiction of the fine clothes. The very fabric of the work of the university supports the sham in Jane's account. Its regulatory systems, including its heavy focus on summative assessment, rigid disciplinary boundaries, positioning of teachers and learners, the way it differentiates what is real and valuable from what is not, and the way it demands that questions be framed are all based on an understanding of learning that obviates risk and encourages frightened compliance. As a mature learner, Jane can see these structures and boundaries for what they are, and she condemns them.

She portrays the discipline itself as both shamful and shameful:

> People are sitting there saying to me "you need evidence,"...and that's somebody's quote from sitting in an office. That's opinion, it's not evidence.

The university thus engages in its own reproductive project, forcing its learners to endlessly replicate what stands for reality in a never-ending performance of scholarship that hermetically seals texts and keeps the messy world outside. The way that the university conspires to foist this endless act of cloning on its learners through its reading practices is an idea that is taken on by Sarah Wood in her exploration of the potential for a model of learning that is not based on property (what Jane calls "opinion" and what her tutors call "evidence").[33] She cites Derrida's ideas about academic reading in "Of Grammatology,"[34] in which he characterizes the sort of deferential referencing that Jane's teachers tell her is "evidence," and which is a core feature of academic practice, as operating as "a guardrail." Wood takes the notion of the guardrail further, emphasizing its restrictive function: "Jump over a guardrail and you risk falling, or being swamped. Remain this side and you risk sterility."[35] Jane resists and condemns the guardrail. For her, it does not just exist to prevent learners from taking risks, but it also guards the texts themselves from really being interrogated or even being disturbed by juxtaposition or comparison. The problem for Jane is not just the effort needed to hold on to her honest vision but also how to contain her anger at what the sham produces while still remaining inside the system.

> I spoke to a lecturer and I said, "don't you feel that this is not only indefensible, it's immoral. You're teaching these children that you can learn about something that is as complex as social exclusion in three and a half days..." This wouldn't matter, except these children will be in positions of power where they're making decisions about ordinary people's lives. That's immoral.

As such, the university is operating its own robust version of social exclusion by insisting on closed readings of a restricted range of texts and maintaining that reference to these texts is more valuable than other forms of knowledge (such as the adult learner's own understanding of the world, based on experience). The socially excluded subject includes what can't be said ("the emperor isn't wearing any clothes") or read within the university walls, or at least within the undergraduate assessment framework. Jane objects to the way that the powerful elite (interestingly, she refers to her fellow students as "children," apparently neutrally) are being educated—not just for their own welfare but for society's as well. She has struggled with the "credentialism" and compliance at the university. But there is space underground for the refusal of constraints; potential for resistance lies in the child's ability to ask questions.

> I'll tell you what learning gives to me. What my biggest lesson about learning is. I thought I had come back to education and learned the answers. What I came back to education and found was that I know what questions to ask.

She sees past the veneer to the political purposes and structures that have created the system:

> I mean, it's constructed, isn't it? You know education is constructed. Even by the reading list it's constructed.

The recognition of construction is not a blissful moment of enlightenment. It is painful, and it leaves Jane in a place of struggle and anger. She is deconstructing the façade, but she still depends on it, and that combination leaves her stranded in a horrible place. She is deconstructing a system that has the power to award or take away symbolic capital at the stroke of an assessor's pen on the mark sheet, while at the same time trying to remain resilient within that system.

To return to the metaphor that I used at the beginning of this chapter, volcanic eruptions can be constructive as well as destructive. In addition to the sudden and violent eruptions that blow the sides off mountains and are recorded as historical events, volcanic activity is slowly and constantly constructing land, often on the seabed, without much attention being paid to it. Even the destructive volcano creates new landscape. Jane needs to angrily resist the nonsense, but she also needs the time and space to construct new meanings and lay down new cognitive ground. Deconstruction alone can't protect her, because there is no space for *jouissance* in a system that insists on "24 essays in two eight-week terms" and in which only a narrow range of "academic skills" is rewarded. Deconstruction without reconstruction keeps the learner in a place of opposition. She survives her degree and is successful by learning enough to succeed, but the process has left her feeling constrained and angry. She needed to find time and space for new construction and reconstruction in order to develop resilience. Partly this happens through the supportive community of the hall of residence. There is also some sense that, for Jane, this process of reconstruction happens in her writing and in the relationships she develops with her interviewees at dissertation stage. Metamorphic activity takes place as she learns independently, without the competitive pressure of the examination system, but even this is not without its problems. Evidence itself is highly suspect; of her own dissertation she says, "it's very easy to read the story in sound bites for interviews." There is a strong sense that lived reality is not usefully represented in academic discourses. She contests not only the way that knowledge is conveyed and communicated but also the nature of the knowledge itself, drawing attention to the dishonesty of the epistemology of the evidence-based disciplines ("Social Science and Education research"), much of which is gathered by sitting "in a corner with a clipboard." Jane has escaped the corner once—learning has provided her with an alternative to the place in which other divorced friends remain, "sitting in a corner, crying"—so the last thing she wants to do is to sit in another corner, with a clipboard as protection. So she leaves the empirical emperors to it, taking her good from the university and embarking on a new, successful career. It is with some dismay, though, that she reflects on the nature of her learning: "I have learnt to read a lot of stuff and [how to] speed read."

3. Assessment

Jane is angry about the assessment system, which she details as involving huge amounts of writing under pressure with a reliance on summative assessments gathered through examinations. What parades as assessment is actually wholly concentrated on attainment. When I ask her, "are you scared of exams now?" she replies, "Oh yes. That's what it's all about. To scare you. It's a psychological thing." The pedagogical function of fear prevents the learner from ever gaining independence and from ever being transformed in any way other than through the acquisition of cultural and social capital. Submission of the learner is guaranteed if the learner is always a guest in disciplines which are not her home.

> Now, that's difficult. So you're changing the way you write and the way you present. The people who are giving you supervision are expecting different things.

Two processes come into play: the pressure to stay in the habitus and the need to submit to a very narrow version of the potential for writing. Instead of enjoying writing, with all its potential for transformation and adventure, Jane has to learn how to perform academic tricks, "churning out" essays that are bound by a very tight structural straitjacket: "cracking great introduction, three black, three white, cracking great conclusion." She studies political social anthropology, social psychology, and sociology in the first year. Each discipline demands that its own protocols be adhered to and reproduced. Interdisciplinary work, by its very nature, gives the learner the privileged insight into the sham if she is prepared to take it. She identifies rigidity of genre boundaries (which operate like national borders, artificial, man-made constructs grafted onto the earth's surface) and the constraint of academic monolinguality within the disciplinary fields as constraints.

Jane's own account of her resilience throughout this system involves notions such as diversification and strategy. Resilience and resistance dance around each other, at points replacing each other. She also clearly identifies the fact that she needed a change and that running away drove her on ("my motivation was the alternatives"), and she identifies her ability to analyze the situation as a strength. She also uses a meta-learning discourse to describe her preferred learning style. Life course and life stages are identified and moved on from: "29 years of my life was down the pan. All my adult life, certainly."

Finally, she sees failure as performing a protective role. The dark side of the whole assessment framework is, paradoxically, the thing that opens the potential for resilience for Jane as an adult learner. Recounting an incident when a young medical student who had previously failed had a revelation while talking to Jane, she says,

> These kids have been the best everywhere. What's helpful from a mature student's point of view is that we've failed before. It's not the first time we've failed. That's what is helpful to us. But some of these kids have never failed. And she said, "I was really surprised, Jane, people still liked me." She had been defined by her academic ability all her life. And she was an attractive girl, but that was how she defined herself. I didn't say it to her, what I thought to myself was that people like you rather more if you fail now and again.

So the maturity of the adult learner enables her to encompass failure as part of life's course. Resilience is borne out of the recognition that a single identity—be it high-achieving academic or deserted wife—is never protective and that multiplicity and diversity need to be embraced as survival strategies. A more relaxed narrative begins to emerge in which failure, including failed marriages, need not be written off as "29 years down the pan" but can be incorporated into a successful learning autobiography as valuable components of resilience. She is able to move to a more extended space beyond the binaries: "the one thing that you learn in life is that...there is no such thing as black and white." At this point in the transcript, too, she begins to break down her own fixed points, portraying her fellow students as complicated learners with their own reserves of resilience, rather than merely being a homogenous group of "children." She articulates what she already knew: that real, lived experience is never what can be represented in the narrow confines of evidence-based academic discourse in which the illiterate mistake "the pretence of existence for life."[36]

As I explained at the end of Chapter Five, I take the same approach to the analysis of the interviews in both Chapters Six and Seven. Reflection on the usefulness of the developing analytical technique is therefore provided at the end of the next chapter.

CHAPTER 7

Sarah

Throughout this book, I have sought to apply Hélène Cixous's celebration of the emancipatory potential of *l'écriture féminine* to a way of reading and understanding the possibilities for transformational adult learning. An issue that emerged from the interview with Jane was that resilience can be constituted in the ability of the learner to allow herself to be transformed and to survive the process within an academic system that expects compliance in return for the benefits it bestows. For Cixous, the corresponding problem, which it is almost impossible to resolve, is how to write in a way that refuses to grant power to the masculine game of academic and philosophical discourse, while at the same time having only the tools of the master[1] with which to work. As Toril Moi puts it, "Her whole theoretical project can in one sense be summed up as the effort to undo this logocentric ideology...and to hail the advent of a new, feminine language that ceaselessly subverts these patriarchal binary schemes."[2] Cixous's own later expansion of *l'écriture féminine* in her essay "Coming to Writing" points the way to the potential benefits that might be reaped by its wider application and specifically to its use in the field of education. It is clearly a view of writing that undermines much that is taken to be inherent in the sort of theoretical mastery that dominates academic writing in the social sciences, though, because it defies attempts to pin it down and define it—Cixous often defines it in terms of what it is not:

You don't seek to master. To demonstrate, explain, grasp. And then to lock away in a strongbox. To pocket a part of the riches of the world. But rather to transmit: to make things loved by making them known. You, in your turn, want to affect, you want to wake the dead, you want to remind people that they once wept for love, and trembled with desires, and that they were then very close to the life that they claim they've been seeking while constantly moving further away ever since.[3]

The basic assumptions of the academic game—that knowledge can be mastered, explained, and owned by the writer/researcher—are turned on their heads. Rather, in the feminine economy, the writer/researcher agrees to a certain passivity—to be written through by what wants to be known and shared. Such writing cannot be theorized or reduced to the rules of the philosophical game; that's the point. It can only survive in a different economy, one in which the old rules are exposed and disregarded. There are other costs to the writer/researcher who chooses to take Cixous's path, as well as risks involved in rebellion. There is also the necessary submission on the part of the writer/researcher to "being 'possessed,' which is to say, dispossessed of herself."[4] This has significant implications for the way the writer/researcher, the text, and the subject are positioned in relation to each other. Writing/research becomes an inherently pedagogical activity, not in the traditional sense of exposition, but rather as a way of awakening readers to a new reality. The text becomes the site that is written *through* by the subject of the writing, and the text subsequently writes itself through the author. Unlike in the masculine economy, with its strong box and its keys, here the subject (or the knowledge, to put it another way) is not a stable, unchanging entity that is up for grabs. Rather, it is a dynamic and fluid force that works through the text.

In order to pursue the possibilities of a model of research that can both honor the principles of the feminine economy and survive in the masculine economy, I am less interested in pursuing the essentialist nature of resilience "in" the interviewee and more interested in the way that resilient and transformational learning is written in the text itself. This is problematic, though, and the problem is one of naming and appropriation. As soon as I attempt to capture resilience, it dies, like the butterfly. I want to find a way of letting it live in and fly through the text. The text needs to exert its authority through me and through the interviewee in ways that will prevent me from attempting to atomize it and to own any knowledge that emerges. As Cixous puts it,

As soon as the question "What is it?" is posed, from the moment a question is put, as soon as a reply is sought, *we are already caught up in masculine interrogation.* I say "masculine interrogation": as we say so-and-so was interrogated by the police.[5]

In Chapter Two, I pointed out that Eliza mistook Higgins's academic interest in her accent for the hostile note taking of a policeman or police informer (as the bystander puts it, "a copper's nark"[6]) on their first meeting in Shaw's *Pygmalion*. In the same way, I am constantly aware of the policewoman in me that wants to seize the evidence for resilient adult learning as soon as I encounter it—*to take it down* and put it in the cells. The struggle runs throughout the work—how to find a way of finding and preserving resilience without killing it in the process. My concern with the analytical approach that I took in relation to Joe's interview was that the vibrant and complex Joe whom I met is somehow lost in my rendition of the interview. Eliza's anguished cries to Higgins on their first encounter, "How do I know whether you took me down right?"[7] could justifiably be the articulated concerns of every resilient learner in this study. So, how does the investigating researcher who wants to write resilience while avoiding the two roles that are sure to kill the subject dead—the entomologist with his net in one hand, his killing jar and his ethyl acetate in the other, or the policewoman with her tape and her right to remain silent—find a way of understanding and communicating resilience in the subjects studied? The text needs, somehow, to exert its authority through me.

The context for this writing (as an academic book) demands results—categorizations, names, and definitions—but language itself forbids the real energy that is resilient adult learning from emerging, because "there is almost nothing left of the sea but a word without water."[8] In other words, the act of naming at once destroys what it preserves. Silver-spotted Skipper, Duke of Burgundy, Purple Emperor, and Brimstone all die on the paper that preserves them. And it is the same for all the important words in the study—learning, resilience, death, and love. Moi argues that "Cixous's work bases itself on a conscious distinction between 'poetry' and 'philosophy,'"[9] and this would suggest that the poetic discourse offers a middle ground. There are real consequences of refusing to play by the logocentric rules, though, not least the threat of exile and non-validation by the academic community. A place must therefore be found in the margins between language and what lies outside of it.[10]

My misgivings about the analysis of the first interview in this section are based on the reductive nature of the theme-based analysis. I suspect, therefore, that the language of the poetical will be more fruitful in this attempt to understand resilient learning in this interview with Sarah. Moi goes on to say that for Cixous writing is "ecstatic self-expression."[11] This implies that there is a stable self that wants to "get out" and is capable of expressing itself. A "philosophical" problem is immediately stumbled upon. The philosophical must be appeased, though, and I can't afford to drift off into poetry entirely; any space for ecstasy in this book must necessarily be fought for. The language and form I use need to correspond closely enough to the dialectical discourse for the book to reach an academic market and therefore gain recognition for the experiences of the resilience of adults included in the study.

My own philosophical problem is that I want to find a way of representing resilience in adult learning in a way that evokes the elusive, energetic (and even numinous?) quality of the experience of transformational learning, but I am caught in an academic system that can operate in ways that desiccate and undermine truly transformational learning. The tension between capture and suffocation has been sending tremors throughout this section of the book. It remains in play here and the tension is unresolved. As my interview with Jane in the previous chapter showed, the academic management system must be appeased as well as escaped from—it rewards, but it also oppresses. How does resilient adult learning write itself? How can transformation be represented in a language that is necessarily academic and intellectual, even if it strives to not be "scientific"? There is a connection, therefore, between the aspirations of *l'écriture féminine* and the inevitable compromises that are necessary in order to enact it on the one hand, and the desire to write about resilience in the context of transformational adult learning and the compromises that are necessary to write it within an academic context on the other. Acknowledgement of the tensions and possible contradictions inherent in the enterprise, however, is not sufficient reason for abandoning the project. It is within the deconstructive energy of those tensions that the thing itself is able to emerge. I want to read the way that resilience is inscribed in the text and how it breaks through attempts to impose conventional and closed readings of it.

Any deconstructive energy in the text emerges in the spaces between two opposites. Moi argues that Cixous's interest is in the radical potential of "I/you" relationships, and these notably include "some variety of the teacher/student or prophet/disciple relationship."[12] The radical rewriting of relationships between men and women, writers and readers, teachers and learners is at the heart of Cixous's thinking about the possibilities offered by the realm of the gift. My examination of the I/you relationship in terms of resilient learning in this text happens in a way that is threefold: the I/you relationship between Sarah and her teacher(s); the I/you relationship between me as interviewer and Sarah as interviewee; and the I/you relationship between me as reader and Sarah writer of the text. The following analysis, then, is an attempt to represent the energy between reader, writer, and text about a resilient adult learner.

We met in the members' restaurant of a London art gallery. We sat by the window with big, open views of the Thames in both directions. London surrounded us; it also featured prominently in the interview. Sarah talked about her family's history in the East End, about exploring the Docklands as that area was being developed, and about how the tutor's visit to the local library enticed her to return to learning and to apply for a place at Kingsley. Sitting in the restaurant overlooking the Thames made the interview very immediate. Talking about the place that we could also see—the river and the view to the east and Docklands—had the effect of grounding the narrative as well as opening it up. The surroundings seemed to echo the content of our conversation.

As an account of resilient adult learning, the interview text works on two levels; or rather, two forces are at play within the text. The first is a rational and sensible account of the strategies and sources of support that Sarah employed in order to gain her certificate and then masters degree in history. I can play entomologist with this discourse, neatly catching each theme (institutional support/resistance of peer group pressure outside the institution/understanding of self as one who doesn't give up). Each butterfly dies quickly, and I line them all up neatly. Behind it, or within it, or below it, is another account, which is far more difficult to capture and categorize. The policewoman wants to exclude it, because it won't fit any of the butterfly frames. Whereas the first account is earthborn, the second is cosmic. The first one employs familiar language to describe what is known, the other struggles to find a language—it trails off, it hesitates, and it exclaims, "It was like star-gazing!"

What mediates these two discourses is the interview itself. My questions form a boundary fence right down the middle of the conversation. Of all the interviews I conducted, this is the one that initially disappointed me the most. Later Sarah and I had lunch—a glass of white wine and a bowl of soup and bread. We continued to sit by the big glass window overlooking the Thames, and she told me about her learning and her life in much more detail. She talked about the impact of reading Adrienne Rich's poetry and of her exhilaration at hearing her own heels clicking on the Ashenden Library courtyard. We talked about Karen Armstrong's book *The Spiral Staircase*.[13] I looked forward to working on the transcripts, but when I did so I realized that this really rich data happened off tape, after the interview had finished. The restaurant was quite packed on the day of the interview and the tables were close together. I had to speak more loudly than I would have liked and I think I might have been anxious about the tape recorder not picking up what Sarah was saying. Whatever the reason was, my contribution to the interview initially disappointed me. It is faltering; I speak too much, and

Sarah speaks too little. Initially I seem tongue-tied and nervous; my first question is syntactically odd and convoluted:

> Can you help me to see the concepts of your learning? The most recent learning you've done. Tell me, how did you start, what were you learning?

It contrasts sharply with Sarah's clipped and taciturn responses. I have no memory of consciously feeling nervous, but perhaps I was. I seem to give her less time to develop her answers and I don't appear, at times, to be listening very sensitively. I liked Sarah immediately and I was very interested in what she was saying, so I am confused by this nervous and edgy performance on my part—as it appears in the transcript. It does, however, make for an energetic, deconstructive text.

Sarah's second, electrically charged discourse keeps emerging from behind the fence I have erected. The fence is, as Cixous puts it, "in the process of being undermined."[14] The more I try to patrol the fence by attempting to herd the conversation to one side of it, the more the second discourse breaks though. The energy of the text is born out of the pull and resistance between a logocentric discourse about resilient learning, framed by my questions that correspond to my semi-structured interview plan and partly complied with by Sarah's responses, and the second, wilder discourse that Sarah leads and to which I respond. On the second point, for example, I take up Sarah's extended metaphor of opening up, and I ask her to elaborate on it. On the other hand, though, the important notion of connection and connecting is left underdeveloped by me. It is Sarah who insists on bringing it back in. At one point, I close her joyful articulation of it down, when she states that learning

> makes connections, but it also leaves something open for me to continue. That's opened up more and more and more and more...It's really exciting!

by following it up with the leaden and unimaginative

> You mentioned some of these a little bit already, but what are the challenges of learning?

Here the glorious sense of boundlessness inherent in Sarah's answer is met with narrowness and closure. I wonder why I tried to close her answer down. Why did I work so hard to patch up the holes in the fence? I seem unwilling to let the text develop into areas that I feel are straying from the script. Every time Sarah gets a bit frisky, I bring her back into line.

If this were a social scientific reading of the interview, I would provide a more extended reflexive account of my performance as a novice interviewer here. I might develop the idea that this was something of a lost opportunity in terms of data gathering, but an essential component in my own development as an adult learner and reflective practitioner. But this is not a conventional social scientific text. Perhaps if I could have slowed the pace and asked Sarah to explore some of the key ideas in a little more depth—especially her notions of connectedness, discovery, and rediscovery, and the idea that "you can never be lost"—a deeper understanding of Sarah's experience of learning as a transformational experience could have emerged. However, I think that, as a text, it is more interesting for the struggle than it would have been if these issues were more fully resolved. It is, in that sense, an elliptical text. To hunt for what is lost in it would be to collude with what Jacques Derrida calls "the phantom of the center."[15] There is a kind of benign violence in the transcript—it moves backward and forward, resisting closure. What is thinkable and sayable appears at times to be sovereign, but at other times it gives way to something far more fluid, open, and dynamic.

When I constructed the questions for the semi-structured interview, I was thinking in terms of oppositions—those "dual, irreconcilable" building blocks of logocentric thought.[16] I imagined my resilient learners in terms of what they were clearly not (those unresilient learners with whom I also worked), and I also thought in terms of challenges/benefits, teachers/learners, and carrying on/dropping out. What I had constructed, therefore, was a logocentric framework into which I tried to drive Sarah. She complies with this in that she provides answers on the first level. But she challenges and undermines it at a second level in the way that shows that, as Cixous puts it, "she is not attached to herself,"[17] and she resists all my attempts to put her back in touch with material explanations for her resilience.

In this sense, then, the text itself performs an undulating transition between a position in which "ordering intervenes"[18] and one which is "cosmic" and "world-wide" in its scope.[19] The first position is in the process of being undermined by an energy that is excessive—it goes beyond language. This second discourse is produced by the gap between Sarah and me. In this sense, the interview is not so much an illustration of the work of a novice interviewer who achieves less than she might have later in the study, and more an illustration of what Roland Barthes calls a "text of bliss,"[20] because it discomforts and unsettles. It performs a potential for rupture in the book as a whole, as Cixous puts it, "one in which it seems possible that the classic structure might be split."[21] Indeed, by the end of the interview, the impending split has happened. Although the character I play in the text (the interviewer and therefore first reader) has not reached a *jouissant* position by its end, there is a sense that things are about to change. This is a deliberate attempt to read the interview in a way that is informed by deconstructionist, feminist, literary theory, such as that practiced by Cixous.

After I had finished work on assembling the transcript, I sent it to Sarah for approval. She returned it with a very warm letter, wishing me well with my research and telling me that the experience had made her think about going back to do some more learning. At the end of the interview, both she and I are learners at a threshold. What follows is the analysis of a text that takes us to that position.

Level 1—Organized Account of Resilience

The first account of resilient learning is rooted in a rational and sensible framework. The questions concern the opposition between the challenges and benefits of learning, and the answers provide apparently tangible explanations of the strategies employed by Sarah to remain resilient in the course of obtaining her certificate and then MA in history. This account can, itself, be divided into two sections that overlap. The first concerns the support for the learner that she accesses from structures and networks around her. The second concerns the qualities and capabilities that Sarah ascribes to herself as a particular type of person and learner.

External Support

Sarah attributes some of the credit for her resilience to the support she receives from the agents and structures around her. She recognizes that her style of learning and researching will be validated by her teacher on first meeting. She had already been interested in family history, and this led her to attend the two-day history course at the local library, run by Kingsley College's Janet Green.[22] She had initially been intimidated by the thought of attending for two reasons: the academic status of her tutor ("I first thought, Oh, I can't do that, I'm not...You know—Dr. Janet Green!") and her perceived notion that she would have to conform to a systematic approach to history that she did not share ("a lot of people who do family history have it beautifully laid out—very efficient").

The teacher, though, endorses Sarah's own way of learning and thus provides important intellectual validation:

> and there was Janet talking about things, memory, looking at things, in the way I do it.

From the start, then, Sarah is consciously resisting order and categorization. For her, history is much more about life—air and ground, "It's the streets they lived in, the smell of the air. Did they walk here?"

Sarah resists the restrictive/logocentric, academic discourse with its efficiently laid out family trees and file cards. Instead, she is drawn to the messy and the real. This understanding of history is endorsed by the academic, who models it in her own teaching. As such, the teacher is able to confirm the way in which the learner is working, and she gives it validity and encouragement. Sarah is thus able to properly begin to contemplate learning again. Although she is still apprehensive, her doubts are allayed by the support of friends:

> And I debated, should I? And then, with a couple of friends, over a couple of bottles of wine, they said. "You go for it." So I did.

Friends are presented ambiguously throughout the interview. Here, these friends are totally supportive. They are like the open-minded and erudite friend in her 80s, whom Sarah talks about, and the friend she mentions who connects Karen Armstrong's account of Catholicism[23] to her own experiences of Judaism. Other acquaintances are presented as something to be escaped from via learning. The people in her neighborhood whom Sarah has known since they were all young parents greet her adult learning with apathy, and this results in her understanding that adult learning has the potential to marginalize and to position the learner differently. She acknowledges that

> People I had known for years. We'd all started the kids at school. They weren't interested at all. Suddenly you're on the edge. You're not one of them anymore, and they weren't involved.

This reads in a matter-of-fact sort of way; I do not get the sense that Sarah was distressed by being marginalized. It is common to many of the accounts of the effects of adult learning that are represented in this study. There is a whimsical sense that things might have been easier with the support of an interested peer group outside the study group, but it would be overstating the case to suggest that the lack of such peer support was the cause of a significant setback for Sarah.

There is also some sense that Sarah behaves in gleeful way as a result of this marginalization: "I'm dodgy," she tells me.

She does find support inside the learning community itself—the history course involves working with "a very close group." However, even in this group of adult learners, she is on the edge, as they all are.

But they were an individualistic group, and even though I'm not a group person, person, per se, it wasn't that sort of camaraderie, you know. "Oh I'm worried about this and that."

Peripherality reflects as a commonality that emerges across the data, and it is reflected in the second of the five capabilities that emerged from the first section of this study—the ability to perceive and negotiate the tension between exclusion and inclusion. The ability to inhabit a position that is half inside and half outside a community is one of the key capabilities that I am suggesting is performed by resilient adult learners. Beyond the teacher and other learners, it is the institution itself that provides the most support, as Sarah says: "But I would say Kingsley, really, that was my support. And one or two other friends."

She mentions the librarian in particular, but it is the whole setup that supports her resilience. The learning is not provided purely as the achievement or the responsibility of the learner—it is achieved instead in the structure of the institution.

"Internal" Reasons for Resilience

Sarah places the account of being a resilient adult learner in the context of certain aspects of her life story, which is itself placed in the context of the second half of the twentieth century. Women's history features both as the content of Sarah's study—she writes her 20,000 word dissertation on Jessie Stevenson, a lesser-known suffragette—and as the context for that study. She reflects explicitly on the impact of growing up as girl in a time when the expectations were that "you would be a wife and you would be a mother," for example. Within this particular social and historical context, Sarah presents herself as a resourceful and resilient person. She has previously gone against the grain in striving for a successful career, and so she places the fatigue and inconvenience of travelling to study in the context of an understanding that in order to be successful it is necessary to work hard. The idea of dropping out is an anathema to her: "I would regret and never forgive myself if I did it. If I dropped out."

Pride also plays an important part in the account. In addition to bringing up a large family, Sarah was a senior nurse and outpatient manager in the health service. She is self-reliant and successful, saying of herself and her fellow adult students at Kingsley, "all of us really don't want sympathy."

She quickly realizes that a passive and narrow retirement is not for her. Her attempts to be part of a local social learning group end quickly. She recounts a story of how she challenged a political candidate at one of the meetings:

> And I think I stood out, they know I'm dodgy . . . I thought, "I'm going to be lynched." And I think that made me . . . it was so boring and narrow.

So although Sarah presents her decision to embark on adult learning as part of her frustration with the narrow alternatives on offer, she does not appear to regret that splitting. On the contrary, she seems delighted to be rejected. She rebels against the unchallenging activities associated with respectable retirement. Learning is presented as a necessary form of escape, in contrast to the closing down associated with aging. Resilience is partly constituted, therefore, in her understanding that despite the challenges of learning, the alternatives would be much worse.

Level 2—Free Account of Resilience

The second level of the interview is entirely disruptive of the first. The logocentric aspects of the text proceed with caution and clear, chronological markers, with natural causal links: for example,

> I was 60ish and I suddenly started doing my family history, and it was through reading a book that I discovered that my grandparents were German.

However, the other discourse butts in, gasps and exclaims,

> It just amazes. It's almost like a Disney: star gazing!

Whereas at the first level, resilient learning is a product of the interaction between learner and institution, and learner and teacher, in this second discourse, "It" amazes. "It" exists independently. At this second level, Sarah is much less concerned with herself as an individual and much more concerned with her attempts to name her experience. The text writes itself—the logocentric discourse that orders and explains is ruptured, and the text becomes excessive—its nouns and verbs limp along after what Sarah is attempting to express.

Sarah tells me about her research project, the subject of which was a suffragette who is not very well known. Sarah portrays herself as the historian who becomes increasingly passive in the writing of Jessie's story: "I also got taken over by Jessie."

The writer is taken over by her subject; it is an act of possession. Cixous categorizes such ability to be possessed as a fundamental aspect of *l'écriture féminine*: "It is true that certain receptivity is 'feminine'."[24] But whereas "History" has exploited such passivity by alienating the possessed, Cixous sees this as a remarkable ability to allow the story to be written.

A woman, by her opening up, is open to being "possessed," which is to say, dispossessed of herself.[25]

The notion of being taken over thus opens up a completely different language with which to discuss the adult learning experience. Hughes's reading of Ovid's *Pygmalion*[26] has the sculptor being possessed by the sculpture and, as I discuss in Chapter Two, the analogy (after Shaw) is of a teacher being possessed by a learner. Here the learner is, herself, possessed by her subject; the historian is possessed by history. This makes my practical questions about how the learner deals with the difficulties of learning (travelling, tiredness, marginalization from home community) redundant. The notion of possession calls into question the ontological assumptions about resilient learning that inform the basis of the interview. If the learner is possessed by learning itself, then resilience is neither a capability (in the sense that I have previously set out in my five-point model) nor an attribute that is particular to the learner. If the learner is possessed (by learning itself or by the subject that wants to "get learned") in the way that Hughes's Pygmalion is possessed by the spirit, then she doesn't have any choice but to carry out the mission, once her autonomy is surrendered. The only resilience needed is the confidence to surrender to the possession itself. This is, of course, a mighty sort of resilience, because surrender to the unknown takes enormous courage. Read in this way, though, subsequent resilient learning is simply the inevitable consequence of what Sarah allows herself to be possessed by; Jessie possesses Sarah so that her story can be told. In order for this to happen, Sarah has to open herself up in the same way that Hughes's Pygmalion submits to the spirit that enters him and sculpts herself a body through his hands. The idea of opening up as a consequence of learning is returned to several times during the interview—"everything has just opened up" and "That's opened up more and more and more and more. It's really exciting." Here opening up is not just a consequence of adult learning; it is a prerequisite for it to take place at deeper levels.

For Cixous, the opening up is a necessary preliminary for possession. It allows a different kind of history to be written. The historian and her subject are therefore bound together. Sarah is thus engaged in "keeping alive the other that is confided to her."[27] It means that opening up is a confident act of love, not defeated surrender, because "there is a nonclosure that is not submission but confidence and comprehension; that is not an opportunity for destruction but for wonderful expansion."[28]

So, by possessing Sarah, Jessie allows her to be opened up. She provides her, in other words, with the resources she needs to be resilient. The author—a feminine historian—is written through by a campaigner for women's right to vote. The authors of the text—Sarah and I—are spoken through a second time. This is a feminine text that is breaking through the first-level discourse ("the system is already letting something else through"[29]) regardless of our attempts to keep the fence in place.

The benefits of learning are presented as utterly transformational, in a way that ridicules the stingy set of skills that underpins the superficial, sociologically inspired "benefits to society" that I suggest. After Sarah's passionate declaration that if she didn't start to learn again she would die, I try to re-present the sentiment to her in a diluted and sanitized way: "The very tangible feeling that you need to do something more at this stage?"

The anodyne reduction of what has been a powerful statement is thin and tiny when juxtaposed with Sarah's explanation of the complete loss of self:

It's expanded. Even coming here (to do the interview) it's just—everything has opened up. That's what I really do enjoy. And I just feel so privileged. It just amazes. It's almost like a Disney: star gazing!

Here again, the "self" of the learner, all the institutional structures that support her, and all her wider networks are portrayed as insignificant in comparison to the vast universe that opens up through learning. The scope is infinite. Like Cixous's feminine writer, the reach is "cosmic" and "worldwide." The effects of learning are to lift Sarah out of the small, separated, and compartmentalized world.

It makes connections, but it also leaves something open for me to continue. That's opened up more and more. It's really exciting.

This metaphor is central to the text—it is an open text, and Sarah's amazement and exhilaration are palpable. Elsewhere in the book, I have drawn the analogy between transformational adult learning and *l'écriture féminine*. Here the comparison is particularly apposite. Sarah's account of the way she has been transformed by studying history reads in ways that are resonant of Cixous's explorations of the potential to develop a new kind of writing in *Sorties*. The key ideas—opening up, making connections, the endless potential for further learning, discovery and rediscovery, and wonder are all familiar ideas. As a writer of a biography, Sarah has been subjected to "the dwelling place of the other in me—the other that I am not, that I don't know how to be, but that I feel passing, that make me live...which is indeed what gives me the desire to know and from which all life soars."[30] By learning history, the stories of the dead who are spoken through her, Sarah is transformed.

The refrain "only connect" occurs throughout the early part of *Educating Rita*.[31] It is an explicit intertextual reference to E. M. Forster's *Howard's End*,[32] a subplot of which is the sad case of the unresilient, working-class learner. Connection is a quintessential feature of the resilient adult learning experience. The connections in Sarah's text, though, go a long way beyond intellectual, social, and cultural ones. She can certainly now go to a historical pub and imagine its origins, or she can read an article in a weekend newspaper about John Berger or Virginia Woolf and link it to what she knows, but there is a far deeper philosophical sense of connection at work:

> I think I came to a point in my life where, how can I put it, where I suddenly noticed connections in my life. You seem to know that you—this is something you have to grab hold of, or at least try it.

The subject is thus propelled along by a stronger force. She goes star gazing, and resilience comes from this deep understanding. But this was going on before the formal learning began. Before she even started to learn history, she was already walking on the edge—tapping into something that allowed her to delight in danger while knowing that she was completely safe. When she retired in her late 50s, she had time to herself:

> And what I did when I first gave up work, now this is another odd thing, I suppose. Well, I don't think it was odd, but I would have what my other friends would call my destiny. I'd come up to London on the travel card and I'd hop on a bus. And sometimes I did go to one place and I'd end up in another, because you can never be lost. I walked toward Docklands as it was being developed. Sometimes I would think God, nobody knows where I am. If I was mugged, killed, anything, nobody would have a clue. But it opened up a lot.

There are echoes here of Virginia Woolf's (1925/1976) *Mrs. Dalloway* and her pedestrian tour of the capital and the resultant thoughts about herself. Whereas Sarah is reveling in the opening up (sorties) and the expansion, Mrs. Dalloway's experience is portrayed as a loss:

> But often now this body she wore...this body, with all its capacities, seemed nothing—nothing at all. She had the oddest sense of being

herself invisible; unseen; unknown; there being no more marrying; no more having of children now, but only this astonishing and rather solemn progress with the rest of them, up Bond Street, this being Mrs. Dalloway, not even Clarissa any more; this being Mrs. Richard Dalloway.[33]

Whereas Woolf explores the loss of a woman's identity beyond the traditional scope for it as the angel of the house (this is a study as much of the invisibility of the middle-aged woman as it is a meditation on the loss of self in an ideological context), Sarah delights in the dissolution of herself. The two accounts could be read as illustrations of the contrasting theoretical feminist approaches to self—the Anglo-modernist approach of Woolf compared to the Franco-post-structuralism of Cixous. Sarah's account is celebratory. The loss of self is supported and also celebrated by Cixous:

I am under the cosmic tent, under the canvas of my body and I gaze out, I am the bosom of happenings. And while I gaze, I listen…I am invaded. I am pushed to the limit. A music floods though me, inculcates me with its staves.[34]

There is a sense of joyful annihilation here—the loss of self is intrinsically bound up in the thrill of opening up. A profound sense of cosmic safety that goes well beyond any notions of physical or psychic danger underpins the statement. This precedes her ability to get lost in learning. When it is transformational, learning allows (insists that) the learner get lost, be in danger, while at the same time letting her know that she is completely safe.

Returning to learning therefore crystallized what was already going on for Sarah. The alternative would be to succumb to a kind of death:

Now this sounds very dramatic, but it's almost as if I didn't do something, you know inside you, when you know…you don't know what it is, you know you've got to do that, or you almost feel you'll die if you don't.

Learning is, in the final analysis, the alternative to death. By learning history, Sarah is able to refuse to collude with the deaths of others, such as Jessie. She is learning, alive, excited, open, and available to them. She learns and lives. It is a clairvoyant text.

The analysis of the text in this chapter has helpfully illuminated some methodological issues that have application to the whole investigation. To a certain extent, the tension in the interview text is mirrored in the analysis. That is to say, the struggle between the poetic and the analytic ways of writing remains unresolved. My own use of metaphor initially felt self-conscious and effete, but I persevered, and the final version serves an important purpose in the reading of the text. I have reached an understanding that the tension between the academic and the poetic, or the logocentric and the feminine ways of writing, need not finally be resolved on one side or the other. In fact, this interview has been served well by their mutual coexistence.

Overall, the analysis of the interviews has led me to understand that the five-capabilities model was successful as a developing theme to support ongoing analysis. When applied to *The Winter's Tale*,[35] the categories worked well—opening up a text that would normally be read through the lens of literary criticism to a more playful reading with direct practical applications. When applied to Joe in the first chapter of this section, the model was more limited, though. Instead of opening the text up, it tended to compartmentalize and stagnate it. The clearer Cixousian reading of Jane and Sarah was more successful. They live as unique people "alive with the elastic of life," as Hughes puts it, whereas Joe remains a subject of this investigation. This is a cause of some sorrow for me, because of all the learners I interviewed, Joe stood out as perhaps the most remarkable. The analysis did serve a necessary methodological purpose for the study overall, because it moved me into a new way of writing that gets closer to a happy balance between academic and poetic. The concluding comments for this section echo those for Sarah. The approach taken in the interview with Joe allowed a particular understanding of resilience to emerge. It feels constrained, though, and mechanistic. The approach taken with Jane and Sarah leads to better writing, and the interviewees more fully emerge as living agents. The understanding of resilience as a whole may be less well served by the analytical approach adopted in relation to Joe, though. There is a clear argument emerging, therefore, for a coexistence of two approaches. I will not abandon the capabilities altogether. They endure as themes, and they are reconsidered at the end of the book in the light of all the evidence gathered.

The next part of the book involves an appraisal of my own autobiographical experiences of resilient learning. It begins with the final biographical interview included in the main body of the study—an interview with Lilian (my mother). In the analysis of it in Chapter Eight, I move closer to *l'écriture féminine* than I have done so far. It builds on the freer use of metaphor, which I have experimented with in this chapter.[36]

CHAPTER 8

Her Mother's Voice

The analysis of the interviews in the previous three chapters provided new readings of resilience. The functions of love, resistance, and possession in the performance of resilient adult learning emerged strongly from the data. These ideas support and amplify the findings from the analysis of the literary texts. Previous chapters of the book have considered the representations of resilient adult learning in other people—fictional and real. In the following two chapters, I consider resilient adult learning from my own perspective. This next section of the book is directly autobiographical. It includes a creative piece of autobiographical writing and a reconsideration of the overall themes of the study in light of it. But first, this chapter features an interview with my mother. The purpose of this chapter is to enlighten and problematize my understanding of my own resilience by thinking about myself as a learner in the context of the rest of the investigation. In order to gain access to those years, I decided to interview my mother. The interview was carried out midway through the investigation. At the point at which I interviewed her, I was still working within a broadly Bourdieusian framework. The intention for the interview, therefore, was not psychoanalytic but rather was based on the somewhat simple notion of capital that I later rejected. The result could, of course, be read in multiple ways—not least through a psychoanalytic lens. My own reading, however, is consistent with the Cixousian approach which has influenced the rest of the work.

My mother's presence in the text opened up my thinking and writing considerably and helped me to find a way through the apparent closure that is a feature of Pierre Bourdieu's work on education. The allowance of space for the mother in the text has a long history in women's writing, as Linda

Anderson points out: "Woolf experimented all her life, in both her autobiography and fiction, with this problem of how to allow the mother's presence into a writing that has traditionally not permitted her a place."[1] Giving my mother a place in the text liberated my writing from the academic discourse. It also helped me to understand more deeply the interchange between resilience and resistance identified in the previous chapters.

The auto/biographical perspective in this chapter and the autobiographical perspective in the next one are provided as important discourses that add to the accumulating representations of resilient adult learning in the study. As Linden West puts it, the autobiographical narrative is useful in the study of adult education because it is "a powerful and natural resource to be used to understand others' life histories and that empathy and relatedness are essential to telling stories."[2] There is a necessary and helpful link, then, between the fictional, biographical, and autobiographical narratives contained in the work. The mixed genre way in which the study is constructed supports the use of the auto/biographical narrative in this text. For reasons I go on to explain, I have deliberately departed from a conventional write-up of this interview. West argues that his own auto/biographical writing has been conducted in "ways which [appear] closer to the work of the novelist, poet and story-teller than the conventional social scientist."[3] Here those links are deliberately pushed even further in order to open the interview into new ways of seeing and writing.

At the point at which I decided to interview my mother, my motivation was to find out what she could tell me about the years between 1971 and 1976 (the first five years of my life, leading up to compulsory education) in terms of my own development as a learner. What emerged halfway through the interview was much more interesting, though. For some of that time she had been an adult learner herself—indeed, a resilient adult learner. Adult learning was vitally important to her; she had left school at 14 and missed out on a selective school place because her parents had said that they could not afford the uniform. The interview, therefore, serves two structural purposes in the context of the overall book: it provides a way into thinking about the construction of a successful learner identity in the early stages of life, but it also provides a narrative for what it feels like to be an adult learner in circumstances that test resilience. Resilience in this final interview is dyadic, being performed in relation to the adult learning undertaken despite bereavement (the loss of her husband, my father, three months after I was born), while at the same time the adult learning itself is a fundamental component of the development of a more profound resilience, the effects of which are intergenerational. My original purpose for the interview—to problematize my earlier restricted reading of my own resilience as a learner—was therefore superseded by a far more important imperative. The direct link between participation in adult learning and the development of hope and resilience is strongly articulated in the interview. The most significant findings would seem somewhat romantic if they were not so firmly rooted in this account—that adult education and the specific acts of reading and writing can perform a deeply protective function for the learner and that the ramifications of that learning reach into adulthood for her daughter. It is a compelling story that illuminates the book.

My father died three months after I was born. The interview with my mother about the first five years of my life is a powerful text about resilience and survival. Resilient learning is constituted in the account of the aftermath of my dad's death. Mourning, love, reading, writing, and adult education all play their part in the construction of hope. These are all strong Cixousian themes, and the text would certainly give itself up to a Cixousian reading in the style of Chapters Six and Seven. The story speaks for itself, though. The narrative is so compelling because the language is both raw and intensely figurative. The text has a purity about it that might be weighed down and compromised by being tightly framed in an "intellectual" reading, no matter how fluid or deconstructive it is. Life and afterlife, death and near-death, hope and resurrection all feature strongly in the interview. For these reasons, I decided to take a more creative approach to the analysis.

Given the intimate and revelatory nature of the material in this section, as well as the highly experimental way in which it is analyzed, I went further in terms of gaining ethical approval from my mother than I did with any of the other interviewees in the study. In general, I take my cue from Laurel Richardson, a writer who I greatly admire for her commitment to crossing the literary/sociological divide and for writing with integrity. She describes my general approach in this study:

> When publishing about other people my ethics require that I subject my writing to a fine-mesh filter: do no harm. What should I reveal? To whom should it be revealed, when, and how? Of course, no matter how painstakingly we filter what we say and how we say it, we cannot know the consequences of our work. We can only do the best we can. One way to help us do the best we can is to give the people we write about a chance to preview what we have written—but not necessarily the right to alter or delete the text...keeping control of the text with its author, I think, is especially important when one is writing personal narrative such as memoir or daybook. It is the author's story, after all.[4]

While I go along with all of this for the rest of the work in this book, in the construction of this chapter I went further than she suggests. I did ask my mother to review the whole chapter as well as the transcript and I gave her the right to alter and to delete aspects of the text. Her eyesight is poor, so I read it to her. She was moved, but she liked it a lot. She did ask for two details to be removed, though—one detail about her own childhood and another about mine. I complied with her wishes and they were removed from the chapter. I felt that this was completely acceptable, given her immense generosity in what she shared with me in the interview as well as her support for the original and radical way I have used the data. Apart from peripheral people in it, this interview is not anonymized in the way that the other interviews are—it seemed pointless to do so, given the direct references to me and members of my family. I therefore sought additional permission from my brother and sister to include the references to them in the text. With my mother's permission, I asked my brother and sister to read the transcript and to approve any references to them in it. My discussion with my sister about the interview text was particularly helpful in supporting my developing understanding of the links between ethical considerations and the ontological nature of the book itself. She found the transcript interesting but was concerned that one friend of the family was absent from the text. My sister remembered a man who had worked with my dad as being quintessential to my mother's resilience in the desperate months after my father died. The practical and emotional support he offered Mum was outstanding and unfailing, she told me, and yet he is nowhere in the text. Up until that point, I had not seriously considered the ethical and political consequences of what is left *out* of a biographical account of resilience, which is ironic, given the way that the interview with Joe so ably highlights the links between underwritten history and personal resilience. We discussed the notions of representation and distortion that pertain to auto/biographical material, and my sister made the following statement in relation to this omission, and she agreed that I could write it down and include it in the study because, I think, it helpfully encapsulates the ethical dilemmas that I have faced. She said of the interview in general,

> To me it is like being at the fairground when you look at a hall of mirrors. Some of them make you fatter, some of them make you thinner, some of them make your image curved. But they all distort the thing itself, which is the person standing there.

My response was that the readings of resilience presented here are no more and no less than the images provided by the mirrors. Open and plural readings of multiple mirrors helpfully present us with a range of understanding of the thing itself—resilient adult learning, or, in my sister's terms, "the person standing there," but what it cannot do, and certainly must not pretend to do, is have privileged access to that phenomenon.

As with any writing, the final sequencing of the work belies the messy and simultaneous nature of its progress. Although this chapter makes the most theoretical sense here, the interview was actually conducted more than a year after the main tranche of interviews. Once I had conducted it and finished working on the transcript, I knew that the whole book had to change in order to accommodate the text. It was obvious that its themes of life, death, love, and survival were better served by the language of myth and poetry than the cold vocabulary of data analysis. Although the location for all the action described takes place in the terraced house just off the seafront in Sheerness—a small seaside town in the southeast of England, where I was born—and the time frame is 1971 to 1976, the imagery spans this world, the underworld, and the next one. The ferocious love that is given voice in the interview is diminished by the label "social capital." The political and personal empowerment afforded by learning to read (at all levels) is attenuated by the vocabulary of cultural capital. The subject matter is too powerful, too majestic, for mainstream social scientific categorization. The categories of capital appear restrictive, puerile, and artificial alongside it (and anyway, as my mother herself says, "they all run into one another"; in other words, the divisions between types of capital belie the complexity of lived experience). The fluidity and profundity of the text demanded a different kind of reading.

The interview had a transformational effect on the way in which I thought about the investigation as a whole. The decision to rethink the epistemological basis of the work that came out of this interview was not just a stylistic rejection of Bourdieu. I have alluded to my "decision" to take on *l'écriture féminine* as a theoretical framework throughout this book. In fact, my attraction to Hélène Cixous was far more instinctive than that, and it came about as a direct result of working with the data in this chapter. What my mother said about our life together in this interview left me feeling exposed and let down by the social scientific discourse within which I was working. I needed help in order to represent the transcript with integrity. I needed the guidance of a writer who was strong enough to handle a text as incendiary and as fragile as this one, and whose work was courageous enough to accompany me into the dark places in the interview and was capacious enough to accommodate its love. I remembered Cixous, in the Platonic sense.[5] My real mother took me to a literary one. Her influence on the evolving writing was maternal in the way that a wolf is maternal—with bare teeth and blood on its coat. She led me into a wild new intellectual terrain. When I reread her work, I received the protective textual love that she writes about in relation to those (variously, Jean Genet,[6] Heinrich von Kleist,[7] Clarice Lispector,[8] William Shakespeare,[9] and others) whose work has shielded and nurtured her—as she says, "I have never known equal to such generosity."[10] I no longer had to write in isolation and undercover after I remembered Cixous.

Cixous's work had a transformative impact on the book as a whole and on me as a writer of it. The text ruptured from the moment her work became involved, and it could never return to its original shape. Her influence changed my earlier view of resilience, because I understood that it had been predicated on the simplistic notion of the resistance of the effects of disadvantage. I had not questioned the death of my father as anything other than a loss up until the point that I read the work of Cixous in relation to the transcript of the interview with my mother. My father's death was certainly a structuring absence[11] throughout my childhood, and it had real, material consequences in my life. Apart from the obvious effects in terms of lack of economic capital, I carried his death with me throughout my childhood. I had to restate it in every new official, social, and institutional environment I found myself in ("What does your father do?" "He's dead"), and I had to carry the burden of other people's horror of death in response. The construction of childhood in modern, Western society predicates against a benevolent reading of this sort of loss and absence. The association of death and childhood is dangerous and challenging for many people,[12] and it was difficult, therefore, to read my own loss as anything other than disadvantage and tragedy. The tragic discourse took on a nastier dimension in the 1980s in the United Kingdom when a strong, political rhetoric developed around single mothers and made dangerous, unsubstantiated links between social breakdown and absent fathers.[13] After reading Cixous, I realized that the effects of the clinical and compartmentalized versions of social science (even in their feminist and post-structuralist forms) that I had hitherto accessed were simply replicating this by forcing me to concentrate on presence and deny absence other than as disadvantage. Such an approach restricted me to regarding resilience in terms of what Jacques Derrida calls "the determination of Being as *presence*."[14] Thus the metaphysics of presence could only characterize death as lack, and this simplicity was limiting. My previous construction of resilient learning, therefore, had presented death as uncomplicated loss. The impact of reading Cixous's work insisted that I reread that disadvantage in a more problematized way, thus perplexing my understanding, not just of myself, but also of resilient learning. Cixous echoes and illustrates my own position in her essay "School of the Dead":

For a long time I lived through my father's death with the feeling of immense loss and child-like regret, as in an inverted fairy-tale: Ah if my father had lived! I naively fabricated other magnificent stories...And I said to myself that I wouldn't have had death if my father had lived. I have written this several times: he gave me death. To start with.[15]

From this point on, then, resilience had to be rethought away from the simplistic binaries of loss and gain and absence and presence. "Surviving is not what we think,"[16] writes Cixous, implying that the unproblematized application of popularly understood notions of resilience is unlikely to lead very far. The following interview therefore sets out an account of resilient learning that reconsiders death as a feature of resilience. This premise provided the space in which to rethink the binary between presence and absence, and this rethinking opened up the possibility for a freer way of interpreting the relationship between death and resilience. Before I explore the text in more detail, I want to frame it in a little more depth in terms of Cixous's thinking about the links between death, writing, and survival. The analysis that follows is an attempt to place these complex theoretical ideas in a creative reading and writing of an auto/biographical narrative of my own mother. Deciding how to write the chapter was a significant dilemma, and I experimented a good deal before I found an approach with which I felt happy. Amy Hollywood has noted a similar concern in her own attempt to provide a thematic reading of Cixous's writing. She notes that her own analysis of Cixous's work inevitably reduces it and "does violence to Cixous's complex textual practice."[17] This was exactly my concern regarding how to represent the interview with my mother—how to find a way of integrating it into the study (because what emerges from it is vastly important) while not *doing violence* to the incredible beauty and profundity of her words. Given that I play a major part in that narrative, I have risked an approach that is more radical than I would normally take were this a purely biographical interview with another participant. The creative response that follows, then, was found as a way of resolving artistic, ethical, and theoretical dilemmas. It also represents an important stage in the development of my own writing, toward the "naked" and creative writing in the next chapter. It seems to me to be a text in transition between writing that is anchored by academic protocols and writing that is crafted in an artistic sense. I think this sense of two forces pulling against each other is theoretically important, and so I have resisted the (strong) temptation to refine the text in retrospect by making it conform to literary expectations, by, for example, unifying my use of the past and present tense. The sense of movement and struggle runs very deep in this chapter, and I want to expose that in its raw state.

Framework: Death and Resilience

Cixous rarely writes explicitly about *resilience*, but she is always writing about resilience. Survival is a major theme in her writing. She writes about survival in ways that are always quixotic, always undercutting essentialist/performative separation. Her autobiographical account of growing up without a father in French colonial Algeria drives her call for resisting oppression in *Sorties*:

> I am looking everywhere. A daughter of chance. One year earlier. A miracle. I know it; I hate it. I might never have been anything but dead. Yesterday, what could I have been? Can I imagine my elsewhere? I live all my childhood in this knowledge: several times I have miraculously survived.[18]

Her survival is a miracle—she is a *miraculé* but not in the sense that Bourdieu uses the word. For Cixous, the miracle is always a result of both momentous significance and mundane luck.[19] This means that she will never comply with an understanding of self that is important, unique, and intentional; she could just have easily been dead. She emphasizes the arbitrariness of who survives and who doesn't, but she follows it with a narrative about her own survival and resilience which is accompanied by an incantation for other people to do the same and to become liberated through writing and reading. Resilience is within everyone's grasp, it is implied, if we are prepared to walk her path.

In her paper "We Who Are Free, Are We Free?" this is complicated further by her refusal to close down the central contradiction of who survives and who perishes in the quest to understand resilience:

> I was born a survivor, I escaped by the skin of my teeth. I need not have been born a survivor. I resemble those who escaped and those who did not escape.[20]

Resilience is always undermined by its opposite, and therefore always contingent on luck and the rolls of the dice. This lends a humility to her writing that undercuts the deliberate mythological and biblical implications of the immense significance of her survival. To this effect, she democratizes survival in *Coming to Writing*,[21] in which she offers a detailed account of what it is necessary to do in order to be liberated into the realm of *l'écriture féminine*. She develops the centrality of this experience of total loss in relation to survival most fully in this text. The death of her own father is repeatedly referred to by Cixous as the source of her writing. As Ian Blyth and Susan Sellers point out, death in general is "central to Cixous's entire writing project."[22] Mobilizing the dreadful effects of death toward the creative project involves progression through a chain of events that begins with death and proceeds through mourning to a position of total loss. Then love—radical and transformative—can penetrate, allowing for real writing to take place. I quote the whole section because the pattern that leads to writing (survival) is most fully set out in this passage, and it is therefore quintessential to my understanding of resilience in this study in general and in the interview with my mother in particular. She begins by considering the desolation left by death and goes on to suggest that this famished, barren land is the place in which writing can begin. It is a loving reading of perfect absence:

> And this tissue from which your pains tailor this body without any borders, this endless wasteland, this ravaged space, your ruined states, without armies, without mastery, without ramparts—you didn't know they were the gardens of love. Not demand. You are not jealousy, not calculation and envy because you are lost. You are not in touch. You are detachment. You do not beg. You lack nothing. You are beyond lack: But you wander stripped down, undefined, at the mercy of the other. And if Love comes along, it can find in you unlimited space, the place without end that is necessary and favourable to it. Only when you are lost can love find itself in you without losing its way.

In this sense, the complete loss of self, created by death, is necessary for survival. Writing is an "act" of complete passivity and surrender to love, and love itself is a mutable force that makes its home in the self but is stronger and greater than it. This undermines the notion of resilience as an active agency or performance, explored in simplistic terms early on in the study. Rather, these actions are non-actions or consents to be invaded by a vigorous force that is attracted to the space left by death. Here love is not an emotion but a being—a metaphysical force that exists independently from its subject. It has its own agency, and it is stronger than its recipient. There are echoes here of Ted Hughes's reading of *Pygmalion*[23] and my application of it to transformational adult learning. The idea that love can "find itself in you" is comparable to Hughes's portrayal of the way that Pygmalion the sculptor is possessed by the spirit so that she can find a way of being. His art is a result of his possession rather than his will. According to Cixous, this is what love does to the writer, but it can only do so when the writer-to-be has been wiped clean by death.

Death is a major theme for Cixous, and it is at the heart of her case for liberation through writing. It is prismatic, though, and it evolves across time. In the four works used here (*Sorties*, 1975; "Coming to Writing," 1977/1991; "School of the Dead" (in *Three Steps on the Ladder of Writing*), 1993a; and "We Who are Free, Are we Free?" 1993b), there is an identifiable progression through her positions on death across two decades. In *Sorties*, the essential imperative for writing is cast, and this idea underlines all the other works—writing is an activity that provides the opportunity to reverse the work of death. Death is associated with passivity, giving in, and collusion with the enemy. As she says in the autobiographical section, "I cannot inhabit a victim, no matter how noble, I resist: detest a certain passivity, it promises death for me,"[24] and death is continually portrayed as something to escape from; it is masculine and colludes with the destructive forces of logocentric power, oppression, and hierarchy. "Death is always at work"[25] in the binary system that assigns to the other the subordinated, dominated position through language. There is a chink through which a radical rereading of death appears, though, and with it a suggestion of the complexity that follows in her later works, in her assertion that death threatens a man differently than it does a woman.[26] Two years later, in her essay "Coming to Writing," death has moved to the center of her thinking about liberation. She still places the death of her father at the center of her work, and it is still cruel (she watches it, from the earliest times "disfigure, paralyze, and massacre"[27]), but it is coming to be associated more closely with writing. Death has become feminine, a second mother, who precedes and antecedes the brief interval of life:

> And from this period of death, one retains the greatest fear and the greatest benefit: the desire to remain as close as possible to Her, death our most powerful mother, the one who gives us the most violent push of desire to cross over, since one cannot *stay close* to her, she desires and incites desire; and this desire is split, it is simultaneously its own opposite, the desire to approach her close enough to die from it, almost, and to hold oneself extremely far back from her, as far as possible.[28]

This is an important shift in which the common noun has become a proper one, a name. Death, being its (Her) own opposite, transcends the violent work of the binaries previously portrayed as the work of death in *Sorties*. Here death nurtures as she destroys, seduces as she repels. She is kind and deadly—"our most dangerous and generous mother."[29] The feminine personification of death opens up the potential for a rereading of the mythological associations of the underworld—it can be rewritten as a wild, deconstructive kingdom in which presence and absence coexist and which resists simple identification as life's dangerous supplement. Instead of the realm of the oppressor, death has become the hopeful place that undermines (and under-mines—it is, after all, a battlefield out there) all the outposts of logocentricism. The imagery ("the one who gives us the most violent push of desire to cross over") echoes Cixous's previous concern with birth in earlier texts. Death is another birth, then. Only the brave can get close to death—to learn to love the mother. The possibilities of *jouissant* living can be entered into only with the acknowledgment of Death and with Her full support. Cixous adopts an authorial voice that echoes the Psalms on the one hand and the lullaby on the other. She speaks to the reader *as* Death now, not just about her. The voice is comforting; at once practically maternal and benevolently divine:

> In the beginning, there is an end. Don't be afraid: it's your death that is dying. Then: all the beginnings. When you have come to the end, only then can Beginning come to you.[30]

Death as a benefactor is developed much more robustly in the 1993a work "School of the Dead." Here Cixous portrays death as the first education for writing and living authentically. Death is necessary and real, a deconstructive playground that allows for the "inaugural scene"[31] to take place, and this is the birthplace of writing. Early experience of death has become "an act of grace."[32] Death provides the door to another world, it undermines everything from then on—all the games of presence and of certainty are never true for the one who has experienced early loss:

> The dead man's death gives us the essential primitive experience, access to the other world, which is not without warning or noise but which is without the loss of your birthplace. So it gives us everything, it gives us the end of the world; to be human we need to experience the end of the world.[33]

As such, the benefit of early experience of death is spelled out—the binaries around presence/absence are undermined by it and, from then on, forever scrambled. They can never again carry weight for the subject. It is a tough and cruel benediction, though, and this is always acknowledged. The references to her own autobiographical struggles constantly remind the reader that the bereaved child has a desperately unhappy childhood.

By the time she writes "We Who Are Free, Are We Free?" in 1993b, Cixous is moving on again from this position of Death as our first mother and recasting her as the benevolent fairy godmother, who is simultaneously the wicked witch who provides us with the poisoned fruit of knowledge. Her quest is to visit particular individuals who are singled out by her because they are able to particularly benefit from her gift. Playing on the German/English translation of the word "gift" she writes,

> And then there are those who received the desert in the cradle. It is a poisoned gift, both poison and gift, and sometimes the poison is a gift—an endowment, the terrible gift granted to some, a sort of curse that is a blessing, a natal desertion, and that condemns and brings them up to poetry.[34]

Poetry occupies a privileged position in Cixous's universe because it is a form of language that resists the ordering of logocentrism. Death therefore presents the bereaved infant with a different possibility for language. It does so by exposing the infant to "perfect absence,"[35] that is to say, absence beyond words—pure desertion. The early poisoned gift opens the door to an alternative; there is a different way of being, of giving, and of loving. Perfect absence undermines the kingdom of presence, and it therefore engenders disbelief in the subject. She is able to know that this world, which is so unfair and so cruel, is not true, is not real, is not the only possibility. By this stage then, Death has been recast as both gift and gift-giver, not without Her poison; Cixous does not romanticize it or sentimentalize the effects (the implications are monstrous), but it is a gift nonetheless. The gift can open the door to another world and, in doing so, it provides resilience. When loss through death is total, it allows access through the rare portal—it allows the bereaved to go beyond language. Previously she had written,

> As soon as you let yourself be led beyond codes, your body is filled with fear and joy, the words diverge, you are no longer enclosed in the maps of social construction.[36]

Now death provides the gateway through which this might happen. So this is the gift of death—it allows for a fundamental doubt in the world as it appears with its hierarchies and its binaries, all of which are founded on the great taboo, the fear of the final dangerous supplement. Those who have received the gift know that it doesn't have to be this way; beyond it is a different kingdom—the home of our Other Mother.

What follows is an attempt to put these ideas into practice as an interpretative technique for the interview with my own mother. It is also a conscious attempt to move into a new way of writing that transgresses the academic/creative binary. As such, there is a tension in it between letting the interview speak for itself and reading it playfully in the context of the rest of the study. The mythopoetic themes are deliberately invoked and death is personified as a way of illuminating this tension.

The Interview

Birth

The interview with my mother (henceforth referred to as my mum to reflect the intimacy of the text) is founded on the movement between death and resurrection, but it is not a simple progression between two poles. The movement is kinetic and concurrent—it allows both states to exist within each other, while at the same time oscillating between the two. Death-in-life and life-in-death are persistent ideas throughout the text, as is the corresponding play of absence and presence. My dad, who died three months after I was born, is an absent presence throughout the text, whereas my near death at birth is a present absence—the specter of what could have been underlines the account. There is a sense that events unfold as a result of casting dice between these alternate positions, or rather, alternative readings of the same position—life in death. A different story is always hovering on the blank side of the paper of the transcript. I just made it; dad didn't. It could have happened the other way around just as easily. Resurrection binds death-in-life to life-in-death because it takes place in a realm where presence and absence coexist inside each other—the realm of my Other Mother.

The account starts before my birth, with the shock of my mum, aged 45, finding herself pregnant. She already had two grown-up children. My sister was 23 and married, and my brother was 20 and away at university. Immediately life and death are starkly juxtaposed. My mum resists death from the beginning. There is a hefty censorship in some of her female friends' reactions to her pregnancy: "One or two of them cried when I told them," and another offers to arrange an abortion for her. "She said, 'why don't you have an abortion?' She said, 'I know a district nurse, she can abort.' I thought, oh yes, so she might—but not me!" I have always understood that death was just as viable and possible an identity for me as life. Absence is just presence inside out. I have never quaked under the sudden realization of my own mortality—I have never unrealized it.

I was born at home just down the road from the seafront in the middle of January 1971. My birth is written through with the very real threat of death—because of the "dreadful breech birth."

The interview sets out what happened in the early hours of that January morning:

1. My mum's doctor was not on duty, so I was delivered by another one who had a severe asthma attack halfway through the birth, rendering him incapable of helping much;
2. I was a breech birth, so he had to pull on my arm to get me out—in so doing he broke it;
3. When I did emerge, the cord was wrapped around my neck;
4. I turned blue due to lack of oxygen;
5. The midwife called for an ambulance, but when it came it didn't have an oxygen mask on board;
6. So they sent out for one and it did arrive, just in time;
7. Once they had the oxygen mask, I got the oxygen and I started to breathe;
8. The unbroken arm was paralyzed for the next 18 months, but I survived. It was four days before my mum's 46th birthday.

My mum summarizes these events as follows:

I was having you, you were being born at home, but the doctor had to send for the ambulance to get you to the hospital...And in the meantime you had two broken arms—no, one broken arm and one paralyzed arm...you were a breech, so they sent for an ambulance. And he, when it came it hadn't got this resurr...not resurrection, resuscitation thing they should carry on the ambulance all the time.

The slippage between *resurrection* and *resuscitation* releases the possibility for death in life—the word itself becomes the difference. Existence continues inside the text, inside the word. This central slippage of what are conventionally regarded as opponents drives my mum's construction of resilience throughout the interview. Resilience is constituted in having access to the resurrection/resuscitation equipment. And I very nearly died, "'Cos the cord was round your neck as well as these broken arms. Wonder you survived, isn't it? But that shows how strong you were," she says.

It must have been so hard for Death—my Other Mother—to let me go. She tries everything to keep me with her for as long as she can. She can't bear to let them take me away. First she clings onto one arm, but they break it free from her. Then, in desperation, She hangs about my neck, but she isn't strong enough. I am lost to her. Poor thing! She must think I was going forever—She cries and cries. But She manages to keep hold of one hand—She won't let me go into the darkness alone, so She holds on.

So I survive—thanks to the resurrection equipment. I am born into resilience. And Death contributes generously to my survival.

As he left, the ambulance man told my dad that he didn't think I would survive the night. When I ask my mum if she thought I would survive, she says, "Well, I did. I thought if I prayed enough you would."

Later in the text, her ability to pray temporarily fails her, but here it serves her well.

Owing to the fact that I had one paralyzed arm and one broken arm, I had to go to the hospital repeatedly for the first 18 months of my life. The first of these visits took place a week after I was born, when my sister and dad took me to the hospital. There is a preempting of the disappearance that will follow in my mum's reaction to them going.

"And when they walked out the door, oh I cried and cried. I thought you were going forever, you know?"

From the beginning, then, the possibility of walking away and never coming back is a reality and a serious consideration that governs everything. But they do come back, and I'm okay. I can't move my arm, but that is because Death still has hold of my hand very tightly. But I'm okay.

Death

I know Death before I know language. My dad dies three months later, on April 21, of a heart attack. Just after Easter in 1971. The terrible, cruel irreversibility of sudden death leaves my mum wasted, in complete shock:

> It was a terrible shock, because he was putting in, erm, double glazing in the front window.

This time they don't have time to call out for the resuscitation/resurrection equipment. He leaves a big hole in the front of the house where the windows were. It is his last loving act—he opens up the space for something else to get in. The house is cold and desolate and open to the raw sea air.

He is just gone.

Death gets as close to me as She can without taking me back. She is devastated by my absence but won't give up on me—She is resilient, after all. She gets into the space that dad occupied and holds me close. She can't believe that this daughter of Hers has gone forever. She has to work fast before language can contaminate things for me, so She messes up the chronology of the "natural" order—Dad's funeral precedes my christening.

This presents my mum with a sense of unreality that is still evident in her speech:

> He hadn't been ill or anything before. Just couldn't believe it was happening to me. But there it was, it did.

Death's work is momentous, monstrous, and devastating. The mourning takes a long time, and my mum "cried and cried and I cried and cried." She is lost, ruined, and she has a baby, of all things, who depends on her, to look after.

The terrible legacy of death is understood in its raw state, language is inadequate, and crying is the only reasonable response. She "just couldn't get over it, you know. I missed him so terribly much." We cry together, my mum and me; she knows total loss, and I know perfect absence. My mum slowly begins to accommodate this new reality by focusing on the mundane tasks of every day—getting us up, feeding herself, breast-feeding me, and going to bed. What surprises and dismays her, though, is death's social effects, rather like her late pregnancy. It is an extravagant act, death, (completely over the top!), and it leads, of all things, to embarrassment; some people just don't know what to say. She says of friends that she and Dad had as a couple,

> Funny though, they sort of dropped me socially after your dad died. I suppose it embarrassed them. I was on me own.

And of Dad's boss's wife:

> And she couldn't face me. You know...I saw her across the road one day and she just turned and went in a shop. I knew she'd seen me. She was so embarrassed.

It is just too much for people to take in—an older mother pushing a pram, with a baby with a teddy bear in one hand and Death clutching the other one. They just can't find the words. "We walked that seafront over and over again," up on the seawall, past the shelters and the arcade and along to the jetty and back again and again and again. On one side the streets where we live and the house with the hole in it where Dad used to be, on the other, the sea, changing shoreline, and somewhere else. She resists the simplistic underestimation of the magnitude of her loss from those people who do try to use language rather than giving up altogether:

> I mean a woman across the road said to me "oh now your husband's dead you can have a completely new life." What a thing to say! I said, "I don't want a new life. I was quite happy with the one I'd got."

Her loss and mourning can only be supported by those who offer love in a way that goes beyond language, like the old lady in the church who tells her, "There's enough of us praying for you." Life, it seems, can never be the same again because life—her life—is at an end: "I just, my life, I felt that my life had ended."

At this point, she has reached the nadir. My dad's death not only meant that she lost the man she loved, but it also had significant material consequences on our lives. My dad had not been wealthy—he was a television engineer working for a local electrical appliances shop—but his income was regular and there was a stability about our existence. After his death, she received £9.00 a week in benefit.[37] She supplemented this by taking in lodgers and looking after children. The prognosis was not good in terms of educational achievement. But I did survive, and so did she. Her resilience, as it is narrated in the interview, can be read as corresponding to the following agencies: love, reading, writing, and adult education.

After Life

Love

Life does not end when my dad dies. Life goes on—my mum has a baby to feed and love has been present, and it continues to be.

> But your dad he loved you very much. I can see him now, laying on the floor with you, playing with you...I mean, before you were born, he said, "It's going to be a girl and we're going to call her Elizabeth." He had all that input into it, you know? He really did.

Language takes the place of Dad that Death has caused him to vacate. What he leaves behind is a word—a name. That word will always be linked to him, and what is counted lost forever can be found again in it. Love has made its presence felt by inhabiting a name before Death can take it away, and as we know, naming is an act of love.[38] It means promise in Hebrew, this name I am given. It promises something else, something beyond language. It promises that Death will not have the final word—it promises different names, magical ones instead—like the star with the singing horses.[39] You would have to go over the moon to find a word like that.

> And as I say, your dad, the first three months before he died, he was so over the moon with you. He adored you, you know, played with you. As I say, he chose your name, he chose your sex...It was lovely.

There is no way around it, though. Death is terrible in what She does. I have no language with which to make sense of what has happened. I just know absence and severe separation. This house into which I am born is a world of suffering and of grief, and I have no understanding of time or of language. I don't yet know that it will pass. I have known adoration and I have adored, and now that is ruptured. My poor mum suffers, and so does the rest of the family. I learn to smile, to walk, and to speak in a household that is grieving. It's a hard, hard start to life, but I am loved and love is so protective. And my mum makes up for the lack of physical contact with my dad by continuing to provide it herself. She presents this act as protective—and therefore fostering resilience—for herself and for me. She juxtaposes her need to breast-feed with her drive to survive:

> What kept me going initially was I was determined to breast-feed you....And that kept me going. I'd got to eat. I'd got to drink. I'd got to do anything because I wanted you to have a good start in life.

There is presence in absence from the start. She will not let the dead father die because he lives on in me. Love is also a feature of other relationships. My dad might have been dead, but there were alternative male figures around, and there was a good deal of love. She says of my relationship to my brother, for example,

> But you adored Bob, right from the beginning. When he used to come home on a Friday night, you know, if he was home for the weekend.

A lot of the support that my mum receives comes from the community. Love is active and it busies itself in the day-to-day realities of supporting her. She gets real financial support from my grandparents and from the ministers at the Methodist Church, and the members of the congregation there are immensely helpful to her:

> But the people who were at the church were excellent. Dear old Mrs. Beale, she was lovely. She said, er, I said, "I can't even pray." "Oh, don't worry about that," she said, "there's enough of us praying for you." And she said, "Ring me, don't matter if it's day or night, if you want someone to talk to, if you can't sleep, ring me up." And I didn't, although I knew I could.

The effect on her is profound.

> You see, 'cos I'd got that sort of boost there, someone to give me a bit of support, I didn't need to do it.

The real conversation doesn't need to take place because the offer of the conversation suffices. The community provides material and literal support freely and generously. Two members of the church give my mum money, and the neighbors are "always there" babysitting, giving her a break, being in the house. Love is therefore not a feeling that is understood as emanating from individuals, rather it is a practical activity; it prays, it gives, and it babysits. Love informs all other developments of resilience and all the other categories that allow it; reading, writing, and education are functions of love.

Love for me was also an ongoing love for my dad. My mum continues to keep him alive by building my resilience, and that is why it is so important to her that we go on.

> But you see, that's why you were such a blessing to me, because you were part of your dad and he was going to live on in you.

There has to be a future, therefore, and love allows it to happen. It means that life can go on, and it does so through the acquisition of language and reading.

Reading

Reading emerges as a function of resilience in two ways in the interview. As it is for Cixous, it is a crux in the way resilience is constituted for my mum.[40] First through language, books become accessible, and through them the portal to other worlds is opened. Second, she resists closed and oppressive readings of her own life.

a. Reading to Survive

Much of the account of how my mum survived the months and years after my dad's death centers on the way that she spent time teaching me to read. Even before my dad died, I was read to every day:

> Right from when you were read to. You know, you wouldn't be able to comprehend, I don't suppose, but you were always read to.

After Dad died, the business of teaching me to read and to talk occupied much of my mum's time, and it helped her to structure a resilient response in herself as well as supporting my own resilience. She used pictures of animals in the Kays Catalogue[41] as a way of helping me to construct meanings from words and pictures.

> We'd go through the catalogue. At one time there were a lot of teddy bears in the catalogue and you used to look for "teddy." "Teddy," you know, you used to look through all the pages there was a teddy.

It is an example of co-construction: "You know, you sort of helped to teach yourself really."

This activity provides both of with us with an opportunity to develop hope and the reasons to go on. There is love in this teaching of reading; it is all part of the same maternal project.[42]

Imagination is key to the relationship between the text, learning, and resilience, and this is as true for her now in her 80s as it was then for her in her 40s. My mum sees reading as the opposite of "playing silly games" (although she does see linguistic games such as crosswords and Scrabble as something to be taken seriously) and as a way of staying alive. It is also a source of pleasure:

> It was the only pleasure I'd got—well, apart from you—it was the only pleasure I'd got you know.

My mum still looks up each new word she comes across (the latest is the word for the sea at its most powerful—"Tsunami") and in doing so she avoids the abyss—she continues to find her own mind rather than losing it to old age. She still spends hours of each day reading narratives of imaginary worlds. Reading for her is a resistance to demise, decline, passivity, and death. She knows that it is possible to read one's way out of heartbreak.[43] She introduces me to texts ranging from Ladybird books to the Kays Catalogue. Reading and language acquisition, for both of us, take on the roles of purpose, a future, and agency. When I ask her what my learning to read meant to her, she says,

> It meant everything to me, didn't it? It gave me something to do. It gave me an aim in life: to make sure you were really well educated.

My achievements become an enormous sense of pride for her because they validate her success as a mother:

> My cousin Betty was there one day. She was absolutely flabbergasted when she see what words you recognized.

The link between reading and survival—both for me as a child and for her as an adult—is very clear in the text. She remembers her grandfather reading her stories from the Bible: "I remember sitting on his lap and hearing the— the Prodigal Son." Reading is an act of love, and it presents the young reader with hope for survival. The space between the reader and the text is a place in which those without capital are as powerful as those with it. "And I always saw that Prodigal Son coming up the hill and his father coming to meet him. See? That was the picture I'd got in me mind." That particular text opens up the possibilities for turning around, for rereading and being read anew. Death operates as a metaphorical concept in that story in a way that allows for rebirth—because this son was dead and is alive again; he was lost and is found. And they began to be merry! The parable opens up the possibility of joy and reversal of apparent finality. The text calls home the reader and liberates her. Like the father in the story, the text was there all along—waiting for her to return to it. The story of the prodigal son offers ways out, forays, sorties. The text is about love and hope, but the act of reading it is also a simultaneous action of love and hope. The prodigal son is provided with the space in which he is read differently, anew. A second way that reading leads to resilience is the way that my mum resists closed readings of texts and of herself as a text.

b. Resistance of Closed Readings

A mocking skepticism of authority runs strongly throughout the interview. It manifests itself in relation to the police ("That's when I lost all respect for the police"); the teacher of child psychology in the adult education classes ("She wasn't of the real world. She just lived in her little bit"); the health services in general ("You were supposed to go every week to get your babies weighed. I never did"); the representative from the benefits office from whom she asked for help to supplement her income of £9.00 a week ("So I sent for this bloke. And he come. And he was obnoxious to me. And in the end I told him to go"); and most notably in relation to the health visitor[44] ("She wore a navy blue mac [raincoat] and a navy blue coat and she looked like Satan)."

She also resists the narrow and unperceptive understanding of my reading ability displayed by the teachers at my first school. All are characterized as intrusive, unhelpful, and condescending. When I ask her how social services knew about my paralyzed arm, she says that someone must have "informed them."[45] "Informed," with its connotations of spying and betrayal, gives an insight into the deep lack of trust that she feels in the system. At the heart of this is a conviction that the main function of the welfare state should have been not about surveillance but about the securement of economic capital. Ultimately many of the struggles that she faced in the years between 1971 and 1976 were a product of the fact that her official income (without the work she was able to do at home) was £9.00 a week.

> But I mean what they should have been helping me with was getting me that money, more money so that I wouldn't have to…

Perhaps the end of the sentence would be about dividing her attention away from child care. She resists any intervention and surveillance that she sees as a threat: "And there they were interrogating me like that."

This disdain for embodied authority is also evident in the way that she resists authoritative and closed readings of texts—including other people's lives and her own life as a text. Whereas she revels in the indeterminacy of meaning afforded by fictional and spiritual texts and is emboldened by the way that she, the reader, lacking in so many other forms of capital, is able to be powerful in the realm of the text, she ridicules the glib, closed reading of child behavior that her child psychology teacher presents her with. The assumption that an adopted girl must be trying to find her biological parents when she runs away is revealed as trite and closed.

> And this woman said, "Oh she's trying to find her parents." She said, "No she's not, she just a little monkey."

Such closed meanings represent not only a restricted understanding of life but also an oppressive one, because they disempower—mapping out failure in preordained plots and endings. She similarly resists the same predictive reading of my life when the same woman tells her that my life will be harmed by the death of my father and therefore my mum should remarry:

> [She said,] "But the child'll be disadvantaged." I said, "No she won't." I said, "Because when she was christened my son and his girlfriend and my daughter and her husband all said—they were her godparents—they said she hasn't just got one parent, she's got five."

This resistance of authoritative readings persists to the present day. She begins the interview by questioning my decision to impose a sociological reading on her life according to Bourdieu's categories. She objected to the rigidity. Before the interview began, she told me that the attempt to separate her experiences into the various forms of capital was artificial:

> *EH*: And, erm, I talked about these categories of Bourdieu, and, erm, I agree with the point that you've just made about the fact that they all go into each other.
> *LC*: They all run into one another, yeah.

Well before I had understood that I needed to find another way of reading that allowed for fluidity and openness, my mum had understood it first. Such closed readings are presented not only as unimaginative and restrictive. Prescribed criteria that are imposed on a text or a life are presented as deeply dangerous and limiting. There are consequences to such readings, she seems to be implying, and the one she must have dreaded most would have been my being taken into the care system. So the health visitor who misreads our lives according to narrow medical and psychological criteria is dismissed angrily:

> The last time she got in touch, she [said], "Is she still wetting the bed?" [I said] "She never did wet the bed!" You know? That's when you were about four! Stupid woman.

My mum insists that she is permitted the space to read in playful ways, and she refuses to be a closed text for others; she demands to be read differently. There is an inherent evil in such a practice; it is the opposite of love, and such a reader represents the common enemy—Satan (she says of the health visitor "She wore a navy blue hat and a navy blue coat and she looked like Satan"). Satan, whose name means "the accuser" is invoked to illustrate those powerful forces who employ closed readings to blame and to categorize people. Such forces are dangerous, because their activity prevents resilience from flourishing. Satan represents the final closed binary between good and evil, blame and redemption, knowledge and ignorance. And my Other Mother is just as wary of Satan. To Her, he is the great pretender, Her impersonator who has pulled off the biggest con trick in history—he has convinced the world that he is She. What big teeth he has! But we got it wrong. Death is a grand mother after all. And the wolf is terrified of the little girl who can see through his clothes because he knows full well that she reads him differently. There is something dangerous about a little girl, dressed like that. He looks at her and he sees red/read.

In order to keep the wolf at bay, my mum has to do something else.

She begins to write.

Writing
After my traumatic, dangerous birth, my early life is punctuated by visits to the hospital, because for the first 18 months of my life one arm is paralyzed. On the last of these visits, I reach up and take the pen from the doctor's breast pocket.

> The last time we went you looked at the doctor and you put your hand up and you pulled the pen out of his pocket. And he said, "She's alright now, you needn't come any more." Yeah.

Death lets go of my arm. It has taken Her 18 months to relinquish it, but She knows now that She needs a scribe. Sick of unbeing, othered on the one hand, impersonated on the other, She craves representation. She has been cast as unfit and dangerous for so long that She frees my arm in order to write herself a text. But She will have to wait a long time. I go prodigal first.

Taking hold of the pen fulfills a symbolic as well as a historical purpose in the text. Writing signifies and facilitates survival in both my mum and in me. My mum writes in the evenings after Dad dies, when I am asleep. Instead of going to bed early, she writes about her life in the past and the present. She writes "reams and reams" of file paper every time she has a spare minute. For her, writing is a lifesaver; it is a way of leaving no space for death.[46]

> I wrote this diary of your first years and I sent it to a magazine called "Mother" and they said it wasn't their sort of thing.

She writes compulsively in the evenings when I am asleep, and sometimes, when our neighbor across the road takes me to give her a break, "I filled it page after page." The act of writing exerts a healing, transformative effect on her that more than compensates for the lack of available readers: "I don't think anyone else but me ever read it."

She tells me it was the act of writing that was so important to her because "If I was writing I couldn't be crying, could I?" And I must have seen her writing, I must have made the connection that when she was writing she wasn't crying. I must understand at some level that it is possible that writing provides a way out of misery.

Writing allows my mum to find her textual self, to make sense of and to articulate suffering in a way that allows her to be present within it while seeing beyond it. More importantly, it is a way of dealing with her own grief and the fact that I would not have a father. For my mum, the gap allows her the space to develop a sense of the real within the sanctuary of her imagination. It is necessary for her resilience, "just to get it out of me system."

She laments the fact that that text was lost, "destroyed in one of the moves," but its place is taken by another text—this one. The death and absence that gave rise to the earlier one has, on revisitation, allowed this one to be born. That text was a way of keeping away from the edge of the abyss. This text does the work of excavation and resurrection.

Education

What my mum does after my dad dies is audacious. In the middle of her grieving and with a small baby to feed, my mum returns to her adult education class, seeing it as something that offers hope, not just for herself but for her whole family:

> I mean because I did all my own educating after I left school—[in the hope] that it would come to something eventually. I didn't realize how it was coming to fruition in you three. But it did. It gave me an aim, to ensure that you were going to be educated.

As such, she makes a direct link between her own continuing education and my own initial education. It allows her to continue her faith in education that was supported by my dad. She mentions my dad's experiences of adult education, "'cos he went to classes, he went to night school, to learn all about radios and stuff, you know." In addition to existing independently as transformational activities, reading and writing are formalized in the act of education. Education is both a function of love and a realization of resilience. She studies on "Monday nights at the library" and the subject is English literature: "We were doing a whole series on H. G. Wells and I really enjoyed it." I had no idea that my mum had done this when I arranged the interview—the focus was initially about the development of my own resilience. When she revealed that she had begun an adult education class before I was born and then carried on after my dad died, the interview took on a new, important dimension as a text about adult learning. What it provided for her was hope:

> Hope that there was a future. Hope that there was something…It gave me an aim—to ensure that you were going to be well educated.

Learning as a form of resistance and survival emerges strongly from the text. In the desperate months and years after my dad dies, she is adamant that her son (my brother, who was 20 at the time) should return to university. Another woman in the same situation who was left at home with a baby in difficult material circumstances may well have thought that the presence of an adult son would have eased things. But her commitment to education did not allow this to happen:

> He came home when your dad died and he wanted to give up university and I wouldn't let him. That was the last thing that your dad wanted because he was so keen on you all getting a decent education…'Cos he'd missed out on it and I'd missed out on it.

The continuation of education is a way of surviving and of not giving in to death; it is a way of keeping alive and of keeping my dad alive, "Because it was your dad's wish as well as mine," and because, "It gave me an aim in life. To make sure you were really educated."

The literature to which my mum is introduced at the night class she attends includes works by Jane Austen and H. G. Wells. She loves H. G. Wells in particular—*Kipps* and *The History of Mr Polly* seize her interest. Her immersion in those books allows her to occupy an anti-land[47] in which she is the powerful, strong, and competent reader in possession of cultural capital. The content is less important to her than the act of reading, discussing, and writing about the books, she tells me.

At the same time that she pursues her own reading, she succeeds in teaching me to read and ensures that I have a good start in life. This means that when I go to school I start in a class higher than my chronological age would suggest:

> Because remember, you were in an extra, a higher class than you should have been right from the beginning. That's erm, I mean, that time, when you were a baby, I started the classes.

The connection that she makes is fitting: her own learning had facilitated mine and enabled me to achieve. Adult education for my mum allows her to "get out of the house," to be with people that she could "be on a par with," and to be intellectually stretched. She reads in preparation for each class and she writes essays for the tutor. She enjoys the experience and, like lots of adult learners, it opens doors for her and allows her to revisit her own impoverished early education. There is something about the nature of what she learned—English literature—that enables her to survive and to grow. Such learning legitimizes complex readings and it promotes reflection. Other worlds exist.

Resilience and education are therefore closely bound together. She survives bereavement by engaging in education as a learner but also as my first teacher. It was as important to her that I had "educational toys" as that I was healthy. She saw her purpose in life as being to ensure "that everything was geared to you because your dad, we both loved you so much that we wanted you to get on in life." In this sense, education is an act of love; it goes hand in hand with breast-feeding as a way of ensuring not just my own resilience as receiver of the love and education but also of her resilience as provider of it.

> And I mean, right until you were weaned. That was the first thing that kept me going. And then, always there was a thing about your dad wanted you to have an education.

Finally, then, education (with its particular focus on advanced reading and writing) and love provide hope and the means to develop resilience. She sums up resilience as being about purpose: "My purpose was you. Making sure you were educated, fed, clothed, and that you weren't going to miss out just because you hadn't got a father." Her own resilience is ultimately bound up with mine. Having something to provide for takes her out of her own misery, and education structures a future. "I mean...that's all I can say about your resilience because I'd got you and I'd got to keep going for your sake."

The interview with my mum provided depth and yet more layers of unknowing in the study. In it, the fiercely transformational nature of love and its relationship with resilience is highlighted. This develops the theme set up in Ovid's[48] version of the Pygmalion myth, in which love is the agent that finally gives life to Galatea, but even more so in Hughes's version, in which both artist and art are helpless in the massively transformational action of love itself. Joe's account of his own resilience relies heavily on the love of his wife. Cixous's blending of death, love, and writing (art) forges links between all three. My early taking up of the motif of resurrection as part of the miracle with relation to the five capabilities (and particularly the exploration of it in relation to *The Winter's Tale*) as a metaphorical treatment of the experience of the adult learner is made far more complex and profound in this chapter. Death exists here in the raw—it is not a cozy metaphorical construct for either Cixous or for my mum. The real relationship between writing and learning and real death is brought sharply into focus here. The first, rather obvious thing to say about what this chapter has revealed is that it has made the relationship between resilience and learning much more dyadic than it was previously. In the other interviews, the concern was simply with how learners performed resilience despite setbacks. Here the concern is two-way—the learning itself lends the resilience that allows the learner to carry on living. In terms of the research and the writing, this chapter took me to a far more threatening place than I have been to previously. It was certainly far more exposing, and the sense of stripping away academic clothing is starting to be felt here. Other clothes are available, though, and the references to literary, mythological, and spiritual texts fulfill that function. I struggled with the dilemma of how to write the interview for a long time. There is a sense that it gets closer to a raw understanding of resilience than previously. There are costs to this sort of writing, though. It was emotionally exhausting to write, certainly, and it provokes a range of (sometimes extreme) reactions in others that I did not anticipate. I think these costs are worth paying. There is a stronger movement in this chapter toward *l'écriture féminine* than has been demonstrated anywhere else in the book.

The content of this interview forced me into areas that would normally be deemed as falling outside of the confines of a social scientific piece of work. My imaginative engagement with those issues has served a methodological as well as an epistemological purpose. I needed to take the creative and personal risks that are embedded in this chapter in order to prepare the way for the complete vulnerability of what follows. A direct and immediate experience of vulnerability in learning is essential if I am going to convey anything like the lived experience of resilience in the face of it. The following chapter contains writing that aims to do just that.

CHAPTER 9

Autobiographical Writing

So far this book has considered a range of representations of resilience in poetic, dramatic, biographical, and auto/biographical contexts. The exploration of the nature of resilience in those learners who survive and thrive in higher education, despite all sorts of obstacles that might reasonably be predicted to prevent them from doing so, has provided a number of readings of resilient adult learning. I am simultaneously inside and outside of the study; I am both a resilient learner myself as well as (apparently) an expert *on* resilience in adult learners. A commitment to the "principles" of Hélène Cixous's understanding of *l'écriture féminine* has meant that there has been a movement away from conventional academic writing toward a freer, more creative way of writing throughout the book. This has been accompanied by the deliberate stripping away of what Laurel Richardson calls the "authority moves" of academic writing.[1] A second ecdysis runs parallel to the theoretical shedding that was outlined in Chapter One. In this second shedding, the devices and protocols associated with academic language are shed to reveal fresh flesh. Each new skin is closer to a literary form of writing that is distinctive because of what Celia Hunt and Fiona Sampson describe as its "margin of excess, latency, and plurality."[2] The point of this second shedding is to take me as close as possible to a position of intellectual vulnerability in order to understand resilience from the "inside," as it were. The shedding of clothes also reveals the constructed narrative that is academic writing. It is revealed as a sham. Perhaps it is no more of a sham than any other narrative, but it is certainly not as honest as those narratives that so openly declare their shammery—such as fiction and drama.

In this penultimate chapter, my own narrative of resilient learning is unveiled; I take off my academic clothes altogether. But what is it that remains? Roland Barthes (1972/2000) draws our attention to the paradox of the "truth" of the naked body:

> The end of the striptease is then no longer to drag into the light a hidden depth, but to signify, through the shedding of an incongruous and artificial clothing, nakedness as a *natural* vesture of woman, which amounts in the end to regaining a perfectly chaste state of flesh.[3]

So although this is *naked* writing, deliberately stripped of academic referencing and protective authority moves, I cannot pretend that it was behind or below or within all the other readings of resilience all the time. It is simply another one, curiously chaste in the sense that it seems to stand alone, briefly illuminated in its own spotlight, untouched by the other learners in the study. This is nakedness in the context of a study that has enjoyed dressing up and disguise, though. The academic clothes are still on the stage, and they will be picked up at the end of this chapter. I will therefore resist the temptation to claim any more validity for the naked chapter than I do for the other chapters in the book. This chapter serves an important methodological purpose as well as an ontological one. On one level, the writing allows me to fictionally inhabit an episode that called for resilience in order to survive and to remember clearly what unadulterated vulnerability in an educational setting feels like. On a second level, the performance of that episode in a piece of autobiographical creative writing, placed as it is in the context of an academic book, puts me in a highly vulnerable position and therefore calls for the same kinds of courage and resilience that were developed by and performed in the first episode. The chapter therefore denotes what it seeks to describe—it is in the process of what Jacques Derrida might call "redoubling."[4] This is not merely an intellectual exercise in post-structuralist writing, though. This writer has a body, and writing the chapter has been undeniably traumatic.

This writing was borne out of frustration as well as a philosophical engagement with the idea of *l'écriture féminine*. I felt angry with, and isolated from, the dominant research community in education, and I was frustrated by the numerous attempts to make me and my writing conform to a safer and more conventional model of social scientific writing. The initial intention was therefore to explain how I had developed and demonstrated resilience in light of what I read as opposition. The time was right for me to move into a new way of writing. I had had enough of fighting with my opponents and the struggle involved in writing against a dominant form, and I was keen to find a more creative and affirmative response. Richardson's summary of the crossover in her own writing (with some reference to Woolf's idea of writing against the current) is helpful as a way of illustrating this stage:

> Writing "against" the current tied me to the "mainstream," always aware of its speed, eddies and whirlpools, displacing the power and centricity of my own "current." I no longer desired to position my work as "counter" or "anti" or "against"...I wanted to write through the "personal" binaries (me/them, good/bad, for/against) that were my walls, invisible to me then, bracing and constraining.[5]

So I was committed to exploring a new type of writing, and I knew that the autobiographical perspective should be necessary to any notion of validity for this particular piece of work, given its subject matter and its theoretical framework. Therefore I was keen to represent my own experience faithfully, but I found that reality infuriatingly slid away as soon as I tried to frame it within academic language. So I decided to take on board W. B. Yeats's assertion that "there's more enterprise / in walking naked."[6] In other words, it is more courageous and more productive to shed our theoretical "clothing" once in a while in order to write authentically. For Yeats, this meant dispensing with his rich mythological framework in order to write about his own life. For me, it meant shedding the disguise of academic language and theoretical references in order to be honest about what resilient adult learning actually feels like. As a result, I did indeed cross over into a kind of writing territory that allowed me to creatively and honestly represent my own story. The first section of this chapter ends with the realization that this would be necessary. The present tense in which the piece was originally written is maintained in order to preserve its immediacy.

In the second section of this chapter, I move beyond a depiction and exploration of the present to a creative response to it that is arranged in two parts, entitled "Towards the Event Horizon" and "After The Fall." Neither the nature nor the content of this writing were anticipated, much less planned. Cixous prefaces *The Book of Promethea* with an epigraph that expresses the fear of the writer before the writing has been formed:

> I am a little afraid for this book. Because it is a book of love. It is a burning bush. Best to plunge in. Once in the fire one is bathed in sweetness. Honestly: here I am, in it.[7]

As I started to "walk naked," I felt overwhelming terror. Hunt's assertion that the type of writing featured in this chapter "is arguably more exposing" than academic writing[8] is absolutely correct. The sense of exposure was dreadful, but there was something much more profound and energetic at play at the same time. I had an accompanying portentous sense of getting near to the brink, to the edge of the abyss, as soon as I started writing creatively. I have tried to evoke this idea in the first part of the creative section of this chapter. It is a sincere attempt to convey the fear I experienced before I surrendered to the pull of annihilation in the second part of the text. Something crosses over in this chapter. Galatea finally wakes up. It is an independent piece of creative writing that is born out of the rest of the book, but it was the shock and terror of removing my clothes that allowed it to come about. This piece of writing is therefore written with the "courage" that Hunt and Sampson (2006, p. 70) emphasize as intrinsic to the creative writing process.[9] I had to "abandon (my) need for certainty and security"[10] in order to follow the writing to where it needed to take me, in order to deepen my knowing/unknowing crystalline understanding of resilient adult learning. There is a departure in this chapter, then, from the secure boundaries of the preceding chapters. Although that sense of safety has been receding as the book has progressed, it has always been present. Even in the previous chapter—in which I have deliberately confronted the boundaries of what is acceptable in an educational research text by exploring allegorical and mythical themes in the interview—even there, the basic confines of the auto/biographical interview hold fast. In this chapter, though, the safety harness is dropped altogether. This is writing in free fall. The chapter is notably different from all the others because it is characterized by what might be regarded as features of literary texts as opposed to documentary or analytical ones.

A Methodological Note on "After the Fall"

I did not know what point in my life would make it onto the page until I started writing the scene in the first paragraph. My original intention was to provide a purely autobiographical piece of writing in the second part of the chapter. In other words, to write through memory in as accurate a form as I could muster. As soon as I attempted to do this, though, I found the blocks regarding what was true and what was fabrication almost impossible to negotiate. So in order to begin writing, I adopted Hunt's instructions for "writing with the voice of a child."[11] I began by collecting nouns pertaining to visual and auditory images from the time in my life that I was trying to evoke. As soon as I started to do this, the stranglehold of my critical instinct was loosened. I shifted my methodological expectations of the writing and accepted, instead, Hunt's reassurance that "the point of the exercise is not to find the 'objective truth' of the past"[12] but rather to understand more deeply the tension and play between vulnerability and resilience. In order to move beyond images into prose, I used Margaret Atwood's *Cat's Eye*[13] as a model.

What attracted me to Atwood initially was the sharp specificity of her visual images and the way that she uses objects to ground experience and memories. The story of *Cat's Eye* (an account of the effects of the experiences of an eight-year-old girl on her life as an adult artist) was clearly also helpful in the construction of the narrative. As such, Atwood's work provided an initial framework for "After the Fall." *Cat's Eye* turned out to be a pertinent choice of text as a writing frame for the draft work for reasons that were not obvious to me when I selected it. As Ben Knights points out, Atwood's "protagonists seem drawn back to a search for origins, looking for the missing bits of the jigsaw in the past,"[14] and this seems to be an apt description of the function of the piece of creative writing that eventually arrived on the page.

By way of contrast with the preceding text, "Towards the Event Horizon," was written more freely and easily and without recourse to specific frameworks, other than some generic allusions to science fiction. David Bowie's 1969 song "Space Oddity" resonated, and it helped me to situate my feelings of terror and being cut adrift.

What follows is an introductory piece of writing that restates the intention to write in a way that is "naked" and then a naked account of the challenges of working in this interdisciplinary space. Embedded in the account are examples of my own resilience. The account ends with the realization that those strategies have taken me so far, but that I have arrived at a crossover point. The next piece of writing, "Towards the Event Horizon," is an attempt to capture the feelings that such a point in learning evokes. Then the crossover happens, and I move into the third piece of autobiographical fiction, "After the Fall" (discussed above). I decided to leave the chapter as it ends, without any further analysis. I am reluctant to close down the text by providing a close reading of it along thematic lines. More fundamentally, I offer the creative and naked writing in this chapter *as* a reading of resilience. It does not adhere to any analytic conventions, but it is a serious reading of resilience that attempts to speak for itself, without a secondary commentary attached to it. The decision to let this chapter work as a reading, unencumbered by secondary analysis, is entirely deliberate.

Part One

Resilient Adult Learning and the Study

Isolation is the biggest challenge that I have faced, and continue to face, as a result of taking this research approach. Other aspects of the experience have certainly tested my stamina, my patience, and my nerve, but they have not required me to be resilient in quite the same way. I've had to knuckle down and bare my teeth at times over the last couple of years, but that wasn't so bad—I've always had to look after myself. What is much, much worse than any of this is coping with the intense loneliness that accompanies the process.

I understand, of course, that completing any piece of single-authored research is always a solitary experience. By definition, any piece of work that aims to make an original contribution to the academy must be created independently and must go beyond what has gone before it. This piece of work, though, has put me in a particularly lonely position for two reasons. First, I am working in a space between and beyond two disciplines: education and English literature. This does not give me two homes; it makes me homeless. It has also meant that, whether I liked it or not, I have adopted a subversive position, because I have ended up challenging some of the fundamental precepts of both disciplines. Secondly, I have developed a methodology that combines biographical interviews with literary criticism and autobiographical writing, and that uses writing itself as a form of enquiry. I am not "writing up" some other piece of research that is going on elsewhere in the conventional way. My decision to go down this path was not based on a whim or the desire to be flamboyant. I have made these choices because, early on in the study, it became apparent to me that human resilience in learning situations is too complex and too elusive to be pinned down and explained by the application of either conventional, evidence-based approaches to research or by the pure critique of literary texts. Neither discipline alone seemed to be capable of providing a language that could adequately describe some of what began to emerge from the study about resilience—questions of love and loss, of death and resurrection, and of hope. This was difficult. I like to think that I am an articulate person, and my original disciplinary home—English literature—is constituted entirely of the written and spoken word. To find myself in a place in which words were inadequate was challenging. I have had to find a space beyond the confines of the two disciplines that would allow an adequate language to emerge. I have therefore put myself in exile. Exile is dangerous and lonely, but like other voluntary migrants, I have chosen it because I understand that the risks of staying at home are far higher than those I will encounter abroad.

There have been three particular aspects of isolation that have tested my resilience. These are the lack of safe readers, the search for home, and the loss of my academic faith.

1. *Lack of Safe Readers*

No reader is completely safe, but some are much more dangerous than others, and this is particularly true for the sapling text. The sapling is fragile and needs space to breathe and grow. All readers take the text and make something else from it. For safe readers, this is a quiet, questioning, and imaginative act of reading. Safe readers understand that the text needs shelter but not control, and that it is both connected to them as readers and to the writer, but that it also has a life of its own. They are teacher/readers and they are recognizable by their tentativeness and encouragement. It is a lot to ask of a reader, and there aren't many of them around. By way of contrast, the dangerous readers see the text as alien and therefore as something to be mastered or dismissed. They are definite in their responses, and they put a lot of energy into responding to what is *not* in the text. They are either noisy or silent. The silent ones are the worst—those readers who choose not to engage with the text at all. I have found the silence of readers who refused to, or who were not able to, engage with the text very challenging because, when I was on shakier ground than I am now, I found it difficult to read that silence as anything other than rejection or disapproval.

The struggle to create something while it is under surveillance (from the academic management system), and particularly to answer endless questions about its linear direction while it was still evolving, made me very defensive of the writing. And yet, as a writer, I have needed readers to validate my work. Negotiating this paradox has been very demanding. The repeated demands to account for where I was going (the research committee: "As part of your proposal tell us what you will find out at the end of this study before you begin") seemed to me not only a pointless waste of time but antithetical to any understanding of transformational learning that is, well, transformational. That is to say, learning that has the potential to be a force that is beyond the control of the teacher and the learner.

In the middle stages of this work, I was most vulnerable to the dangerous sort of readers because I desperately wanted affirmation and to talk about the thing that was taking up so much of my time and playing such a big part in my life. Now I am much more secure. I am happy with my group of safe readers whom I trust and respect, and I also work with another group of virtual safe readers in my imagination. These are the authors of books that I find very helpful and encouraging. Their writing feels like home to me. They haven't read my work yet, but I know that when they do, they will be safe. Ironically, now that I need them less, and now that I have developed a stronger writing style, I am attracting more safe readers to the work. The text has developed its own energy; the sapling has become a living thing to be reckoned with. As it grew to be a tree, it started to look after itself and it needed me less. And later, it started to shelter me. Earlier on, though, protecting the sapling work from the dangerous readers was tiring, and relationships have been damaged by the process (in the words of Virginia Woolf,

I have had to upset some very good fellows[15]). This sense of writing in the desert has been isolating, and it required resilience in order to keep going. There are benefits to spending so long in the wilderness, though—I can see that now. Deserts are arid and frightening places, but you can hear more clearly under the bare night sky. And some trees grow there.

2. *The Search for a Home*

In recognition of the lack of safe readers who were available to me, I spent a lot of time attending conferences and seminars and presenting papers in order to find like-minded souls. Early on, when the work was nascent and vulnerable, I thought that if I looked hard enough, I would find a ready-made community of people who understood what I was doing and who would encourage me in it. I looked in earnest on conference Web sites and journal listings but to no avail. What tested my resilience in this period of the work was that I felt compelled to behave in relation to the study in ways that I never would in other aspects of my life. I am confident and grounded and I have a strong group of close friends. I am not accustomed to feeling needy and asking people to be friends with me, but that is how I felt academically as I made contact with people after conferences and forced myself to network. And like all needy people, it made me very vulnerable to other people, who might choose to get back to me or not, to respond to my work or not (see previous section). It was the academic equivalent of sitting at home and waiting for the phone to ring. The attack on my pride and self-concept as a successful and confident person was a real challenge to my resilience, and I hated it.

So I ended up in some remote and desert place. What I found there was not exactly a community, but a loose affiliation of other hermits and the odd prophet in the wilderness, who could offer support, who understood what I was doing, and who encouraged me. I met some excellent people who were selfless in their support of me and of the work. This made it a helpful exercise, and it made me reappraise what I understood by community. Communities exist in the desert, but they are moving, nomadic, and loosely affiliated. The guarded citadels behind city walls could never provide a home for me—besides, even if I wanted to get in, the gatekeepers wouldn't let me pass.

My 18-month tour of the desert also taught me to be as wary as a fox about whom to trust. I was not prepared for the aggression and hostility that the work would ignite in some quarters of the educational research establishment. At one conference, a senior professorial figure in that world took strong exception to the concept of using drama as a way of looking at anything educational. "You're in danger," he said most sternly, "of using something that has been written by a male playwright and comparing it to interviews with real women!" That was exactly what I was doing. What shocked me about that for a while was not the grilling—of course I understand that some people think that that is what gatekeepers are supposed to do—but the way that my understanding of a theoretical position could be so different from another one that was apparently inside the same (post-structuralist) stable. The incident has stayed with me, and it taught me an important lesson, in that there is a need for caution in working with those who appear to provide a home in terms of content but might be miles away in terms of approach or philosophical position. It was a valuable lesson learned and, in retrospect, I realize that it was a very lucky encounter early on; but it did underline, again, that I was isolated with regard to mainstream educational research and, in particular, with the wing of it that might look like home.

3. *Loss of My Academic Faith*

As I searched for a community in which I could feel supported and at home, I became increasingly disillusioned with both disciplines—English and education. Education because of its heavy reliance on a narrow version of evidence-based sociology (and to a lesser extent, cognitive psychology) and English because of its disconnectedness and introspection. The things that had made me feel frustrated with the discipline as an English literature graduate in my early twenties resurfaced. And worse than that, I was starting to regard the very process of literary criticism (as opposed to English teaching) as something that was parasitic, indecent even. It felt like voyeurism. The idea that hundreds, maybe thousands, of people were making their living out of other people's creativity without ever putting themselves on the line or facing the fear of exposure that comes with any sort of personal or creative writing now seemed to me to be bizarre and wrong. Being on the outside of both disciplines was making me see the sham of each of them. But now there was something deeper still. It *all* started to appear as a sham to me; *all* of it seemed to be a parade of the emperor's new clothes. Academic writing seemed to be a masquerade and a distraction from the really difficult thinking and writing that happens without frameworks—a guard to protect people from engaging in what is real, difficult, and authentic.

In the winter of 2007, as I was moving out of the middle stage of the work and into the final stage, I wrote a play with a colleague who works in initial teacher education. In the play, we were attempting to use Boal's notion of theater of the oppressed to dramatize some of the most difficult problems faced by student teachers in their encounters with high school students. So we wrote a play[16] that dramatized the course of a disastrous English lesson on war poetry, taught by a student teacher to a group of 15-year-olds. Inhabiting the characters' voices was so challenging, and yet so liberating, that it allowed me to write in a way that I never had before. This was so much harder than anything I had done until then—it didn't come easily to me at all. The creative writing of the play crystallized a set of latent concerns and it made me question my faith in the whole system. *All* of it—the referencing, the peer reviews, the methodology debates, the hypothesizing, and the concluding (the certainty, in fact)—all of it was starting to appear to me as a gigantic sham, designed to keep people in their places and to screen academics off from what is messy, authentic, and difficult. Like an atheist in a seminary, I was aware that I had lost my faith, and I was angry with the others who couldn't see through the hocus-pocus. But militant atheism is an unimaginative and simplistic stance, forever locked into a binary with a restricted version of theism, forever trapped by language into denying the existence of what can't be described. I now need to move on from angry disbelief to find a kind of academic writing that is authentic and that acknowledges a space for other writers who can allow me to develop my ideas, while at the same time allowing that raw, risky revelation of the self to emerge.

Part Two

Toward the Event Horizon[17]

So I find myself here, now, in this dark, silent, nebular place, trying to write about resilience with words that are different from the Formican certainty of academic language. I can't move. The anger that got me here, that propelled me through the early and middle stages of the work, has burned itself out, leaving me here on my own, without gravitational pull either to the academic language I have left behind or to anything else that might be up here with me. I am petrified by the silence and the dark. I can't go back to where I have come from, but I am too scared to move forward—I can't retreat or advance, I am just here, still.

I have three choices now. This is the first. I can go back to where I have come from, to what I felt I needed to leave so urgently and what I was so certain was a sham. I could crawl back through the wardrobe and emerge, covered in coats, to a room full of gowns, and they would be so pleased to see me. They would be kind to me, I think. They would offer me a glass of sherry and ask me to share an abstract, and I could get a book out of it. It would take some tweaking, and I'd have to add in some statistics and go back to the journals, but I could do it. It would be called "Success and the Nontraditional Adult Learner in Higher Education: A Case Study Approach."

I can't do that; it would be inauthentic and cowardly.

This is the second choice. I could just stop. I could stay here, tethered to nothing, motionless, in exile, listening to my too-fast heartbeats breaking up the silence. I know that I am getting dangerously close to the edge of something, and for that reason I must not move a muscle, breathe too deeply, or close my eyes. I must stay awake and still, hyperaware and filled with terror. I can't stay here in this merely pulsar state; this fear will kill me eventually, and then who will know what I have been thinking and what will it all have been for? Just another far out, failed attempt to discern patterns in the chaos.

This is the third choice. I could surrender to the event horizon. I could exhale and expand into the starry space where I would be subject to a pull that is far stronger than me or anything I have left behind. I know there is something else up here, but I can't see it. We think we know about it because its existence is based on academic modeling, but that sort of knowledge has its limitations, after all. There is no evidence, so it's not necessarily true. Is it? We don't know what it is, but we know that when objects get too close, they spin faster and faster around its edge until they vanish and are either annihilated or transformed, into what we cannot imagine. It goes without saying why I wouldn't want that happening to me.

Those are my three choices.

No wonder they tried their best to save me from this in the early stages, the good people of Ground Control. No wonder they wanted to tie me to the floor! This, after all, is what all those administrative hurdles—the proposals, subcommittee meetings, methodology plans, time lines, peer reviews, the insistence on accessing the evidence base and ethical clearance codes—were designed to do: to save me from this. They knew that this is what could happen, that I could end up here, alone, in pain. They were trying to save me from facing this and they were trying to save themselves from the knowledge that anybody else ever gets this far. Poor things! I thrashed and kicked against them until they couldn't hold me down and then I launched myself out of there, with a blazing tail. I didn't look down—too busy fighting free and too contemptuous to feel scared. Fire and anger have been easy for me; I am so proud and I wanted to prove them wrong. But now those rockets have dropped off and Ground Control has gone quiet. Are they watching me on their screens or have they tuned out? No one is pulling me down, no one is arguing me out of this. I wish they would try to stop me now. I wish someone would insist I come home before it gets too dark.

I don't want to do this surrendering thing. I don't want to give up those references and frameworks and theories. I don't want to lose my cover of all those other lives through which I have been looking at resilience. This is terrifying and I need something to hide behind; I need some opaque phrases and some sturdy footnotes to help me recover. But I let that go and I can't go back to it. I am suspended up here, a reluctant stargazer, frozen but still alive.

What on earth possessed me and made me think I could hack it up here on my own?

Something is traveling through me that is so fierce and so forceful. I am fragmenting. It seems to be inside me and outside at the same time. It's migrating me. I can hardly breathe!

Did I say that out loud? Words are failing me now.

Now, what was I thinking about? It's immaterial now; it doesn't matter. It isn't matter. There's nothing for it now, I close my eyes and I let myself go.

Black Hole. Exotic Dark Star. Mighty Naught. I surrender.

This is it.

Part Three

After the Fall

At the front of the classroom is a blackboard with the date, *October 17, 1979*, written in the top right-hand corner. The handwriting slopes to the right and is joined up. In the middle of the board are the words *Poetry Test* in the same writing, and this is underlined. In front of the board is a plinth, and on the plinth is a teacher's desk, at which sits the writer with the slanted handwriting, Sister Kathleen. I am sitting in the middle of the middle row with girls on each side dressed in the same bottle-green blazers with the same *The Convent of the Holy Cross* badge on the top pocket. The lids of our desks flip upwards and backwards like sparrows with broken necks. Inside my desk are all my exercise books and textbooks and pencils and money for break and lunch. Inside the flip-up lid is a timetable that I copied out in the first week of term, taped to the wood. It looked quite good in September, but now the tape is peeling a bit and the paper is going yellow. It tells me what subject I do at what time and with what teacher. Sister Kathleen's name features a lot, because she is our class teacher and takes us for nearly everything apart from Physical Education, which would be ridiculous as she is an old nun with a bustle and a veil and she wears a black leather glove on her diseased right hand. We don't know what is wrong with that hand.

I reach into my desk to take out my blue poetry book. I am feeling sick with fear because I have not done the homework. This is unusual for me, unheard of even. My school reports say that I am a hard-working, well-behaved, and very shy little girl. Polite is a word they use a lot in these reports. The only time I have been sent out of a class was for crying and the only time a teacher has shouted at me was last year when I did not cross myself during the prayers. I do my homework. I say please and thank you. But there is something about this homework that has prevented me from doing it. I just haven't been able to do it and now I will be found out. The homework was to learn the spellings and meanings of all the difficult words in a poem for a test.

I have it written out at the back of my poetry book, and on the next page are all the words that I should have learned for homework but have not. They are *dirge, bleak, wailing, boughs, shroud, array, bier, sepulchre, knelling, blithe*. I have tried to learn them, but it has been no good; they just won't go in. I have not asked my mum to test me on them like I normally would. I am unprepared.

Sister Kathleen tells us to open our books at the back and get ready to do the test. My stomach is all churned up. So far I have managed to keep my head down and avoid Sister Kathleen's attention. I am not one of her favorites, but I wouldn't expect to be. She has only shouted at me as part of the group. We were all terrified of going up into her class. There are rumors about her. Every year she picks on a girl and she Makes Her Life Hell and you don't want it to be you. There are rumors that she takes naughty girls into the cupboard off her classroom and beats them. I have seen a film on the telly about rail safety that was supposed to teach you not to play near trains. In it, some kids go into a tunnel to muck about, but they don't know that a train is going to come through it. Then it does and they are left splattered like birds' mess on the sides of the walls. You don't get to see them splattered, but I have been imagining it ever since. I feel now like they must have felt when they heard that train coming down the track.

Just before the test is due to start, a small queue of girls forms in front of her desk. The girls are asking to be excused from the test because they have been ill. A chink of light appears in the darkness. I hurtle toward it. I see clearly what I need to do, so I get up and join the queue. When I get face to face with her I say, "I am sorry that I haven't done the homework, Sister." My thinking goes like this. This is the right thing to do because it is honest and honest is good. It is good to tell the truth. So if I just come clean then she will understand why I am about to get such a bad mark—a 4 or even a 2. After I have said this sentence, something weird happens to time. It splits into two.

At home, I have a telescope that my brother and sister-in-law bought me for my birthday back in January. They also got me a book called *Stars and Planets* to go with it. I love space. Every night I go to bed and I listen to my *War of the Worlds* tape until I fall asleep. *War of the Worlds* is based on a book by H. G. Wells. I have read in my *Stars and Planets* book that if you were to fall into a black hole then you would vanish in an instant, but for everybody watching you on earth (if they had strong enough telescopes, that is) you would appear suspended on the edge of the hole for ever after. That is because of what the black hole does to time, and this is what happens to time now. On the one hand, events no longer happen in order, in the way they used to, and the classroom and everything in it is spinning quickly around me as if it has been whipped up and carried away by a gigantic, intergalactic twister. On the other hand, I am doing what she is shouting at me to do, which is to empty my desk of all the books and pencil case and my bag and to put them all by her on the floor in the corner. She calls these things my *belongings*. I am doing all this as if in slow motion. I feel sick.

From that moment, time is swallowed up and I disappear. At exactly the same moment, I am suspended forever, sitting on the floorboards below her desk with all my things around me and my desk is open and empty. My hands and feet have gone numb, and my ears are blocking out large bits of her voice, so I know she is still shouting at me, but it is coming from a long, long way away. *Light years* away. I know that my crying is making her angry, but I can't stop. I seem to have been removed to somewhere else and I am hearing it all as if it is happening to another person. She tells me that from now on the floor will be my home and that I am not to have a desk like the other girls. She also forbids the other girls to speak to me or have any contact with me because I am BAD. After a period of time that is both a second and hours, she starts the test. When I reach for my book she shouts, "Not you, you will get a naught." This makes things much, much worse, because a naught will be filled in the mark book and the head teacher, Sister Mary, as well as all the other teachers, will see that. Naughts hang over you like black halos. I have become the sort of girl who gets naught. I am naughty. While the test is going on, I must sit in silence, writing nothing, trying to swallow my sobs so that my throat aches. At the end of the test, all the books are collected in apart from mine. The bell for break goes. I already know what is coming. "Not you," she shouts. "I haven't finished with you yet." She tells me that from now on I will only have time to go to the toilet at break times and to eat my lunch at lunchtimes and that I must immediately return to her for the rest of the time. We will start this now. I go to the toilet. When I come back, she locks the door. This is the way it will be from now on.

At home that night, I sit on my bed looking through my *Stars and Planets* book. I am blank and scrambled at the same time—like a television screen that has lost its picture. I stare at the pages. At the back of the book there is a section called "Far Out Theories" where it tells you all about the crazy scientists who have their own ideas about the universe. One of the Far Out Theories is about *transversable wormholes*. The idea is based on Albert Einstein's theory of time travel through wormholes. One scientist reckons that you could make a machine that would allow you to travel through space and time. What you would need is enough *negative matter* to turn a black hole into a wormhole. That would hold both ends of the wormhole open and, instead of being *annihilated*, an object would come out the other end in another time and space entirely. This is what it actually says:

> We just don't know whether it would be possible to go through a wormhole without destabilizing it or dying in the attempt.

I would go through a wormhole now, given half a chance. I would take that risk. I might even settle for a black hole.

I don't tell my mum that night. My mum cries a lot and I have a strong need to protect her. My mum never really got over my dad's death. She sometimes wishes she had died with him. I also feel such incredible shame that I can't put what is happening into words, even if I wanted to. The next day, I hope it will all be forgotten and that I can go back to being the sort of girl who gets 7s and 8s out of 10 and who is described as polite and well behaved on her report. But it doesn't get better—it gets worse. Everything I do now seems to carry a dark message about my sinfulness to Sister. Every piece of work I hand in has a terrible mistake in it that needs to be shown to the class and for which I must be punished. Sometimes the punishments come immediately, but sometimes they are delayed, which is much worse because I am tormented with worry about what will happen. Sometimes these delayed punishments don't come from Sister at all. "God sees," she tells me. I desperately want things to go back to the way they were. I want her to like me, or at least to not hate me. I try to be watchful. I try to be on my guard for mistakes that I am yet to make, but it is so exhausting because I am clumsy and inept and I don't know what will annoy her until it happens. "Trust you to mess it up," she says, "Trust you to try to be different." I spend a long time doing my homework and I make sure it is all written as well as it can be, but then she throws the book back at me because I forgot to underline the title. After that, large bits of time are missing for me. I start to lose touch with reality. Before, events seemed to be more-or-less tied to outcomes, but now things are rubbery and unreliable. There is a cupboard behind her desk which locks from the outside. It is a black rectangle of nothingness into which that year disappears.

I spend hours and hours alone with Sister Kathleen that year, behind the locked door. She lets me help her with her teaching because she lectures me about my sin and she uses me as an example to the other girls of sin and badness in the lessons. I start to take a pale blue plastic washing-up bowl to bed with me each night because I am sick most nights. I like the relief that throwing up brings. I like the reassuring smell of disinfectant and the violent contraction of the muscles in my stomach. And afterward I feel empty, rested, and clean. Every day my mouth is full of ulcers. I dread school and I think it will be better to be dead than to have to face her day after day; I think life can't get much worse.

Tinsel and fairy lights start to appear, very small at first, in the distance through the dark. I commence countdown. Christmas will mean three weeks without school. Three whole weeks without seeing Sister. I draw big pictures of Father Christmas with his sleigh at the back of my Rough Book and I color him in with optimistic red and black marker pens. But on Christmas day my grandmother dies. My brother finds her dead body when he goes to pick her up and bring her over to our house. We are still unwrapping our presents when he arrives with the news. My mum goes to pieces. That is the phrase that keeps coming back to me as I sit with my toys in front of the fire in the quiet. She has gone to Pieces as if it is a place, like Lourdes or Purgatory. If I had any thought of telling my mum about Sister Kathleen, then it is taken away from me. Winter carries on.

From February, my weekends are taken up with practicing for the Methodist Sunday Schools Bible Reading Competition. I have to read with expression the following passage to a room full of people:

> While he yet spake, there came from the ruler of the synagogue's house certain which said, Thy daughter is dead: why troublest thou the Master any further? As soon as Jesus heard the word that was spoken, he saith unto the ruler of the synagogue, Be not afraid, only believe. And he suffered no man to follow him, save Peter, and James, and John the brother of James. And he cometh to the house of the ruler of the synagogue, and seeth the tumult, and them that wept and wailed greatly. And when he was come in, he saith unto them, Why make ye this ado, and weep? the damsel is not dead, but sleepeth. And they laughed him to scorn. But when he had put them all out, he taketh the father and the mother of the damsel, and them that were with him, and entereth in where the damsel was lying. And he took the damsel by the hand, and said unto her, *Talitha cumi*; which is, being interpreted, Damsel, I say unto thee, arise.

And straightway the damsel arose, and walked; for she was of the age of twelve years. And they were astonished with a great astonishment. And he charged them straitly that no man should know it; and commanded that something should be given her to eat.[18]

I have the passage marked in my proper, old-fashioned, leather-bound Bible. But inside the open pages I have written it out in my own writing, underlining all the words that I need to stress and with pauses where I need to take a breath. I practice with my mum in the evenings and at Sunday School. On the day of the competition, I get up and I read it out. I am nervous, but I am so used to feeling sick most of the time that there isn't much difference. I wear my green-checked dress with the velvet collar. I know it all by heart, so I only need to glance at the page occasionally. I don't look at the people in the audience; I just look around the room as I speak clearly and loudly. I win the heats and I get a certificate for it. It means I have to go into the bigger, district competition, where I win again. Finally I end up in the whole regional finals. I don't tell anyone at school about my success—school and church are very separate. I keep it to myself. But it is the beginning of a successful new venture (I nearly call it a "hobby," but it is far too serious for that). It becomes an important feature in my life over the next few years. I have found something I do very well in. I win prizes in Bible-reading competitions.

In the early summer term, something changes. At school we do our exams in the period of time after the gardener puts the netting across the top of the huge statue of Jesus in the courtyard to stop the birds nesting in his crown and before the older girls play tennis on the courtyards. I have messed up my Scripture exam—as usual. I had worked hard for it, but Sister Kathleen can't read my writing. I will have to write it all again in my lunchtimes, on my own with her. She gives out all the marks to the rest of the class and leaves a gap when she gets to my name on the register. "You will have to do it again," she says, and the class all look at me. They have been expecting it. Then she goes through all the answers and tells the class what they should have put.

I wait behind that lunchtime in the cool classroom. The white sun is not quite blocked out by the blinds and the backs of my thighs are sticking to the wooden bench in the heat. She sighs. "What are we going to do with you?" she says. She seems lost, defeated somehow. She gives me the question paper and I read the bright purple ink from the script duplicator machine. I know the Bible; I am at home with these old purple words.

There are different sections in Sister Kathleen's exam paper. Section 1 tests us on the meanings of the parables, and in section 2 we have to choose a miracle and write it out by memory and then write out what it means. I'm not afraid of the test—I'm in my element when it comes to miracles. As I go through my script that she has given back to me, I change all my answers to incorporate the correct ones she has given the class. I put down all the meanings for the parables that she has told us are the correct ones. And then I write out my miracle—word for word—about the resurrection of the dead girl and I add the following as an explanation:

> The miracle shows us that Jesus has power over everything because he is the Son of God. His power was so great that he could bring a dead girl back to life. Everybody else saw that she was dead but to him she was only sleeping. When he spoke the words "Talitha Cumi" he brought her back to life. All this was possible because he was God's only Son who came to forgive our sins and save us.

I do not entirely believe what I have written.

I finish quickly and I give it back to her.

The next day she reads out the marks, going down the register. I get 86%. I have done very well. The rest of the class look surprised when she says my mark. I have learned something, at last. For the first time, I know the protective comfort of contempt. After that, my marks start to get better. As my marks get better, my behavior gets worse. Something seismic happens: I start to metamorphosize. I scowl and I saunter.

I have been transformed, I think.

I have become that creature that academic systems find it most difficult to categorize and to control. A truculent high achiever.

CHAPTER 10

Exposed Nonconformity: A View from Hopi Point

We have arrived at our destination. I find myself at the edge of an abrupt precipice, overlooking a vast, grand canyon. So this is where the snake has led me to—back to her ancestral home. It is like nothing I have ever seen before. Beautiful chasm! Wild aching hole of two-billion-year-old naked Earth. We lie down and gaze at it, the snake and me, watching the sun set over Isis Temple. She said she would bring me to a point of knowledge. So this is what she wanted to show me. This place in which words—the words available to me at least—fail and fall into the interspace before us. But for all its gigantic beauty, I feel that the snake has deceived me somehow. We have reached the end of the road! After all the struggles of the journey and all the resilience that has been required of me to follow her path over the past five years—we have ended up at a geological road block. How could she lead me here, to the point of no return?

But there is something else as well. I have a funny feeling in my stomach—excitement, maybe—as if we are on the eve of something. Maybe it was something I ate? We make a funny couple, me and my serpentine friend. Me tired, forlorn, burnt out. Her, basking, with one eye open, watching and waiting for my next move. It seems to me that we have reached the final binary. On one side of the canyon, this side, is knowledge of the academy. It is serious, logical; it is guarded by gatekeepers, and uniforms are provided. On the other side, right over there, is another kind of knowing: fiction, drama, art, poetry, and sacred texts. In between lies the abyss. Down there are the rhythms and realities of this planet's history, which we can't begin to imagine, let alone claim to fully understand. It feels as if there is no exit to this final opposition. Do I return to the safe but heavily regulated world of the academy? Try to pull some conclusions out of this study and publish them in the appropriate places? But that is easier said than done. "I find that my academic tools do not work with this writing," grumbles the reviewer for the prestigious American journal to which I submit an article based on the study. "This is beautiful, nuanced, and inspiring writing. But it needs another home," laments another. Conventional, disciplinary-based academic publishing is not really an option for me now. I can't go back.

When two other travelers are faced with their version of the dilemma at the edge of the same canyon, Thelma says to Louise, "Let's not get caught. Let's keep going," before they leap off the edge of the canyon into either flight or suicide, depending on your point of view. Is that my choice now as well—to turn myself into the disciplinary police or to commit career suicide? But I did not travel here in a 1966 Thunderbird Convertible. I was led here by a snake. She promised me a different way of knowing if I followed her path. But snakes, as we have often been told, have a criminal record when it comes to knowledge. Following the desert path of the snake wrenches us out of the apparently safe binaries of the academic world—such as truth and untruth, "real" data and fiction, and research subject and object—into more dangerous terrain, in which the shedding of our academic skin and the blurring of boundaries are inevitable, terrible, and necessary. She takes us to places in which our academic safety harness and protective clothing are no longer relevant. The snake eyes me warily. Has she put all this effort into this journey just for me to cave in and resort to a tired old way of thinking right at the end? No. I owe it to her to gather the energy and courage to reflect on this expedition and to distill from it some markers that will at least provide a trace that this journey has happened. Perhaps it will even form a kind of path through the desert.

I will have to put some clothes on first.

La Recherche Féminine: *An Alternative Methodology*

This book has attempted to demonstrate that the enduring prevalence of "scientistic," academic writing and empirically based research in mainstream social scientific arenas is inadequate and unhelpful, not because the results they produce are deficient or intrinsically wrong, but because they are usually unaccompanied by other forms of knowing. The importance and prevalence imposed on these "masculine" ways of knowing prevent us from reaching deeper, more compassionate ways of understanding the human condition and therefore finding meaningful ways to help each other. I do not want to argue for the abandonment of the logocentric academic project, though. Hugely important discoveries and insights have been arrived at in this way, and that practice should continue. As an educator who passionately believes in, and is committed to, higher education as a force for social transformation, rather than an endless reproductive project that endorses and reproduces inequalities, I frequently return to the work of Bourdieu to support my arguments. His collection and analysis of empirical evidence base powerfully exposes the complacency and inequalities at the heart of higher education to policy makers, managers, teachers, and learners. So I am not arguing for the end of impersonal, empirical studies. Rather, I argue that such research is much more helpful if it is accompanied by other types of texts, which require the researcher to step out of protective academic clothing and write as a vulnerable human being and a member of the community directly affected by the issues s/he is researching. "Feminine" research undermines the serious claim that the only knowledge worth pursuing is academic and detached. It gives prominence to fictional, mythical, poetical, and nakedly autobiographical discourses, and it deliberately marries the scholarly with the poetic. When dramatic and poetic texts are combined with empirical data, the interview texts open up in new and surprising ways. Somehow space needs to be found in academic texts for these understandings to be told. This crossover allows us to confront and understand our own experiences in ways that irreversibly subvert the power structures that underpin the researched and the researcher.

The world is full of survivors—resilience emerges everywhere the marginalized and the disadvantaged refuse to accept the script—the roles and attendant practices that the powerful and the privileged have assigned them. The education system is only one area in which resilience is performed. Readers may know about the resilience required to resist extreme political or cultural oppression, for example, or to continue a rich and generous life despite the diagnosis of a life-threatening illness. It may be that others will want to appropriate this approach and transform it in their hands into something new and living. *Miraculés* exist in all sorts of contexts. I want this study to open up the conversation about how this method might be used, and I will now offer some insights into the way this approach has worked here.

I am, however, cautious about tying down the approach that has been taken in this book—its methodology—to any set "principles," given the epistemological and ontological debts owed to Hélène Cixous. Antithetical as it seems to atomize and systemize a practice that is so heavily influenced by fluidity and transgression, I nonetheless feel it is important to try to articulate in academic terms what it is that I have done here so that others are able to continue the conversation and, perhaps, to consider the application and adaptation of the practice in other areas.

La recherche féminine takes a body of ideas and writings usually associated with literary theory and applies them to a real, "live," educational problem—in this case, an attempt to delineate what makes an adult learner resilient. It involves the incorporation of an eclectic mixture of genres and types of writing, all of which are presented as having equal claims to faithfully represent reality, in order to read the subject in as crystalline a manner as possible. It uses writing as an investigative technique throughout the enquiry, and it uses autobiographical and creative writing as investigative tools alongside data analysis techniques. It applies the work of Hélène Cixous specifically to the investigation of the phenomenon studied. A commitment to her vision for the revolutionary potential of writing, articulated in *Sorties*[1] as *l'écriture féminine*, functions in at least three ways: as a way of writing, which the researcher aspires to and gets closer to throughout the work; as a way of knowing and entering the unknown in relation to the subject; and as an analogy for, and a comparable experience to, the subject—in this case resilient adult learning.

Here, then, are some indications of how *la recherche féminine* works in practice.

1. It resists a linear, objectivized, rational approach to either study design or a retrospective account of progress. It is honest about its messiness and the way that processes overlap and change directions. It reveals its methods throughout.

2. Instead it "radiates"[2] from a single point of informed, instinctive understanding that a particular piece of work may open up to new understandings. The instinctive identification between a reader and a text is taken seriously here as a first point in the research process. In this case, the fictional text (*Educating Rita*) formed an entry point into the whole study.

3. Fiction is taken very seriously in the enquiry, because it is the "anti-land"[3] in which alternative realities—in this case resilience—can be imagined. Cixous insists that it is through imaginative writing that places emerge in which the machinery of the oppressive system breaks down to offer hope for the system's overthrow. This process is illustrated in the way that this study begins with the archetypal resilient adult learners as a way of imagining what could be if the reproductive project could be overturned. In this way, Rita is a central heroine, in both senses of the word. She is "endowed with an individual strength but without authority"[4] and, with Perdita, she represents a model for liberated resilience that sheds light on the

whole study. Together, they are "great, undaunted, sturdy beings, who [are] at odds with the Law."[5] This means that the readings of the fictional resilient adult learners are given an early emphasis in the work.

4. Myth is incorporated into the enquiry and taken seriously. Here it has emerged in the form of two direct versions of the Pygmalion text. Myth is accorded a special place in the work of Cixous because its complex and protean nature allows the reader space to inhabit multiple positions within the same text and because of the enduring effects of mythos on culture. The presence of myth in the study informs and opens up the subsequent literary readings. In this way, the combined study of myth and fiction allows the researcher to ask whether the oppressive system is "impossible to bypass."[6] Both sorts of texts offer ways for the reader to imagine a place outside the depressing order of reality. To paraphrase Cixous, if my resilience is possible, it means the system is already letting something else through.[7]

5. Empirical data—in the form of interviews here, but there is certainly space for other kinds of data—allow for other stories to be incorporated into the enquiry. It needs to be understood that all the data included have equal claims to faithfully representing what is real and that the texts need to be placed alongside each other in order to be read openly. It is the deconstructive energy that is produced by the juxtaposition of a range of generically different texts that produces something like an honest account of lived experience. No one text can do this on its own. Cixous's insistence that generic barriers are deliberately crossed and boundary laws flouted means that interview texts included are read through a literary lens as well as a social scientific one. This kind of enquiry is deliberately of mixed genre, and it deliberately juxtaposes these interview texts with literary analysis and creative writing. What is important is the understanding that no one type of data has preeminence over the others.

6. Relevant aspects of the researcher's autobiography are included in the study as data. There is a requirement of the researcher to walk naked at some point in the study. This forms a crucial function in eroding the boundaries between the subject and object of the research—thus putting forward an alternative form of subjectivity. Of the naked writing, it may be that there is place for the voice of the child, although this cannot be predicted and much less planned for. This corresponds to Cixous's mining of her own experiences in *Sorties* as a way of understanding and explaining the opportunities and difficulties of

achieving *l'écriture féminine*. The child is also the source of writing for Cixous:

> There is a ground, it is her ground—childhood flesh, shining blood—or background, depth. A white depth, a core, unforgettable, forgotten, and this ground covered by infinite number of strata, layers, sheets of paper—is her sun (*sol…soleil*). And nothing can put it out.[8]

My own childhood appears twice, for those reasons—once in an account of it given in an interview with my mother in Chapter Eight, and once in a fictionalized piece of autobiographical writing in Chapter Nine. Both chapters are important components of the work; to leave them out would be theoretically inconsistent, given Cixous's insistence that the feminine writer (researcher) "involves her story in history."[9] In the same way, the voice of the mother is brought into the center of the text and given prominence in this "feminine" version of enquiry.

7. Writing itself is the driving force for the whole work. Its emancipatory and revolutionary properties effect a transformation on the work that is radical, visceral, and irreversible. The impact of this transformational writing is acknowledged as the work progresses.

8. There is an expectation that the researcher will surrender to the unpredictable force of this writing practice from the beginning. In this case, the writing attempts to write resilience in ways that "simple," "linear," and "universalized"[10] versions of research cannot allow. Cixous's use of feminine *jouissance* as an example of an experience that is inexpressible within the symbolic order of logocentric language, and her subsequent urgent question (so "how does it write itself?"[11]) allows the space for other experiences that lie outside the academic text to be taken seriously and granted access. As such, what cannot be said about resilient adult learning in conventional academic discourse can start to be imagined, accommodated, and perhaps written when the principles of *l'écriture féminine* are adopted.

So what of conclusions? Where does a study like this leave us, and what do we know at the end of it? I love Laurel Richardson's use of *crystallization* as the metaphor for validity in her own work:

> Crystallization provides us with a deepened, complex, thoroughly partial understanding of the topic. Paradoxically, we know more and doubt what we know.[12]

To support her analogy, Richardson is drawing on the way light passes through crystal in irregular ways, distorting its apparent transparency. The incredible lucidity of the crystal is interrupted by its ability to refract light, and that is its strength. Its clarity dupes us into thinking it is transparent, but as soon as we look closely at it, we see multiple reflections, endlessly changing images with infinite complexity. We can observe the way that color changes as it hits the crystal, compare the angles, and enjoy its kaleidoscopic effects as we look into its middle. What we can never do, though, is expect to look through it to another object and see that object in a simple and transparent way; being *crystal clear* about something does not mean the same thing as revealing its simple truth. I want to push the metaphor further in the context of *la recherche féminine*. It works geologically as well as in terms of optics. Crystallization occurs when molten materials cool and, depending on their composition and cooling rates, form different kinds of rocks. The material takes a permanent and hard form as igneous and metamorphic rock—its history is written into its fabric. A similar process of solidification occurs with *la recherche féminine*. This text is the final material form of a transformative event, rather than a transparent and retrospective reflection of that event. The understandings of resilience can be discerned in the plural readings that are included here. Each one has the potential to shed new light on the subject of the research. You can read the history of the rock formation, from its volcanic origins onwards, in the side of the canyon. Nothing is stable; everything is subject to marvelous change. Even a substance as hard as igneous rock will ultimately become metamorphic over time. And so it is with feminine research. This text will transform in the hands of different readers. It is intended to be mutable, porous, and open.

The Risks Involved in Dancing with Snakes

I do not, for a minute, underestimate the risks and difficulties of adopting this model of research within the Western academy, and in particular within the social sciences. There are costs to the researcher who chooses to take this path. The first and most immediate is that work written in this way can remain invalidated by an academic community that is largely tied to logocentric writing conventions and to firm disciplinary boundaries. Choosing to go against the rules of the game is extremely risky—exclusion has material consequences in an academic world in which publications are linked to income for both the individual and the institution. The reality is that the majority of peer-reviewed journals work on strict criteria, which are based on logical and rational arguments and the writer's ability to demonstrate that he or she is familiar with the field.

The poor snake, which has tended to be associated with deceit in the Abrahamic religions, here has performed in the opposite way. I have never tried to dupe the reader by presenting a polished version of a stable text that pretends to represent some other piece of completed knowing that exists outside of its pages. The metaphor of ecdysis allowed me to briefly experience, and then shed, two theoretical frameworks before arriving at Cixous. It also demonstrated in practice what deconstruction promised in theory. That is to say, from the outset, the work was decentered and multiple. At the same time, the traces of those other theories remained throughout the work. The image of the snake works metaphorically in other ways as well. Its serpentine motion suggested a way of moving through the research that defied the logocentric, linear approach that I felt I was writing against. Its movement was of a different order; at times side-winding, at times basking, and sometimes darting in for the kill. Judeo-Christian associations between the snake and dangerous knowledge also suggested, from the beginning, that this enquiry would be carried out in a self-confessed and self-consciously dangerous way. We need to fully understand the risks of working in this way before we consent to it. This is not a half-measure type of methodology. It places significant demands on the researcher.

If the risks to one's academic career of adopting such a challenging approach are significant, the risks to the psyche of the writer are perhaps more severe still; the necessary submission on the part of the writer/researcher to "being 'possessed,' which is to say, dispossessed of herself"[13] is a hefty request. The certainties, elegant conclusions, and logical linearities that emanate from conscious composition are no longer relevant or even possible. Where there were solid ladders that took the reader from argument to evidence to conclusion, we find snakes. *L'écriture féminine* posits writing as a form of enquiry—of writing one's way through knowledge and one's defenses to a state of unknowing insight. The very purpose of such writing is to depart from the familiar, logocentric understanding of the world and to find new ways of knowing. Writing as enquiry is not a report on what is already known; rather it takes the researcher to new places. This is a risky business, because writing in the Cixousian sense means giving way to an entirely new way of knowing. This transformational writing experience is wild and profound, though, and it calls for a good deal of resilience to survive it.

But still the snake insists that there is another kind of knowledge, another kind of knowing that it is worth pursuing if we are brave enough to take those risks. It is a way of knowing that draws on the ancient wisdom of stories, the communities of which we are a part, and our own vulnerabilities.

This other way of knowing has the might to save us from getting caught up in the power games, field boundaries, and authority moves that restrict our thinking and separate us from our fellow human beings.

Let's not get caught.

Let's keep going."

Notes

Preface

1. Cixous (1993a, p. 7).
2. See, for example, Radford (2008).

1   Ecdysis

1. Challener (1997, p. 7).
2. In keeping with Pierre Bourdieu, I am using the economic term metaphorically to describe the range of advantages that students bring to higher education. Here the term is used generally, to encompass all forms of advantage that might predispose a student to success in higher education. Bourdieu and Passeron (1977) expand on the precise effects of a lack of linguistic and cultural capital on equality of access to higher education in *Reproduction in Education Society and Culture*, pp. 72–89.
3. Bourdieu's concept of habitus is helpfully and succinctly defined by Moi (1990) as the "totality of general *dispositions* acquired through practical experience in the field" (p. 271).
4. United Nations Educational, Scientific and Cultural Organization (2009). Communiqué: 2009 World Conference on Higher Education: The New Dynamics of Higher Education and Research for Societal Change and Development, UNESCO, Paris, July 5–8, 2009, http://unesco.org/images /0018/001832/183277e.pdf, retrieved on May 21, 2011. P.3.
5. Ibid.
6. Ibid.
7. Such work is ably summarized by Hart et al. (2007). While I acknowledge the excellent contribution to the understanding of resilience that such work has made, this work is an attempt to read resilience from outside the dominant academic field that usually lays claim to it.
8. Rich (1972, p. 23).

9. Richardson (1997, p. 167).
10. Rich (1972, p. 23).
11. "Feminine Writing"—this concept is drawn upon throughout the study, and its meaning and relevance is developed as the book progresses.
12. Although Cixous's work is perhaps more correctly understood as being a version of deconstruction rather than post-structuralism, I acknowledge that across a number of disciplines and publishing terms post-structuralism has come to represent a genre of texts which challenge essentialist readings of reality rather than the technical meaning of the word as that philosophy which supersedes structuralism. At this point I am using the term broadly in the sense that most readers will understand it in relation to educational research and literary theory.
13. Knights and Thurgar-Dawson (2006, p. 55).
14. Ibid., p. 60.
15. Meyer and Land (2003, p. 412).
16. Meyer and Land (2003).
17. Rowland (2006, p. 24–25).
18. Bourdieu and Passeron (1977, p. 73).
19. Skeggs (1997/2002, p. 9).
20. Bourdieu and Passeron (1977/2000, p. 73).
21. Moi (1990, p. 275).
22. Ibid., p. 276.
23. Ibid.
24. Ibid.
25. In an explanatory note in *Reproduction* (1977/2000), Bourdieu and Passeron present the *miraculé* (translated by Richard Nice as "wonder boys") as "the working-class child who succeeds 'against all the odds'; cf., perhaps, in Britain, the 'scholarship boy'" (p. 175, n. 34). There is no direct English translation for the French word *miraculé*. It means "one on whom a miracle has been enacted."
26. Moi (1990, p. 276).
27. Of course, Bourdieu was far more interested in the functionalist nature of the academic system than the individual's experience of it. The way that his work leans towards what is arguably a Marxist view of society means that for him the existence of the *miraculé* is actually an unhelpful diversion from the oppressive class divisions that constitute the system itself.
28. Jenkins (1992, p. 91).
29. Bourdieu (1979/2006, p. 82).
30. Moi (1997, p. 310).
31. Bourdieu (1979/2006, p. 243).
32. Kramsch (2008, p. 36).
33. The ideas drawn on here might be characterized as emerging from those seminal works on textual deconstruction of the late 1960s and early 1970s "Structure, Sign and Play" (1966/2007), "Of Grammatology" (1967), and "Différance" (1968).

34. Derrida (1978/2007, p. 352).
35. Derrida (1976/1992, p. 81).
36. I use the term deconstruction to imply the practical application of the ideas of play and *différance* to texts.
37. Richardson (1997, p. 15).
38. Interview, Derek Attridge with Jacques Derrida, 1989, in *Acts of Literature* (1992), p. 45.
39. As Derrida puts it (1989, p. 59) "the more 'powerful' a text is (but power is not a masculine attribute here and it is often the most disarming feebleness) the more it shakes up its own limits or lets them be thought, as well as the limits of phallocentrism, of all authority and all 'centrism', all hegemony in general."
40. Knights and Thurgar-Dawson (2006, p. 70).
41. Keats (1817/2002).
42. St. John of the Cross, "Entréme donde no supe". As the translator, Willis Barnstone states that "science" here "is used in its primary sense, in Spanish and English, of systemized knowledge." (c. 1578/1972, p. 59).
43. My first degree was in English literature. My masters and doctoral studies have been undertaken in education.
44. The texts which were imported were not particularly representative of the body of work produced by the authors. Derrida's key essays on *différance*, for example, tended not to be taught alongside the work in which he asserts the need for deconstruction to be accompanied by practical ethical applications (see, for example, "Violence and Metaphysics," 1964). This wider range of texts might have changed the way in which deconstruction came to be understood in literary theory classrooms.
45. Knights (2005, pp. 33–34).
46. Ibid., p. 37.
47. Ibid., p. 47.
48. Ibid., p. 43.
49. Ibid., p. 47. There are now many advocates of deconstruction across a range of disciplines who argue against the way Derrida's work was appropriated by the Western, English-speaking academy as a purely intellectual exercise into the movement that became known as "post-structuralism."
50. Bourdieu (1979/2006, p. 495).
51. But not female—most of the examples she provides of feminine writers are biologically male.
52. Hollywood (2002, p. 4).
53. Stocker (2006, p. 185).
54. Hollywood (2003, p. 150).
55. Cixous (1975/1986, p. 92).
56. Hollywood (2003, p. 148).
57. Hunt (2000/2006).
58. Richardson and Lockridge (2004)
59. Knights (1992) and Knights and Thurgar-Dawson (2006).

60. Which might be characterized as "liberal humanist"—I use the term respectfully.
61. Challener (1997, p. 18).
62. It was first performed in 1913 and first published in 1916.
63. Warner (1985, p. 233).
64. Richardson (1997, p. 167).
65. See Susan Sellers's impressive body of work on Cixous, (eg 1994), Renshaw (2009), and Blyth and Sellers (2004) among others.

2 Pygmalion

1. Ovid, *Metamorphoses* (c. 8 A.D./2004). The version used throughout this book is the 2004 translation for Penguin by David Raeburn.
2. As Law (February, 1932) points out, "The name Galatea does not appear in any Greek or Roman versions of the myth and is apparently introduced comparatively late in modern literature" (p. 337). As Shaw uses the name Galatea in his commentary to *Pygmalion*, it will also be used throughout this study.
3. As Denis Feeney (in Ovid, c.8 A.D./2004) points out, Ovid plays with language brilliantly in order to demonstrate as well as describe the dynamics of transformation from the outset: "the Greek word for transformation is transformed into Latin in Ovid's (c.8 A.D./2004) first line: *meta-morphoseis* 'trans-formations' becomes *mutas formas*, literally, 'changed forms'." (p. xxii).
4. See, for example, Mezirow (2000) and Shor and Freire (1987).
5. See, for example, Hooks (1994) and Freire (1969/2003, p. 45).
6. Stoichita (2008, p. 3).
7. Feeney (2004, p. xxiv).
8. Barthes (1973).
9. Stokes (2007).
10. Bronfen (1992, p. 106).
11. Cixous develops her critique of this notion of "god the mother" in relation to Christianity in *Sorties* and elsewhere in her work. For an in-depth analysis of this theme in the work of Cixous (as well as Kristeva and Irigaray), see Sal Renshaw's (2009) book, *The Subject of Love: Helene Cixous and the Feminine Divine*, Manchester and New York: Manchester University Press, in particular chapter two, "Feminist theology: for the love of God."
12. Bronfen, p. 368.
13. Cixous (1975/1986).
14. Perrault (1975/1986, p. 66).
15. Cixous (1975/1986, p. 66–67).
16. Others have done this convincingly by reading the interpretation of the myth, and in particular artistic representations of it—see, for example, Danahay (1994).
17. Cixous, "The School of Roots" (in 1993a, p. 129).
18. Stoichita (2008, p. 20).

19. As Rubin Suleiman (1991) explains, writing past the wall, for Cixous the wall is constituted of "the constraints, both inner and outer" which conspire to prevent one from writing (p. ix).
20. Ovid, *Orpheus' Song: Pygmalion* (from *Metamorphoses* in translation) pp. 394–96.
21. Ovid, line 247.
22. Roos (2001, p. 96).
23. Ovid, line 256.
24. Ibid., line 259.
25. Ibid., line 276.
26. Ibid., lines 282–84.
27. Ibid., line 288.
28. Hughes (1997, pp. 144–50).
29. Hughes (1997, p. 146).
30. Roos (2001, p. 95, citing Havelock, 1995, p. 130) points out that in Ovid's (c.8 A.D./2004) Hellenistic sources, Pygmalion is a king rather than a sculptor. He orders that a statue of Aphrodite be created. She then comes to life *as* herself rather than magnanimously blessing the creation of another female with life, as in Ovid's (c.8 A.D./2004) version.
31. Stoichita (2008) makes the point that a life-size model made of ivory would be practically impossible to execute. So there are two transformations in the original story—the main one when ivory turns into flesh but also a preliminary one in which a doll-sized figure is transformed into the size of a real woman (p. 10).
32. Warner (1985, p. 228).
33. Hughes (1997, p. 150).
34. Hughes, (1997, p. ix).
35. Ibid., p. x.
36. Interestingly, when Ted Hughes won the 1997 Whitbread prize for *Tales for Ovid*, the judges made the following comment: "In contemporary speech Hughes has hacked away as that accomplished master and come up with something rougher and more immediate to a generation not raised on the classics." The comment seems to be evoking the same idea as the comment attributed to Michelangelo. See Clare Garner, writing in *The Independent*, "Hughes Wins the Whitbread Prize" (Wednesday, January 28, 1998, http://www .independent.co.uk/news/hughes-wins-whitbread-prize-1141289.html, last accessed August 22, 2011.
37. Shaw, *Pygmalion* (1916/2007).
38. Shaw, *Pygmalion* (1916/2007), commentary p. 118.
39. Ibid., p. 115.
40. Roos (2001, p. 97).
41. Shaw, *Pygmalion* (1916/2007, pp. 63–64).
42. Ibid., p. 19.
43. Ibid., p. 27.
44. Ibid., p. 28.

45. Ibid., p. 62.
46. Ibid., p. 78.
47. Ibid., p. 80.
48. Ibid., p. 100.
49. Ibid., p. 23.
50. Ibid., p. 26.
51. Ibid., p. 27.
52. Ibid., p. 28.
53. Ibid., p. 22.
54. Ibid., p. 26.
55. Ibid., p. 94.
56. Ibid., p. 53.
57. Ibid., p. 97.
58. Ibid., p. 109.
59. Ibid., p. 105.
60. In an interview with the BBC, the acclaimed British actor Tim Piggott-Smith, who played Frank in *Educating Rita* at the Trafalgar Studios in London in 2010 and Higgins at the Old Vic in London in 2008, confirmed that Willy Russell, who worked closely with the cast inpreparation for the 2010 production, had not read *Pygmalion* when he wrote *Educating Rita*. Piggott-Smith also said that he regarded Higgins and Frank as "completely different characters" ("Tim Piggott-Smith on starring in *Educating Rita*," BBC, August 26, 2010, http://www.bbc.co.uk/news/entertainment-arts-11094806, retrieved May 17, 2011).

3   *Educating Rita* and *Oleanna*

1. Russell, *Educating Rita* (1981/2000).
2. Mamet, *Oleanna* (1993).
3. For example, MacLeod (1995).
4. For example, Glazer-Raymo (2000).
5. For example, Silverstein (1995).
6. For example, Badenhausen (1998).
7. Raymond (2003, p. 53), and Plato (c. 370/2005).
8. Garner (2000, p. 39).
9. Ibid., p. 41.
10. Knights (1992, p. 10).
11. Land (2008).
12. Mamet, *Oleanna* (1993, p. 76).
13. Garner (2000, p. 43).
14. Russell, *Educating Rita* (1981/2000, p. 25).
15. Ibid., p. 71.
16. Ibid., p. 76.
17. Mamet, *Oleanna* (1993, p. 9).
18. Ibid., p. 19.
19. Russell, *Educating Rita* (1981/2000, p. 98).
20. Mary Shelley, *Frankenstein* (1831/2004, p. 39).

21. Ibid., p. 122.
22. Mamet, *Oleanna* (1993, p. 67).
23. Shelley, *Frankenstein* (1831/2004, p. 162).
24. Mackie (2001), reviewing Kereos's (1999) study. The study includes analyses of *Educating Rita* and *Oleanna* within this framework.
25. Ibid., p. 289.
26. Russell, *Educating Rita* (1981/2000, p. 36).
27. Ibid., p. 37.
28. Billington (2004).
29. Mamet, *Oleanna* (1993, p. 79).
30. Ibid., p. 19.
31. Ibid., p. 15.
32. Garner (2000, p. 48).
33. Russell, *Educating Rita* (1981/2000, p.15).
34. Mamet, *Oleanna* (1993, p. 8).
35. Barthes (1973/1975, p. 14).
36. Russell, *Educating Rita* (1981/2000, p. 71).
37. Mamet, *Oleanna* (1993, p. 6).
38. Ibid.
39. Ibid., p. 3.
40. Ibid., p. 9.
41. Ibid., p. 14.
42. Ibid., p. 49.
43. Russell, *Educating Rita* (1981/2000, p. 15).
44. Ibid., p. 34.
45. Ibid., p. 18.
46. Ibid., p. 24.
47. Ibid., p. 24.
48. Shaw, *Pygmalion* (1916/2007, p. 23).
49. Ibid., p. 8.
50. Ibid., p. 19.
51. Ibid., p.v97.
52. Ovid, *Metamorphoses* (c. 8 A.D./2004).
53. Russell, *Educating Rita* (1981/2000, p. 32).
54. Ibid., p. 38.
55. Ibid., p. 73.
56. Ibid., p. 105.
57. Ibid., p. 26.
58. John, *The Meaning in the Miracles*, (2001, p. 11).

4 *The Winter's Tale*

Some of the material in this chapter has previously been published by Elizabeth Chapman Hoult in the Autumn 2011 edition of *Critical Survey*, vol. 23, no. 2, pp. 91–105, published by Berghahan Journals, in an article entitled "...And .., *The Winter's Tale* and Resilient Learners."

1. See interview with Susan Sellers entitled "We must hand our inheritance on" in Cixous, 2008, p. 149.
2. .Blyth and Sellers (2004, p. 52). For a specific comparison, see Blyth and Sellers's commentary on how her plays *The Terrible but Unfinished Story of Norodom Sihanouk, King of Cambodia* and *L'Indiade* make use of Shakespearean structures, with particular reference to Henry IV (2004, p. 52).
3. Shakespeare, *The Winter's Tale* (1623/2007).
4. Cixous (1975/1986).
5. My reading of Bourdieu's representation here is admittedly rather one dimensional, based, as it is, on his work from the late 1970s. For a detailed discussion of Bourdieu's changing attitudes to gift-relations over the course of his career, see Ilan F. Silber (2009), "Bourdieu's Gift to Gift Theory: An Unacknowledged Trajectory," *Sociological Theory*, vol. 27, pp. 173–90.
6. Bourdieu (1979/2006).
7. Bourdieu and Passeron (1977/2000).
8. Bristol (1991), Cavell (1987, p. 200), and Fischer (1985), cited in Parker (2004).
9. Neely (1985).
10. De Grazia (1990, p. 26).
11. Bristol (1991, p. 163).
12. Cixous (1975/1986, p. 80).
13. Ibid., p. 87.
14. Ibid., p. 81.
15. Ibid., p. 83.
16. Ibid., p. 65.
17. Ibid., p. 91.
18. Ibid., p. 97.
19. Ibid., p. 84.
20. Ibid., p. 84.
21. Cixous (1975/1986, p. 78).
22. Jenkins (1992/2002, p. 85).
23. Cixous (1975/1986, p. 80).
24. Ibid., p. 78.
25. Massey (2003, p. 20).
26. Cixous (2007).
27. Rowan (2003).
28. Cixous (1975/1986, p. 78).
29. Shakespeare, *The Winter's Tale* (1623/2007, 1/2, line 4).
30. Bristol (1991, p. 156).
31. Cixous (1975/1986, p. 80).
32. Ibid., p. 90.
33. Bristol uses the notion of the gift economy antithetically to Cixous. He reverses the application of vocabulary that is used in this paper in relation to the contrasting economies of Sicilia and Bohemia (p. 163), "The gift economy that was dominant in the first half of the play now must co-exist with an active and aggressive market in commodities and community exchange (in Bohemia)."

34. Shakespeare, *The Winter's Tale* (1623/2007, 1/2, 108–10).
35. Ibid., line 123.
36. Ibid., line 270.
37. Derrida, (1978/2007, p. 352).
38. Mamet, *Oleanna* (1993).
39. Blake, "Without contraries is no progression" (1793/1975), *The Marriage of Heaven and Hell*.
40. Cixous (1975/1986, p. 64).
41. Mamet, *Oleanna* (1993, p. 67).
42. Shakespeare, *The Winter's Tale* (1623/2007, 2/1, lines 293–96).
43. Ibid., 1/2, line 292.
44. Ibid., 2/1 line 48.
45. Mamet, *Oleanna* (1993, p. 66).
46. Ibid.
47. Shakespeare, *The Winter's Tale* (1623/2007, 1/2, lines 114 and 115).
48. Cixous (1975/1986).
49. Bourdieu (1979/2006, p. 243).
50. Schwartz (2005, p. 11).
51. Derrida, (1978/2007, p. 354).
52. Mamet, *Oleanna* (1993, p. 52).
53. Shakespeare, *The Winter's Tale* (1623/2007, 2/1 lines 100–104).
54. Derrida (1978/2007, p. 352).
55. Shakespeare, *The Winter's Tale* (1623/2007, 1/2, lines 138–41).
56. Neely (1985) p. 325.
57. Shakespeare, *The Winter's Tale* (1623/2007, 2/1, lines 189–93).
58. Snyder (1999, p. 8).
59. Shakespeare, *The Winter's Tale* (1623/2007, 3/2, lines 79–80).
60. Ibid., lines 86–87.
61. Ibid., line 91.
62. Ibid., line 131.
63. Ibid., line 139.
64. Ibid., lines 140–41.
65. Ibid., 2/3, lines 139–40.
66. Bristol (1991, p. 158).
67. Shakespeare, *The Winter's Tale* (1623/2007, 5/3, line 95).
68. Ibid., 4/4, line 135.
69. Ibid., lines 134–46.
70. Ibid., 5/3, lines 45–46.
71. Ibid., 4/4, line 423.
72. Ibid., 3/2, lines 145–46.
73. Ibid., 2/3, line 174.
74. Ibid., line 177.
75. Ibid., 3/3, line 2.
76. Ibid., 3/2, line 99.
77. Ibid., line 97–99.
78. Hopkins (2005, p. 7).

79. Shakespeare, *The Winter's Tale* (1623/2007, 3/3, line 14).
80. Schwartz (2005, p. 6).
81. Shakespeare, *The Winter's Tale* (1623/2007, 3/3, lines 15–18).
82. Cixous (1975/1986, p. 93).
83. Shakespeare, *The Winter's Tale* (1623/2007, 3/3, line 32).
84. Schwartz (2005, p. 6).
85. Ibid.
86. Shakespeare, *The Winter's Tale* (1623/2007, 4/4, lines 140–43).
87. Cixous (1975/1986, p.84–85).
88. Shakespeare, *The Winter's Tale* (1623/2007, 5/1, lines 110–12).
89. Schwartz (2005, p. 16).
90. Shakespeare, *The Winter's Tale* (1623/2007, 3/3, line 105).
91. Snyder and Curren-Aquino, (2007, p. 20).
92. Cixous (1975/1986, p. 72).
93. Shakespeare, *The Winter's Tale* (1623/2007, 3/3, line 103).
94. Ibid., 4/1, line 27.
95. Ibid., 4/4, line 2.
96. Ibid., 4/4 lines 3–5.
97. Ibid., 5/1, line 156.
98. Ibid., 5/2 lines 111–13.
99. Ibid., 4/4, lines 9–10.
100. Ibid., lines 22–24.
101. For a detailed account of sumptuary laws in Tudor England, see Wilfrid Hooper, *The English Historical Review*, vol. 30, no. 119, (July 1915) pp. 433–49. Classes lower than lords were prohibited from wearing certain clothing, such as those made from/incorporating gold and silver cloth, and velvet in crimson and blue (p. 433). A new historicist reading would note that the last sumptuary law was actually repealed in England in 1604. Shakespeare could either be reflecting the newfound freedom to dress in ways that crossed boundaries of social status or reflecting the fear of transgression that still remained in the public imagination. See Linda Levy Peck (2005) for a detailed analysis of society and culture in seventeenth century England.
102. Shakespeare, *The Winter's Tale* (1623/2007, 4/4, lines 134–35).
103. Ibid., lines 562–63.
104. Ibid., lines 424–26.
105. Ibid., lines 623–24.
106. Cixous (1975/1986, p. 96).
107. Bourdieu and Passeron (1977/2000, p. 110).
108. Hughes, *Tales from Ovid* (1997).
109. Freire (1969/2003 p. 45).
110. Ibid., p. 46.
111. Ovid, *Metamorphoses* (c.8 A.D./2004).
112. Snyder and Curren-Aquino (2007, p. 72).
113. Shakespeare, *The Winter's Tale* (1623/2007, 5/3).
114. Robert Greene's *Pandosto* (Snyder and Curren-Aquino, 2007, p. 68).

115. Shakespeare, *The Winter's Tale* (1623/2007, 5/3, line 10).
116. Ibid., lines 17–18.
117. Ibid., lines 21–22.
118. Ibid., 3/3, line 24.
119. Ibid., 5/3, lines 37–38.
120. Ibid., line 83.
121. Ibid., line 66.
122. Ibid., line 91.
123. Ibid., lines 94–95.
124. John (2001).
125. Shakespeare, *The Winter's Tale* (1623/2007, 5/3, lines 104–5).
126. Ibid., lines 96–97.
127. Ibid., line 114.
128. Cixous (1977/1991, p. 41).
129. Shakespeare, *The Winter's Tale* (1623/2007, 5/3, line 155).
130. Paulina's actions can be read as Cixousian here. As Renshaw argues (2003, p. 116), for Cixous, giving and love "becomes an occasion for feminine *becoming*, which is directed toward 'keeping the other alive', rather than masculine *being*, with its implicit affiliation with the death of the other."
131. Cixous (1977/1991, p. 42), "Coming to Writing" in *"Coming to Writing" and Other Essays*, (Cambridge and London: Harvard University Press, 1977/1991).
132. Bourdieu (1979/2004, p. 243).
133. Cixous (1977/1991, p. 49).
134. Warner (1985, p. 233).

5 Joe

1. Shakespeare, *The Winter's Tale* (1623/2007).
2. This is, admittedly, a simplistic reading of Bourdieu's theory of agency overall. The space for agency in his work on education is less well developed than it is in other areas of his work. As Reed-Danahay (2005) puts it, "There are ambiguities in Bourdieu's work about the relative degree of freedom and constraint on human agency, as evident in the gap between readings of his work on education…and his work on the Kabyles" (p. 15–16).
3. Or, as Grant and Wong put it more specifically, "Given that cultural capital values upper-class dispositions, is it possible for education to transform those relations of domination?" (2008, p. 176).
4. Cixous (1975/1986, p. 70).
5. Ibid., p. 71.
6. Ibid., p. 73.
7. Ibid., p. 71.
8. Ibid., p. 71.
9. Ibid., p. 70.
10. Ibid., p. 71.

11. Ibid., p. 78.
12. Elsewhere she uses the metaphor of the hostage in captivity to explain the tension. Although she is resigned to the life of the hostage, writing provides at least some potential to celebrate, "what remains freely human throughout the betrayal or capture of politics" (Alexandrescu, 1999, p. 271).
13. Cixous (1975/1986, p. 72).
14. Ibid., p. 73.
15. Ibid., p. 72.
16. Alexandrescu (1999, p. 281).
17. Such as in her tribute to Gandhi in "L'Indiade."
18. Shakespeare, *The Winter's Tale* (1623/2007, 5/3, line 114).
19. Fictional name for a college of higher education that emerged from the "working men's colleges" movement and that has some links to a university in the same city.
20. An honors degree is the higher level of the bachelor degree in the UK.
21. A redbrick university is a UK research intensive university, normally originating in the nineteenth century.
22. A secondary modern school/education is the term used in the United Kingdom to denote the schools that supposedly provided a technical, that is, non-academic, education in the years after World War II. These schools still exist in isolated patches in the United Kingdom.
23. Cixous (1975/1986, p. 72).
24. Dossing is a colloquial UK term for living a life of leisure while collecting state benefits.
25. Pseudonym for the history tutor and gatekeeper.
26. Pseudonym for ancient library in the University of A.
27. Pseudonym for a library within the Ashenden Library.
28. The Red Cross is a charity which runs second-hand clothes and book shops in the UK.
29. This is an ancient and prestigious debating society with its own premises in the city.
30. Past Times is an English shop selling historic merchandise.
31. Cixous, "School of the Dead" (1993a).
32. Shakespeare, *The Tempest*, (1623/1999, 5/1, line 180).

6 Jane

1. Cixous (1975/1986).
2. Ibid., p. 90.
3. Ibid., p. 88.
4. Ibid., p. 87.
5. Shurmur-Smith (2000, p. 165).
6. Cixous and Calle-Gruber (1994; tr. Prenowitz, 1997, p. 80).
7. Bourdieu (1979/2006, p. 495).

8. Lovelock (2001).
9. Interview Hélène Cixous with Susan Sellers (2004, p. 118).
10. Cixous (1975/1986, p. 95).
11. Ibid., p. 94.
12. Ibid., p. 98.
13. Goulet (2003 p. ix).
14. Richardson (1997, p. 19).
15. Jouve (1991, p. 7, cited in Anderson, p. 2001).
16. In this chapter, the university is one of the oldest and most prestigious universities in the world.
17. Russell, *Educating Rita* (1981/2000).
18. Cixous (1975/1986, p. 77).
19. Cixous (2007).
20. Bourdieu (1979/2006, p. 287).
21. For example, "Same thing/shame thing." (Cixous, 2007).
22. Bourdieu (1979/2006, p. 147).
23. Gilbert and Gubar (1979/2000).
24. Jouve (1991).
25. The university operates a collegial system. This college is a female-only college.
26. Cixous (1975/1986, p. 64).
27. In the tradition of Stanley (1993) and Skeggs (1997/2002), for example.
28. Russell, *Educating Rita* (1981/2000, p. 30).
29. Skeggs (1997/2002) and Bourdieu (1979/2006).
30. Russell, *Educating Rita* (1981/2000, p. 97).
31. Ibid., p. 98.
32. Mamet, *Oleanna* (1993, p. 19).
33. Wood (2006).
34. Derrida, "Of Grammatology" (1976/1992, p. 158).
35. Wood (2006, p. 54).
36. Cixous (1975/1986, p. 98).

7 Sarah

1. Hélène Cixous argues the need to escape the draw to mastery in teaching at length in her interchange with Catherine Clément in the Exchange section of *The Newly Born Woman* (1975/1986); see pages 140–44.
2. Moi (1985/2002, p. 103).
3. Cixous (1977/1991, p. 570).
4. Cixous (1975/1986, p. 86).
5. Cixous (1981, p. 45).
6. Shaw, 1916, p. 11.
7. Ibid.
8. Cixous (1979, p. 412), cited in Moi, (1985/2002, p. 113).
9. Moi (1985/2002, p. 118).

10. Cixous's (1993, p. 213) dire warning that "if you love ritual of truth more than yourself you will be rejected by publishers and academies" is bleak, but her own prolific output and the intellectual capital she enjoys internationally within her own academic field belies the universal application of her statement.
11. Moi (1985/2002, p. 123).
12. Ibid.
13. Armstrong (2004).
14. Cixous (1975/1986, p. 65).
15. Derrida (1978/2007, p. 375).
16. Cixous (1975/1986, p. 64).
17. Ibid., p. 89.
18. Ibid., p. 64.
19. "Her libido is cosmic, just as her unconscious is worldwide: her writing also can only go on and on, without ever describing or distinguishing contours" (Cixous, 1975/1986, p. 88).
20. Barthes (1973/1975, p. 14).
21. Cixous (1975/1986, p. 83).
22. Pseudonym for the same tutor referred to by Joe.
23. Armstrong (2004).
24. Cixous (1975/1986, p. 86).
25. Ibid.
26. Ovid, *Pygmalion* (c. 8 A.D./2004).
27. Cixous (1975/1986, p. 86).
28. Ibid., p. 86.
29. Ibid., p. 78.
30. Ibid., pp. 85–86.
31. Russell, *Educating Rita* (1981/2000).
32. Forster, *Howard's End* (1910).
33. Woolf, *Mrs. Dalloway* (1925/1976, pp. 14–15).
34. Cixous (1977/1991, p. 53).
35. Shakespeare, *The Winter's Tale* (1623/2007).
36. Cixous, 1975/1986, p. 98.

8 Her Mother's Voice

1. Anderson (2001, p. 94).
2. West (1996, p. 19).
3. Ibid., p. 32.
4. Richardson (2007, p. 170–71).
5. As Stephen Rowland (2006, p. 106) puts it in relation to Plato, "Learning is not so much a matter of teaching as of being reminded or brought to an awareness of this innate knowledge."
6. Cixous (1975/1986, p. 84).
7. Ibid., p. 98.

8. Cixous (1993a, p. 5).
9. Cixous (1975/1986, p. 98).
10. Ibid., p. 99.
11. Skeggs (1997/2002, p. 74).
12. In 2006, a woman became pregnant at 62. This caused much negative public comment. Miriam Stoppard's comments (presumably sought to provide a medical perspective on the case) about this pregnancy are typical of the way that the event was discussed (reported on Channel 4 news, "Britain's Oldest Mother," May, 4, 2006): "The last thing that really bothers me is that a child has a great deal of difficulty coping with the fear of death of their parents. Now, when most children ask this question, you can say, 'Oh yes, but it is so unlikely to happen that you don't have to think about it.' With this child she will have to think about it and be traumatized by the thought that her parents may die."
13. The way that this oppositional rhetoric moved from the lobbying of sideline special interest groups such as the Conservative Family Campaign to mainstream Tory policy is charted by Lorraine Fox Harding (p. 120) in Jagger and Wright (1999), "Changing Family Values: Difference, Diversity and the Decline of the Male Order."
14. Derrida (1978/2007, p. 353).
15. Cixous (1991, p. 11–12).
16. Ibid., p. 13.
17. Hollywood (2003, p. 158, n. 9).
18. Cixous (1975/1986, pp. 71–72).
19. "A couple of rolls of the dice, a meeting between two trajectories of the Diaspora…" (1975/1986).
20. Cixous, (1993b, p. 204).
21. Cixous (1977/1991).
22. Blyth and Sellers (2004, p. 37).
23. Hughes, *Pygmalion* (1997).
24. Cixous (1975/1986, p. 72).
25. Ibid., p. 64.
26. Ibid., p. 65.
27. Cixous (1977/1991, p. 2).
28. Ibid., p. 37.
29. Ibid.
30. Ibid., p. 41.
31. Cixous (1993a, p. 8).
32. Cixous, 1993a, p.10.
33. Ibid., p. 10.
34. Cixous (1993b, p. 209).
35. Ibid., p. 209.
36. Cixous (1977/1991, p. 49–50).
37. State benefit (social security).
38. Cixous, "Loving: keeping alive: naming." (1977/1991, p. 3).

39. Cixous: "Die for a word? At least let it be magical and ring at God's door, like the word 'Absinthe' or the word 'Mystical'. At least a quicksilver horse, or the star with the singing horses." (1990, quoted in Sellers, (1994) p. 186).

40. For Cixous, reading, writing, and the death of her father are all interconnected. "Because as soon as we read we forget it, we read and we forget we read to forget and two times to forget, to forget everything except for the book in as much as we are enchanted passengers within it, and then to forget the book that draws its limbs into itself, goes and lays down again in the tomb, that it is alike a beloved dead person ready to return at the call of his name to bring us help when we miss him, him, only that one, there, about which we have forgotten everything but the name, and the power" (from *Lettres de mon Père*, 1997, cited in Hollywood, 2003, p. 149).

41. A shopping catalog for household goods and clothes.

42. "I was raised on the milk of words. Language nourished me." (Cixous, 1977/1991, p. 20).

43. "There has to be somewhere else, I tell myself. And everyone knows that to go somewhere else there are routes, signs, 'maps'—for an exploration, a trip—that's what books are." (Cixous, 1975/1996 p. 72).

44. A health visitor is a state worker with particular interest in young children's welfare and development.

45. A copper's nark, perhaps?

46. For Cixous, writing is "a way of leaving no space for death, of pushing back forgetfulness, of never letting oneself be surprised by the abyss. Of never becoming resigned, consoled: never turning over in bed to face the wall and drift asleep again as if nothing had happened, as if nothing could happen." (1977/1991, p. 3).

47. Cixous (1975/1986, p. 72).

48. Ovid, *Pygmalion* (c. 8 A.D./2004).

9   Autobiographical Writing

A version of Part One of this chapter ("Resilient Adult Learning and the Study") previously appeared in a chapter by Elizabeth Chapman Hoult entitled "Exploring Resilience" in the book edited by Tony Brown entitled *The Doctorate: Stories of Knowledge, Power and Becoming*, published by ESCalate.

1. Richardson, "References are authority moves; disruptions; invite the reader to disengage from the text, like answering the doorbell in the middle of a lively conversation." (1997, p. 167).

2. Hunt and Sampson (2006, p. 119).

3. Barthes (1972/2000, p. 84–85).

4. Derrida (1978/2007, p. 374).

5. Richardson (1997, p. 174).

6. Yeats, from "A Coat" (1916).

7. Cixous (1991, preface).
8. Hunt (2000/2006, p. 50).
9. Hunt and Sampson (2006, p. 70).
10. Ibid., p. 65.
11. Hunt (2000/2006, pp. 23–24).
12. Ibid., p. 23.
13. Atwood, *Cat's Eye* (1988/1990).
14. Knights (1995, p. 128).
15. Woolf, *A Room of One's Own*, (1928/2005, p. 125).
16. Skinner and Hoult, *NoManzLand* (2008).
17. An event horizon is the surface of a black hole. Scientists conjecture that black holes exist because there is evidence of the sorts of effects that they might produce if they did exist. Two of these effects are the severe bending of a light beam and the extreme slowing of time. Using observations of these effects, astronomers refer to objects that are almost certainly black holes as "black holes" despite the uncertainty of their existence (adapted from McClintock, 2004).
18. Saint Mark, (c. 1 A.D./1979). Chapter Five, verses 35–43, *The Holy Bible* (Authorized King James Version) Great Britain: Collins.

10 Exposed Nonconformity: A View from Hopi Point

1. Cixous (1975/1986).
2. Ibid., p. 88.
3. Cixous (1975/1986, p. 72).
4. Ibid., (1975/1986, p. 73).
5. Cixous (1975/1986, p. 73).
6. Ibid., p. 78.
7. "If my desire is possible, it means that the system is already letting something else through" (p. 78).
8. Cixous (1975/1986, p. 88).
9. Ibid., p. 92.
10. Ibid.
11. Ibid., p. 82.
12. Richardson (1997, p. 92).
13. Cixous (1975/1986, p. 86).

Bibliography

Alexandrescu, L. (1999). "Bringing a Historical Character on Stage: *L'Indiade*," in L. A. Jacobus and R. Barreca, *Hélène Cixous: Critical Impressions*. Amsterdam: Gordon and Breach Publishers, pp. 265–92.

Anderson, L. (2001). *Autobiography*. Abingdon and New York: Routledge.

Angelou, M. (1969). *I Know Why the Caged Bird Sings*. New York: Random House.

Armstrong, K. (2004). *The Spiral Staircase: A Memoir*. London: Harper Perennial.

Ashworth, A. (1998). *Once in a House on Fire*. Basingstoke and Oxford: Picador.

Atwood, M. (1988/1990). *Cat's Eye*. London: Virago Press.

Badenhausen, R. (1998). "The Modern Academy Raging in the Dark: Misreading Mamet's Political Incorrectness in 'Oleanna,'" *College Literature*, vol. 25, no. 3, pp. 1–19.

Barthes, R. (1971/1986). "From Work to Text" (trans. Richard Howard), in *The Rustle of Language*. Oxford: Blackwell.

———— (1972/2000). "Striptease," in *Mythologies* (trans. Annette Lavers). London: Jonathon Cape, Vintage, Random House, pp. 84–87.

———— (1973/1975). *The Pleasure of the Text* (trans. Richard Miller). New York: Hill and Wang.

Bates, M. J., and S. Norton (2002). "Educating Rita: an Examination of Female Life Course and Its Influence on Women's Participation in Higher Education," *New Horizons in Adult Education*, vol. 16, no. 3, Summer, 2002, pp. 4–12.

Berkowitz, C. A. (2003). "Paradise Reconsidered: Hélène Cixous and the Bible's Other Voice," in M. Joy, K. O'Grady, and J. L. Poxon (eds.), *Religion in French Feminist Thought: Critical Perspectives*. London and New York: Routledge Taylor Francis Group, pp. 176–88.

Billington, M. (2004). "Review of *Oleanna* at The Garrick Theatre, London," *The Guardian*, April 23, 2004. Available at http://www.guardian.co.uk/stage/2004/apr/23/theatre, accessed on 01/07/2009.

Blake, W. (1793/1975). *The Marriage of Heaven and Hell*. Oxford: Oxford University Press.

Blyth, I., and S. Sellers (2004). *Live Theory*. London and New York: Continuum.

Bourdieu, P. (1979/2006). *Distinction: A Social Critique of the Judgement of Taste* (trans. Richard Nice). New York and London: Routledge Taylor and Frances Group.

——— (1980/1990). *The Logic of Practice* (trans. Richard Nice). Cambridge: Polity Press.

——— (1990). *In Other Words: Essays Towards a Reflexive Sociology* (trans. Matthew Adamson). Oxford: Polity Press in association with Basil Blackwell.

——— (1993/2004). *The Field of Cultural Production* (trans. Randal Johnson). Oxford: Polity Press in association with Blackwell Publishing Ltd.

Bourdieu, P., and J.-C. Passeron (1977/2000). *Reproduction in Education, Society and Culture* (trans. Richard Nice). London, Thousands Oaks, New Delhi: Sage.

——— (1979). *The Inheritors: French Students and their Relation to Culture* (trans. Richard Nice). Chicago: Chicago University Press.

Bowie, D. (1969). "Space Oddity," on the album *Space Oddity*. Philips (Mercury).

Bristol, M. D. (1991). "In Search of the Bear: Spatiotemporal Form and the Heterogeneity of Economics in 'The Winter's Tale,'" *Shakespeare Quarterly*, vol. 42, no. 2, pp. 145–67.

Bronfen, E. (1992). *Over Her Dead Body: Death, femininity and the aesthetic*, Manchester and New York: Manchester University Press.

Cavell, S. (1987). "Recounting Gains, Showing Losses," in *Disowning Knowledge in Seven Plays of Shakespeare*. Cambridge: Cambridge University Press, pp. 196–206.

Challener, D. D. (1997). *Stories of Resilience in Childhood: The Narratives of Maya Angelou, Maxine Hong Kingston, Richard Roderiguez, John Edgar Wideman and Tobias Wolff*. New York and London: Garland Publishing, Inc.

Channel 4 News, (04/05/2006). *Britain's Oldest Mother*.

Cixous, H. (1975/1986). "Sorties: Out and Out: Attacks/Ways Out/Forays" (trans. Betsy Wing), in H. Cixous and C. Clément, *The Newly Born Woman*. London: I. B.Tauris Publishers.

——— (1977/1991). "Coming to Writing," in D. Jenson (ed.), *Coming to Writing and Other Essays* (trans. Sarah Cornell, Deborah Jenson, Ann Liddle and Susan Sellers). Cambridge and London: Harvard University Press, pp. 1–58.

——— (1979). "L'Approche de Clarice Lispector," *Poetique*, no. 40, pp. 408–19.

——— (1981). "Castration or Decapitation" (trans. Annette Kuhn), *Signs*, vol. 7, no.1, pp. 41–55.

——— (1990). *Jours de l'an*, sl: Des Femmes.

——— (1991). *The Book of Promethea* (trans. Betsy Wing). Lincoln and London: The University of Nebraska Press.

——— (1993a). *Three Steps on the Ladder of Writing*. New York and Chichester: Columbia University Press.

——— (1993b). "We Who are Free, Are We Free?" (trans. Chris Miller), *Critical Inquiry*, vol. 19, no. 2, pp. 201–19.

——— (1997). *Or: lettres de mon père*. Paris: Des Femmes.

——— (2007). Comments at *Helene Cixous, Jacques Derrida: Their Psychoanalyses Conference*, June 1–3, 2007, Three Albion Place, Leeds.

——— (2008). *White Ink: Interviews on Sex, Text and Politics* (ed. Susan Sellers). Stocksfield: Acumen.

Cixous, H., and M. Calle-Gruber (1994). *Hélène Cixous, Photos de Racines* (trans. E. Prenowitz). Paris: Des Femmes A.

Cixous, H., and S. Sellers (2004). *The Writing Notebooks* (ed. and trans. Susan Sellers). London and New York: Continuum.

——— (2007). "We Must Hand Our Inheritance On," interview with Susan Sellers. In H. Cixous (2008), *White Ink: Interviews on Sex, Text and Politics* (ed. Susan Sellers), Stocksfield: Acumen, pp. 148–54.

Cohen, L., L. Manion, and K. Morrison (2007). *Research Methods in Education*. Abingdon and New York: Routledge.

Danahay, M. A. (1994). "Mirrors of Masculine Desire: Narcissus and Pygmalion in Victorian Representation," *Victorian Poetry*, vol. 32, no. 1 (Spring, 1994), pp. 35–54.

De Grazia, M. (1990). "Homonyms Before and After Lexical Standardization," in *Deutsche Shakespeare Gesellschaft West Jahrbuch*, Bochum: Kamp, pp. 143–56.

Derrida, J. (1976/1992). "…that dangerous supplement," extract from *Of Grammatology* (trans. Gayatri Chakravorty Spivak), in D. Attridge (ed.), *Acts of Literature* (1992). London: Routledge, pp. 78–109.

——— (1978/2007). "Ellipsis," in *Writing and Difference* (trans. Alan Bass). Abingdon: Routledge, pp. 371–78.

——— (1978/2006). "Structure, Sign and Play in the Discourse of the Human Sciences," in *Writing and Difference* (trans. Alan Bass). Abingdon: Routledge, pp. 351–70.

——— (1982). "Différance" (trans. Alan Bass), in *Margins of Philosophy*. Chicago: Chicago University Press, pp. 3–27.

——— (1983). "The Principle of Reason: The University in the Eyes of its Pupils" (trans. Catherine Porter and Edward P. Morris), *diacritics*, (Fall), pp. 3–20.

——— (1988). "Afterword: Toward an Ethic of Discussion," in G. Graff (ed.), *Limited Inc*. Evanston: Northwestern University Press, pp. 111–60.

——— (1992). *Acts of Literature* (ed. Derek Attridge). New York and London: Routledge.

——— (2007). *Learning to Live Finally: The Last Interview* (trans. Pascale Brandt and Michael Naas). Hobben: Melville House Publishing.

Derrida, J., and D. Attridge (1989). "This Strange Institution Called Literature: An Interview with Jacques Derrida" (trans. Geoffrey Bennington and Rachel Bowlby), in J. Derrida (1992), *Acts of Literature* (ed. Derek Attridge). New York and London: Routledge.

Feeney, D. (2004). Introduction to *Metamorphoses* (trans. David Raeburn). London: Penguin.

Fischer, S. (1985). *Econolingua: A Glossary of Coins and Economic Language in Renaissance Drama*. s.l.: Associated University Presses.

Forster, E. M. (1910). *Howard's End*. London: Edward Arnold.

Fox Harding, L. (1999). "Family Values and Conservative Government Policy: 1979–97," in C. Wright and G. Jagger (eds.), *Changing Family Values: Difference, Diversity and the Decline of the Male Order*. London and New York: Routledge, pp. 119–135.

Freire, P. (1969/2003). *Education for Critical Consciousness*. New York: The Continuing Publishing Group Inc.

——— (2005). *Teachers as Cultural Workers: Letters to Those Who Dare to Teach*. Boulder: Westview Press.

Garai, J., S. E. Haggerty, S. Rekhi, and M. Chance (2006). "Infrared Absorption Investigations Confirm the Extra-Terrestrial Origin of Carbonado Diamonds," *The Astrophysical Journal*, 653: L153–L156. Available at: http://www.fiu.edu/~jgara002/research%20statement/carbonado/carbonado-2006.pdf, accessed on July, 9, 2009.

Garner, C. (1998). "Hughes Wins the Whitbread Prize" in *The Independent*, (Wednesday, January 28, 1998, http://www.independent.co.uk/news/hughes-wins-whitbread-prize-1141289.html, accessed on August 22, 2011.

Garner, S. B. (2000). "Framing the Classroom: Pedagogy, Power, Oleanna," *Theatre Topics*, vol. 10, no. 1, pp. 39–52.

Gilbert, S., and S. Gubar (1979/2000). *The Madwoman in the Attic: The Woman Writer and the Nineteenth Century Literary Imagination, Second Edition*. New Haven and London: Yale University Press.

Glazer-Raymo, J. (2000). "Sexual Harassment in the Academy," *The Review of Higher Education*, vol. 23, no. 4, pp. 491–500.

Gough, V. (2000). "The Lesbian Christ: Body Politics in Helene Cixous's 'Le Livre de Promethea,'" in A. Horner and A. Keane (eds.), *Body Matters: Feminism, Textuality and Corporeality*. Manchester: Manchester University Press, pp. 234–43.

Goulet, D. (2003). "Introduction," in P. Freire (1996/2003), *Education for Critical Consciousness*. New York and London: Continuum.

Grant, R., and S. D. Wong (2008). "Critical Race Perspectives, Bourdieu and Language Education," in J. Allbright and A. Luke (eds.), *Pierre Bourdieu and Literacy Education*. New York and Abingdon: Routledge.

Hart, A., and D. Blincow, with H. Thomas (2007). *Resilient Therapy: Working with Children and Families*. Hove and New York: Routledge Taylor and Francis Group.

Havelock, C. M. (1995). *The Aphrodite of Knidos and Her Successors: A Historical Review of the Female Nude in Greek Art*. Ann Arbor: University of Michigan Press.

Hollywood, A. (2002). *Sensible Ecstasy: Mysticism, Sexual Difference, and the Demands of History*. London and Chicago: The University of Chicago Press.

——— (2003). "Mysticism, Death and Desire in the Work of Hélène Cixous and Catherine Clément," in M. Joy, K. O'Grady, and J. L. Poxon (eds.), *Religion in French Feminist Thought: Critical Perspectives*. London and New York: Routledge Taylor Francis Group, pp. 145–61.

Hooks, B. (1994). *Teaching to Transgress*. London and New York: Routledge.

Hooper, W. (1915). "The Tudor Sumptuary Laws," *The English Historical Review*, vol. 30, no. 119, (July 1915) pp. 433–49.

Hopkins, B. (2005). "Every Man Kills the Thing He Loves: Object Use and Potential Space in 'The Winter's Tale,'" *PSYART: An Online Journal for the Psychological*

Study of the Arts. Available at: www. Clas.ufl.edu/ipsa/journal/2005_hopkins03, accessed on July 3, 2009.

Hoult, E., H. Bryan, K. Goouch, and L. Revell (2006). "A Room of One's Own? How the New Academics in the Expanding Higher Education Sector Are Transforming the Understanding of What It Means to Be a New University Teacher," paper presented at *ISSOTL Conference*, November 9–12, Vancouver.

Hughes, T. (1997). "Pygmalion," in *Tales from Ovid: Twenty-four Passages from the Metamorphoses*. London: Faber and Faber, pp. 144–50.

Hunt, C. (2000/2006). *Therapeutic Dimensions of Autobiography in Creative Writing*. London and Philadelphia: Jessica Kingsley Publishers.

Hunt, C., and F. Sampson (2006). *Writing: Self and Reflexivity*. Basingstoke and New York: Palgrave.

Jenkins, R. (1992/2002). *Pierre Bourdieu (revised edition)*. London and New York: Routledge.

John, J. (2001). *The Meaning in the Miracles*. Norwich: Canterbury Press.

Jouve, N. W. (1991). *White Woman Speaks with Forked Tongue: Critcism as Autobiography*. New York and London: Routledge.

Keats, J. (1817/2002). "Letter to George and Tom Keats, 21st and/or 27th December 1817," in R. Gittings (ed.), *John Keats: Selected Letters*. Oxford: Oxford University Press.

Knights, B. (1992). *From Reader to Reader: Theory, Text and Practice in the Study Group*. Hemel Hemsted: Harvester Wheatsheaf.

——— (1995). *The Listening Reader: Fiction and Poetry for Counsellors and Psychotherapists*. London and Bristol: Jessica Kingsley Publishers.

———(2005). "Intelligence and Interrogation: The Identity of the English Student," *Arts and Humanities in Higher Education*, vol. 4, no. 1, pp. 33–52.

Knights, B., and C. Thurgar-Dawson (2006). *Active Reading: Transformative Writing in Literary Studies*. London and New York: Continuum Literary Studies.

Kramsch, C. (2008). "Pierre Bourdieu: A Biographical Memoir," in J. Albright and A. Luke (eds.), *Pierre Bourdieu and Literacy Education*. New York and Abingdon: Routledge, pp. 33–49.

Lacan, J. (1975/1999). *On Feminine Sexuality, the Limits of Love and Knowledge, 1972–1973: Encore—the Seminar of Jacques Lacan, Book XX* (trans. B. Fink). New York and London: W. W. Norton.

Land, R. (2008). "Overcoming Barriers to Student Understanding: Threshold Concepts and Troublesome Knowledge," paper presented at the International Conference for Educational Development, Salt Lake City: University of Utah, June 12–15, 2008.

Land, R., J. H. F. Meyer, and J. Smith, eds. (2008). *Threshold Concepts within the Disciplines*. Rotterdam: Sense Publications.

Law. H. H. (February, 1932). "The Name Galatea in the Pygmalion Myth," *The Classical Journal*, vol. 27, no. 5, pp. 337–42.

Lovelock, J. (2001). *Gaia: A New Look at Life on Earth*. Oxford and New York: Oxford University Press.

MacGilchrist, B., K. Myers, and J. Reed (1997). *The Intelligent School*. London, Thousand Oaks, and New Delhi: Paul Chapman Publishing.

Mackie, A. (2001). "Popular Identities: Perpetuating Myths, Providing Possibilities," *Pedagogy, Culture and Society*, vol. 9, no. 2, pp. 289–96.

Macleod, C. (1995). "The Politics of Gender, Language and Hierarchy in Mamet's 'Oleanna,'" *Journal of American Studies*, vol. 29, no. 2, pp. 199–213.

Mamet, D. (1993). *Oleanna*. London: Methuen Drama.

Massey, J. (2003). "'The Double Bind of Troilus to Tellen': the Time of the Gift in Chaucer's Troilus and Criseyde," *The Chaucer Review*, vol. 38, no. 1, pp. 16–35.

McClintock, J. E. (2004). "Black Hole," in *World Book Online Reference Center*. Available at: http:www.worldbookonline.com/wb/Article?id+ar062594, accessed on July 3, 2009.

Meyer, J. H. F., and R. Land (2003). "Threshold Concepts and Troublesome Knowledge: Linkages to Ways of Thinking and Practising within the Disciplines," in Rust C. (ed.), *Improving Student Learning: Theory and Practice—Ten Years On*. OCSLD, Oxford, pp. 412–24.

Mezirow, J. (2000). *Learning as Transformation: Critical Perspectives on a Theory in Progress*. San Fransisco: Jossey-Bass.

Moi, T. (1985/2002). *Sexual/Textual Politics*. London and New York: Routledge (Taylor Francis Group).

——— (1990). "Appropriating Bourdieu: Feminist Theory and Pierre Bourdieu's Sociology of Culture," in T. Moi (1999). *What is a Woman?* Oxford: Oxford University Press, pp. 264–99.

——— (1997). "The Challenge of the Particular Case: Bourdieu's Sociology of Culture and Literary Criticism," in T. Moi (1999). *What is a Woman?* Oxford: Oxford University Press, pp. 299–311.

Morrison, T. (1970). *The Bluest Eye*. New York: Washington Square Press.

Neely, C. T. (1985). "*The Winter's Tale*: The Triumph of Speech," *Studies in English Literature*, 1500–1900, vol. 15, no. 2, pp. 321–38.

Ovid (c. 8 a.d./2004). *Metamorphoses* (trans. David Raeburn, introduction by Dennis Feeney). London: Penguin.

Parker, P. (2004). "Temporal Gestation, Legal Contracts and the Promissory Economy in *The Winter's Tale*," in N. E. Wright, W. Ferguson, and A. R. Buck (eds.), *Women, Property and the Letters of the Law in Early Modern England*. Toronto: University of Toronto Press.

Paul Hamlyn Foundation: National Commission on Education (1996). *Success Against the Odds: Effective Schools in Disadvantaged Areas*. London and New York: Routledge.

Peck, L. L. (2005). *Consuming Splendour: Society and Culture in Seventeenth Century England*. Cambridge, New York, Melbourne, Cape Town, Singapore, São Paulo: Cambridge University Press.

Perrault, C. (1697/2004). *The Sleeping Beauty in the Wood* (trans. A. E. Johnson). Ware: Wordsworth Editions.

Piette, A., (2004). "The 1980s," in C. Bigsby (ed.), *Cambridge Companion to David Mamet*. Cambridge: Cambridge University Press. pp. 74–88.

Plato (c. 370 b.c./2005). *Phaedrus* (trans. Christopher Rowe). London: Penguin.

Plummer, K. (2001). *Documents of Life 2: An Invitation to a Critical Humanism.* London, Thousand Oaks, and Delhi: Sage.

Radford, M. (2008). "Prediction, Control and the Challenge to Complexity," *Oxford Review of Education*, vol. 34, no. 5, pp. 505–20.

Raeburn, D. (2004). Translation of Ovid's (c. 8 a.d./2004) *Metamorphoses*. London: Penguin.

Raymond, C. R. (2003). "Rhetoricizing English Studies: Students' Ways of Reading Oleanna," *Pedagogy*, vol. 3, no. 1, pp. 53–71.

Reed-Danahay, D. (2005). *Locating Bourdieu*. Bloomington: Indiana University Press.

Renshaw, S. (2003). "The Thealogy of Hélène Cixous," in M. Joy, K. O'Grady, and J. L. Poxon (eds.), *Religion in French Feminist Thought: Critical Perspectives.* London and New York: Routledge Taylor Francis Group, pp. 162–75.

———— (2009). *The Subject of Love: Hélène Cixous and the Feminine Divine.* Manchester and New York: Manchester University Press.

Rich, A. (1972). "Diving into the Wreck," in A. Rich (1973) *Diving into the Wreck.* New York and London: W.W. Norton and Company.

Richardson, L. (1997). *Fields of Play: Constructing an Academic Life.* New Brunswick, NJ: Rutgers University Press.

———— (2007). *Last Writes: A Daybook for a Dying Friend.* Walnut Creek, CA: Left Coast Press, Inc.

Richardson, L., and E. Lockridge (2004). *Travels with Ernest: Crossing the Literary/Sociological Divide.* Walnut Creek, CA and Oxford: AltaMira Press.

Roos, B. (2001). "Refining the Artist into Existence: Pygmalion's Statue, Stephen Villanelle and the Venus of Praxiteles," *Comparative Literary Studies*, vol. 38, no. 2, pp. 95–117.

Rowan, L. (2003). "Back from the Brink: Reclaiming 'Quality' in the Pursuit of a Transformational Education Agenda," in E. Van Til (ed.), *Educational Research: Risks and Dilemmas, NZARE AARE Conference Proceedings, 2003.* Auckland, New Zealand: NZARE, pp. 1–11.

Rowland, S. (2006). *The Enquiring University: Compliance and Contestation in Higher Education.* Berkshire and New York: Open University Press.

Rubin Suleiman, S. (1991). "Writing Past the Wall, or the Passion According to H. C." (introduction), in H. Cixous (1991), *Coming to Writing and Other Essays.* Cambridge and London: Harvard University Press.

Rushdie, S. (1992). *The Wizard of Oz.* London: The British Film Institute.

Russell, W. (1981/2000). *Educating Rita.* London: Longman.

Ryan, S. (1996). "*Oleanna*: David Mamet's Power Play," *Modern Drama*, no. 39, pp. 392–403.

Sage, L. (2001). *Bad Blood.* London: Fourth Estate (Harper Collins).

Saint John of the Cross (c. 1578/1972). *The Poems of St John of the Cross* (trans. Willis Barnstone). Bloomington: Indiana University Press.

Saint Luke (c. 1 a.d./1979). Chapter Two, verse 45, *The Holy Bible* (Authorized King James Version).Glasgow: Collins.

Saint Mark (c. 1 a.d./1979). Chapter Five, verses 35–43, *The Holy Bible* (Authorized King James Version).Glasgow: Collins.

Saint Teresa of Ávila (c. 1565/1957). *The Life of Saint Teresa of Ávila by Herself* (trans. J. M. Cohen). London: Penguin Classics.

Schwartz, M. (2005). "Loss and Transformation in *The Winter's Tale*—Part 2: Transformations," *PSYART: An Online Journal for the Psychological Study of the Arts*. Available at http://www.clas.ufl.edu/ipsa/journal/2005_schwartz03b.shtml, accessed on July, 1, 2009.

Sellers, S. (ed.) (1994). *The Hélène Cixous Reader*. London and New York: Routledge.

Shakespeare, W. (1623—first folio, performance dated 1610–1611/2007). *The Winter's Tale*. S. Snyder and D. Curren-Aquino (eds.) (2007). Cambridge: Cambridge University Press.

——— (1623/1999). *The Tempest*. V. Mason Vaughn and A. T. Vaughan (eds.). London: The Arden Shakespeare, Cengage Learning.

Shaw, G. B. (1916/2007). *Pygmalion*. London: Longman.

Shelley, M. (1831/2004). *Frankenstein*. London: The Folio Society.

Shelley, P. B. (1824). *Autumn, A Dirge*. Available at: http://www.litscape.com/author/Percy_Bysshe_Shelley/Autumn_A_Dirge.html, accessed on September 9, 2009.

Shipton, G. (2007). "The Annihilation of Triangular Space in David Mamet's *Oleanna* and Some Implications for Teacher-Student Relationships in the Era of Mass University Education," *Psychodynamic Practice*, vol. 13, no. 2, pp. 141–52.

Shor, I., and P. Freire (1987). *A Pedagogy for Liberation: Dialogues on Transforming Education*. Westport, CA: Greenwood.

Shurmur-Smith, P. (2000). "Hélène Cixous," in M. Crang and N. Thrift, (eds.), *Thinking Space*. London and New York: Routledge.

Silber, I. F. (2009). "Bourdieu's Gift to Gift Theory: An Unacknowledged Trajectory," *Sociological Theory*, vol. 27, pp. 173–190. doi: 10.1111/j.1467-9558.2009.01342.

Silverstein, M. (1995). "'We're Just Human': *Oleanna* and Cultural Crisis," *South Atlantic Review*, vol. 60, no. 2, pp. 103–20.

Skeggs, B. (1997/2002). *Formations of Class and Gender*. London, Thousand Oaks, and New Delhi: Sage Publications.

Skinner, P. T., and E. C. Hoult (2008). *NoManzLand*. First performance, Canterbury Christ Church University, June 25, 2008.

Snyder, S. (1999). "Mamillius and Gender Polarization in the Winter's Tale," *Shakespeare Quarterly*, vol. 50, no. 1, p. 1–8.

Snyder, S., and D. T. Curren-Aquino (2007). Introduction to *The Winter's Tale*. Cambridge: Cambridge University Press.

Speer, S. A. (2005). *Gender Talk: Feminism, Discourse and Conversational Analysis*. Hove: Routledge.

Stanley, L. (1993). "On Autobiography," *Sociology*, vol. 27, no.1, pp. 41–52.

Stocker, B. (2006). *Derrida on Deconstruction*. Oxon: Routledge.

Stoichita, V. I. (2008). *The Pygmalion Effect: From Ovid to Hitchcock*. Chicago and London: The University of Chicago Press.

Stokes, J. (2007). "Paris in the 1880s," notes accompanying the National Theatre's (2007) production of *The Enchantment*, "The Programme". s.l.: The National Theatre.

United Nations Educational, Scientific, and Cultural Organization (2009). Communiqué: 2009 World Conference on Higher Education: The New Dynamics of Higher Education and Research for Societal Change and Development, UNESCO, Paris, July 5–8, 2009, http://unesco.org/images/0018/001832/183277e.pdf, retrieved on May 21, 2011.

Van-Rossum Guyon, F., and M. Diaz-Diocaretz (1990). *Helene Cixous, chemins d'une ecriture*, 1 Colloque International: Papers. Presses Universitaires de Vincennes PUV (L'Imaginaire du Texte), Editions Rodopi (Faux titre, 49).

Warner, M. (1985). *Monuments and Maidens: The Allegory of the Female Form*. London: Picador.

Watkins, C., E. Carnell, C. Lodge, and C. Whalley (1996). "Effective Learning," occasional paper for *School Improvement Network*. London: Institute of Education.

West, L. (1996). *Beyond Fragments: Adults, Motivation and Higher Education—A Biographical Analysis*. London: Taylor and Francis.

Winterson, J. (1985). *Oranges Are Not The Only Fruit*. London: Vintage.

Wood, S. (2006). "Beauty and Admiration in Learning: Louise Bourgeois and Paul de Man," *Parallax*, vol. 1, no. 3, pp. 51–64.

Woolf, V. (1925/1976). *Mrs Dalloway*. London: Triad.

——— (1928/2005). *A Room of One's Own*, in *Selected Works of Virginia Woolf*. Ware: Wordsworth Editions.

Yeats, W. B. (1916). "A Coat," in *Responsibilities and Other Poems*. New York: The Macmillan Company.

Index